# Manifestoes

*Provocations of the Modern*

# Manifestoes

*Provocations of the Modern*

Janet Lyon

Cornell University Press    Ithaca and London

First published 1999 by Cornell University Press
First printing, Cornell Paperbacks, 1999

Printed in the United States of America

Lyon, Janet.
    Manifestoes : provocations of the modern / Janet Lyon.
        p.      cm.
    Includes bibliographical references and index.
    ISBN 0-8014-3635-4 (cloth : alk. paper). —ISBN 0-8014-8591-6
    (pbk. : alk. paper)
        1. Revolutionary literature—History and criticism.    2. Politics
    and literature.    3. Avant-garde (Aesthetics)    4. Feminism
    and literature.    5. Modernism (Literature)    I.    Title.
PN51.L936    1999
809'.93358—DC21                                                    98-36507

Cornell University Press strives to use environmentally responsible suppliers and materials to the fullest extent possible in the publishing of its books. Such materials include vegetable-based, low-VOC inks and acid-free papers that are recycled, totally chlorine-free, or partly composed of nonwood fibers. Books that bear the logo of the FSC (Forest Stewardship Council) use paper taken from forests that have been inspected and certified as meeting the highest standards for environmental and social responsibility. For further information, visit our Web site at www.cornellpress.cornell.edu.

FSC  FSC Trademark © 1996 Forest Stewardship Council A.C.
        SW-COC-098

Cloth printing          10 9 8 7 6 5 4 3 2 1
Paperback printing     10 9 8 7 6 5 4 3 2 1

For my parents, Brad and Kay Lyon

# Contents

# Acknowledgments

Michael Levenson and Susan Fraiman guided me wisely in the early incarnations of this project, and Mark Edmundson and Jerome McGann offered important preliminary suggestions. Several of my colleagues at Illinois read parts of the manuscript and offered corrections, critiques, and smart conversation; for these I am indebted to Nina Baym, Carol Neely, Cary Nelson, Bob Parker, Dick Wheeler, and especially Joe Valente and Lori Newcomb. The University of Illinois Faculty Research Board and the Program for the Study of Cultural Values and Ethics generously granted me time released from teaching. I wish to acknowledge and thank those friends and colleagues who have either provided me with copies of crucial manifestoes or participated in discussions that helped to shape this project: Madison Bell, Alice Gambrell, Peter Garrett, Sandra Hammond, Allen Hance, Rosemary Kegl, Dan Kinney, Amitava Kumar (whose photographs are themselves manifestoes), Bill Maxwell, Sonya Michel, Richard Mohr, Mark Morrisson, Melissa Orlie, Rick Powers, Marthe Rosenfeld, Jack Stillinger, Zohreh Sullivan, Michael Thurston, Paula Treichler, Hap Veeser, and Carol Wipf-Miller. Cary Nelson generously opened his modernist archives to me. Elizabeth Majerus talked music with me during manuscript preparations; Carine Melkom-Mardorossian and Kevin Carollo graciously consulted on translations. Rita Felski has been an invaluable correspondent, and Barbara Green has been a wonderful modern interlocutor for lo these many years. I thank my parents, to whom this book is dedicated, and my in-laws, Mo and Anne Bérubé, for shouts of encouragement. I am grateful to my excellent friend Amanda Anderson for all our adventures, and for the insight and time she has given to this project. Love and gratitude also go to my siblings Cynthia, Barbara, Todd, and Bud for unceasing irreverent inspiration, and to my kids Nick and Jamie, members of the next generation of creative collectivity. Finally, my dearest thanks go to my partner, the multiply gifted and adroitly helpful Michael Bérubé, who has seen me through all of this and much more.

Parts of this book have appeared in sections of previously published essays. Grateful acknowledgment is made for permission to reprint passages from the following: Janet Lyon, "Mina Loy's Pregnant Pauses: The Space of Possibility in the Florence Writings," in *Mina Loy: Poet and Person,* ed. Maeera Schreiber and Keith Tuma (Orono, Maine: National Poetry Foundation, 1989), 379–401; Janet Lyon, "Women Demonstrating Modernism,"

# Introduction

## Polemics in the Modern Vein

Since the mid-1960s, historical and literary scholarship has produced a striking number of studies of the avant-garde, as well as an unprecedented outpouring of histories and theories of feminism and women's writing. It is not too much to say that these intellectual projects have redefined our understanding of the modern political subject in the West, the citizen invoked and instantiated by "we the people" of modernity. Nevertheless, neither feminist histories nor contemporary narratives of the avant-garde have produced any sustained theoretical account of the manifestoes, revolutionary discourses, and public polemics that have defined—and often written—the history of Western modernity. My aim in this book is to offer a history and theory of the manifesto, and in so doing provide a comprehensive synthesis of the relations among revolutionary discourse, avant-garde aesthetics, feminist polemics, and the development of modern spheres of public contestation and debate.

*Manifestoes: Provocations of the Modern* is thus predicated on a comprehensive analysis of the manifesto, a ubiquitous yet undertheorized genre in the catalogue of modern discursive forms. In defining and enacting the identities of radical groups, individuals, and parties, the manifesto has galvanized revolutionary movements for the past three hundred years. From its appearance in England during the pamplet wars of the seventheenth century through its reappearances in Europe and the Americas during subsequent moments of profound historical crisis, the manifesto marks the point of impact where the idea of radical egalitarianism runs up against the entrenchment of an ancien régime. The rise of the manifesto is thus coeval with the emergence of the bourgeois and plebeian public

1

spheres in the West: mixing hortatory political rhetoric with righteous rage, the manifesto addresses and at the same time elicits an entity called the People, each constituent of which is hailed as an entitled universal subject of the modern state.

Situating the manifesto form within a larger understanding of the emergence of political modernity—within the "provocations of the modern"—enables me to frame a few key historical moments when the production and circulation of polemical writings became unusually widespread. The early years of the French Revolution, for example, saw the wide circulation of anonymous or multiply authored utopian tracts which recast modern history in terms of natural law and unnatural tyranny; in the course of human events, those broadsides then became a discursive template for the subsequent texts of Chartism, the Commune, Latin American revolutions, and late nineteenth-century anarchism. Likewise, the early years of the historical avant-garde in the first decades of the twentieth century echoed with the revolutionary discourse that was reinflected and redirected in the founding aesthetic texts of early British modernism, the continental futurist movement and the subsequent dada and surrealist movements, and the concurrent agitation for women's rights. And in the late 1960s, the difficult problems raised by universalist revolutionary discourse were addressed directly in the manifestoes of radical second-wave feminism, with its connections to the civil rights and labor movements. In all of these historical moments, manifestoes functioned to circumvent ordinary parliamentarian avenues of public redress, and to challenge the ostensible universalism that underpins modern democratic cultural formations.

One of my broadest claims in this study is that the manifesto form has much to teach us about the problems of modernity: while it may be best known as the no-nonsense genre of plain speech, the genre that shoots from the hip, it is in fact a complex, ideologically inflected genre that has helped to create modern public spheres. Its influence on the history of the modern West, though decisive, has been largely overlooked, perhaps precisely because its apparent rhetorical straightforwardness obscures the degree to which the form is embedded in the contradictions of political representation. On the one hand, the manifesto as we know it from the French Revolution forward is the liberatory genre that narrates in no uncertain terms the incongruous experiences of modernity of those whose needs have been ignored or excluded in a putatively democratic political culture. On the other hand, the manifesto is the genre not of universal liberation

but of rigid hierarchical binaries: on this reading, the manifesto participates in a reduced understanding of heterogeneous social fields, creating
audiences through a rhetoric of exclusivity, parceling out political identities across a polarized discursive field, claiming for "us" the moral high
ground of revolutionary idealism, and constructing "them" as ideological
tyrants, bankrupt usurpers, or corrupt fools.

In Chapter 1, "Manifestoes and Public Spheres," I theorize these two
salient and conflicting aspects of the manifesto form. I argue that when the
conditions of possibility emerged for an ideology of a universal subject
with universal rights and sensibilities—that is, when political and economic developments in post-Enlightenment Europe generated the modern concepts of equality and rational autonomy—the manifesto arose as a
public genre for contesting or recalibrating the assumptions underlying
this newly "universal" subject. In this influential instantiation, the manifesto is the form that exposes the broken promises of modernity: if modern democratic forms claim to honor the sovereignty of universal political
subjecthood, the manifesto is a testimony to the partiality of that claim.
Manifestoes chronicle the exclusions and deferrals experienced by those
outside the "legitimate" bourgeois spheres of public exchange; the manifesto marks the gap between democratic ideals and modern political practice. At the same time, however, the manifesto promulgates the very discourses it critiques: it makes itself intelligible to the dominant order
through a logic that presumes the efficacy of modern democratic ideals.
However paratactic or irreverent or systematic a manifesto may be, it
nonetheless operates by putting the case of a particular group into a context that honors the *idea* of a universal political subject.

As a way of framing my discussion of this double-edged quality, I offer
in Chapter 1 a rhetorical analysis of the form of the manifesto. Here I examine its early prototypes in the tracts of the Diggers and Levellers of 1650
and follow the iterability of the form into its modern incarnations, such as
the 1918 Dada Manifesto and the 1992 Dyke Manifesto. The discussion isolates and explores some of the consistent formal features of the manifesto—its selective and impassioned chronicle of the oppression that has
led to the present moment of rupture; its forceful enumeration of grievances; its epigrammatic style—and then shows how the repetition of these
structures and locutions across myriad political epochs attests to the
form's capacity to serve as a multiaccentual ideological sign, one that can
be evoked in any number of struggles, on any number of sides. Such "multiaccentuality" contributes to the manifesto's continued use as an emblem

of political combat: to write a manifesto is to participate symbolically in a history of struggle against dominant forces; it is to link one's voice to the countless voices of previous revolutionary conflicts.

But the form's atavism also entails its encryption of the gendered inflections of revolutionary discourse. In Chapter 2, "Manifestoes and Revolutionary Discourse," I thus turn to an analysis of the distinct play of gender in some of the prototypical tracts of the French Revolution. The early years of this period saw an explosion of uncensored pamphlets and placards invoking the will of the people and asserting the sovereignty of public opinion; they also saw the emergence of a small number of feminists in France who adopted the new French Republic's revolutionary modes of social activism and political speech. The discursive conditions under which republican feminism emerged, however, were far from propitious. With the development of a revolutionary iconography adapted from a model of Roman fraternity, republican discourse increasingly sought to control the semiotic grounds on which the claims for "natural" law and "universal" rights were made; and although feminist critiques of partial representation in revolutionary government dovetailed with the sansculottes' propagation of the ideal of direct power, feminism per se was increasingly cast as a divisive, anti-universalist, and, ultimately, counterrevolutionary threat to the coherence of "public opinion" in the Revolution. Moreover, revolutionary discourse itself was predicated on a coded distinction between corrupt femininity and hygienic masculinity, and the force of this dichotomy was instrumental in the revolutionary policies that subsequently barred women from public political activity. At this point, "woman" became more or less officially a marker not of a distinct, rights-bearing group of *persons* but of an instrumental adjunct of an ungendered *people*—one for whom actual citizenship was superfluous. In the course of this discussion I draw on the scholarship of Dominique Godineau, Lynn Hunt, Joan Landes, Joan Wallach Scott, and others in my comparative analysis of feminist activity and revolutionary discourse; this analysis, in turn, anchors my discussion of the polemics produced in subsequent revolutionary movements in nineteenth-century England and France. I argue that the gendered imperatives of revolutionary discourse, as popularized and circulated in movements such as Chartism and the Commune, afford contemporary readers a useful magnification of the troubled relation between political avantgardes and feminist agitation. As in the French Revolution, feminism is viewed within the ranks of these movements as divisively anti-republican; even for the most radical of revolutionaries, the universalist ideal of the sovereign citizen requires a political identification with masculinity.

I close this chapter with an examination of what I take to be a decisive moment in the historical uses of revolutionary discourse—that is, the intersection of the political avant-garde and the aesthetic avant-garde, and the role of the manifesto in that intersection. In the decades following the revolutionary activities of the 1871 Commune, the manifesto emerged as the signature genre for avant-garde groups announcing the birth of artistic movements. The aesthetic coteries of the historical avant-garde—from symbolists to vorticists, from futurists to surrealists—adapted the manifesto's revolutionary discourse to signal their own radical departures from bourgeois artistic forms and practices. By articulating their programs to the political history of dissent via its most salient genre, avant-garde groups appropriated for themselves a powerful voice that not only declared the precepts for a poetics of "the new" but also participated in a widespread ideological critique of modernity. Twinning the parataxis of the manifesto form with an aesthetic agenda of abstraction, irony, detachment, and "anti-sentimentalism," avant-gardists of this transitional period developed a complex subgenre that challenged the discourses of reason, progressivism, and universalism associated with the liberal bourgeois public sphere. Their challenge was intensified by the militancy embedded in the manifesto's revolutionary discourse, a militancy that borrowed its edge from contemporary militant workers' movements such as those of the British coal miners and American textile workers. Thus the aesthetic manifesto was a singularly overdetermined form: linking aesthetic practice with political militancy, modern rupture with revolutionary history, and bourgeois critique with aesthetic abstraction, the avant-garde manifestoes of this period posited a prismatic reading audience sundered by the competing claims of modernity yet diffusely united under the banner of dissent.

The importance of this conjuncture can hardly be overstated; the cultural revolution known as modernism has been made intelligible to us primarily through its adaptations of the manifesto form. Modernism's signal crisis—how to negotiate between radical individualism and forms of representation—found its expression in the paradoxes of the manifesto, the form that is at once political and aesthetic, rational and irrational, angry and restrained, and always poised between the violence of the armed insurrection and the stasis of the written word. Accordingly, the focus of Chapters 3 and 4 rests on London, one of the centers of modernism, during the decade 1909–19. For it is in London that an artistic avant-garde emerged simultaneously with a militant wing of the women's suffrage movement. In the first of the London chapters, "Militant Allies and Strange Bedfellows," I reconstruct the tangled affiliations between the

Suffragettes' polemical tactics and early modernist manifestoes. Drawing on writings by futurists, vorticists, journalists, and the WSPU (Women's Social and Political Union), I argue that while these groups were in an overdetermined dialogue with one another, and often constructed themselves in opposition to one another, their identities were also in part produced by a burgeoning popular press that insistently linked Suffragette transgressions of gender roles with the less dangerous but equally threatening challenges to "realistic" representation that issued from the camps of vorticists and Omega Workshop affiliates. In Chapter 3 I trace the relation between the dominant masculinist aesthetic of the London avant-garde— particularly the aesthetic promoted in the manifestoes of Wyndham Lewis and F. T. Marinetti (whose appearances in London produced heated publicity)—and the gendered revolutionary discourse of previous militant movements. In analyzing the "revolutionary" polemics of each group, I emphasize the difficulty of the negotiations made by Suffragettes in their adaptations of revolutionary forms, and the corresponding (and hitherto unremarked) dependence of the aesthetic avant-garde on the anti-bourgeois spectacle of suffragist violence.

Moving from the troubled collectivity of the early modernists and the WSPU to the hallmark individualism of modernism, the second London chapter takes up the work of two vastly different militant writers—Ezra Pound and Mina Loy—in order to examine Pound's de-feminization of modernism and Loy's aggressive feminization of futurism. Pound's personal claim to the invention of modernism is among the best-documented titles in modernist literary history; Mina Loy's work today is largely unread. Yet it is precisely in the figure of Mina Loy that my study finds its decisive pivot to the present. Loy's "Feminist Manifesto" (1914) lays bare for us the obstacles for feminists who arrive at the intersection of aesthetic discourse, revolutionary discourse, and feminist polemic. Her shift from the manifesto form to her more compelling dramaturgy and satires in *The Sacred Prostitute* and *The Pamperers* (written during the same period) provides a sharp look at the prospects for feminist avant-gardism in comparatively "traditional" literary genres. Reading the strictures of Pound's imagism manifesto (which, he insisted, was *not* a manifesto) against Loy's attempts to negotiate the form's universalist imperatives, I show how the dual anxieties of modernism—the disdain for democratic homogeneity and the distrust of mass production—are routed through the modernist use of the form. Pound translates revolutionary discourse into cloistered cipher and produces not a manifesto but a simulacrum of struggle in the name of aesthetic elitism; by contrast, Loy manipulates the manifesto form to challenge parochial, anti-individualist representations of "Woman," even as she invokes, through her use of revolutionary discourse, a normative ideal of republican motherhood.

The intractable relations between identity and difference sketched out in Loy's manifesto characterize most of the polemical tracts produced in the third historical conjuncture of this study, the period of the late 1960s and early 1970s, when the radical left reconfigured itself under the forceful influence of a temporary alliance among student agitators, civil rights activists, Black Power militants, Marxists, anti-imperialists, and several very different brands of feminism. Significantly, the feminist manifestoes produced during this period offer a compelling case study in the gender trouble generated by the limited availability of feminist subject positions within leftist revolutionary discourse. The textual record of this period suggests that if the French Revolution is the mother of all revolutions (as Pierre Bourdieu has argued), then her great-great-granddaughters of second-wave feminism have inherited her ambivalent legacy of universalism.

Chapter 5, "A Second-Wave Problematic," takes as its starting point a pair of early works by Monique Wittig, a writer whose relations to feminism and the political avant-garde are famously uneasy. In 1970 she published the gender warfare novel *Les Guérillères* to widespread critical acclaim; in the same year she also co-wrote an obscure Maoist-feminist manifesto for the politically volatile audience of the Parisian New Left. The novel, an experimental mosaic of litanies and fables, nimbly narrates the overthrow of patriarchy. The long and difficult manifesto, by contrast, tries to locate a mandate for feminism within historical Marxism, but quickly becomes mired in a rhetorical dilemma: it must find a way to critique the left's programmatic exclusion of women while adapting to the universalist conventions of revolutionary discourse.

This strain tells on the pulses of a whole spectrum of 1960s feminist manifestoes—"SCUM," "Redstockings," "The SDS Resolution on Women"—and, even more broadly, in the militant liberation manifestoes of the same period, from the conclusion of *The Wretched of the Earth* to the "Black Panther Platform" to the "Chicano Manifesto." In all of these tracts, "we" is offered as the authentic voice of "the people" even as that entity is confounded and contested; the history of revolution is invoked even as the normative markers of that history are challenged. Yet these are still modern manifestoes, troubled by the modern, and as such they replay the modern dilemma of political subjecthood which can be discerned in all manifestoes that couch their demands in the language of universalism. Indeed, I identify this dilemma and its attendant political-theoretical impasse as the pivot on which the *post*modern manifesto turns, for in those manifestoes (by Jenny Holzer and Donna Haraway, for example), the avant-garde employment of revolutionary discourse is considerably more flexible and revisionary than in earlier incarnations. Nonetheless—and this is diagnostic of the manifesto's textured history—the difficulty of creating subject positions within the manifesto form, even in "postmodern" manifestoes, duplicates the difficulty of collective self-representation in modernity.

Ultimately, I suggest, the manifesto as a genre is constitutive of the public sphere to the degree that it persistently registers the contradictions within modern political life. For while modernity offers ideological assurances of autonomy and individualism within collectivity, it also and at the same time draws on the deferral of those promises. The manifesto records just this breach between modernity's promissory notes and their payment. In order to understand how the manifesto has kept the records of modernity for the past three centuries, therefore, we must first reopen the historical record of democratic universalism in the West.

# 1 Manifestoes and Public Spheres

## Probing Modernity

The literary and political manifestoes that flag the history of modernity are usually taken to be transparent public expressions of pure will: whoever its author and whatever its subject, a manifesto is understood as the testimony of a historical present tense spoken in the impassioned voice of its participants. The form's capacity for rhetorical trompe l'oeil tends to shape its wide intelligibility; the syntax of a manifesto is so narrowly controlled by exhortation, its style so insistently unmediated, that it appears to say only what it means, and to mean only what it says. The manifesto declares a position; the manifesto refuses dialogue or discussion; the manifesto fosters antagonism and scorns conciliation. It is univocal, unilateral, single-minded. It conveys resolute oppositionality and indulges no tolerance for the fainthearted, as a women's manifesto of the Paris Commune aptly demonstrates: in response to spurious calls for peace made by "reactionary" women, this 1871 tract flatly declares, "Reconciliation would be treason!" and then pitches an effort to rouse its besieged audience: "The final hour has struck. . . . The place of the workers is back at their barricades. . . . Action! Energy! The tree of liberty is best nourished by the blood of its enemies!" [1]

Like many manifestoes, the Commune tract embellishes the urgency of struggle through a variety of conventions: angry rejections of half-

---

[1] From "Manifeste du Comité Central de l'Union des Femmes: pour la défense de Paris et les soins aux blessés," May 6, 1871. In Clarétie, 2:440. All translations are my own unless otherwise noted. According to Gay L. Gullickson, the calls for peace were posted anonymously by a *groupe de citoyennes* whose appeal "presented women as united across class if not across geographical lines" (127).

measures, demands for immediate action, and a call to take to the streets. More than a century later, a 1993 manifesto by the Lesbian Avengers of New York uses these same tropes and gestures, albeit in a different key: their "Dyke Manifesto," a polemic against the Christian Right, deplores conciliatory efforts by "straight-acting 'gay people'" and warns, in increasingly bold and exclamatory typeface, "We have no desire to win a battle if it means losing the war. **Now's the time to fight back and fight forward. . . . Join the struggle, take the streets** . . . 1000's OF ANGRY DYKES CAN'T BE WRONG — AND WON'T GIVE IN. EVER." [2] For the Lesbian Avengers, as for the Communards, conciliation is tantamount to treason; dykes too will fight as if to nourish the tree of liberty.

The example of these two manifestoes points up the iterable structure and rhetoric of the form: throughout its historical transformations, the manifesto has shaped passionate political address as a genre at once intelligible and intransigent. Yet it would be a mistake to see the form simply as a vehicle for complaints of all stripes; far from being no more than the scaffolding for expressions of angry dissent, the manifesto's formal contours actually produce and intensify the urgency of its particular imperatives. They do so in part by activating the symbolic force of the form's role in earlier political confrontations: to write a manifesto is to announce one's participation, however discursive, in a history of struggle against oppressive forces. The form must be understood therefore as more than "plain talk": the manifesto is a complex, convention-laden, ideologically inflected genre. It is part of an overdetermined history of modernity that involves the emergence of public spheres and the rise of the modern state. More specifically, manifestoes proliferate at the cloverleafs of class war, gender politics, ethnic identification, and national struggle. In this chapter, therefore, I propose to survey the shape of the genre not only as a formal entity with distinctive features, but also as a historical force in the myriad challenges mounted within and against Western modernity.

My aim in the pages that follow is to sketch a historical backdrop against which to read what will ultimately be the signal relationship addressed in this book: that between the manifesto form and the modernist cultural period. For it is in modernism that Western anxieties about modernity receive their fullest aesthetic treatment. Various familiar critiques of modernity — with its attendant faith in "progressive" democratic reforms and technological innovations — were leveled explicitly in the

---

[2] "Out against the Right: The Dyke Manifesto," ca. 1993. I am grateful to Richard Mohr for bringing this manifesto to my attention and lending me his copy.

work of groups such as the British modernists, continental dadaists, and surrealists. In the same period, however, even those avant-garde groups that enthusiastically embraced the promises of a technologically advanced culture—such as the futurists and constructivists—nearly always modified their faith in modern futurity with a clause of doubt: the spoils of modernity, it was understood, would accrue to those powers that best harnessed the technological means of production. For all of these modernist groups, in other words, the variegated fabric of modernity was spun on a loom of uncertainty. Modernity was a series of conditional promises that could be fully honored only in the future tense; it involved continual deferral and proximal faith.

In order to trace the role of the manifesto in the modern public sphere, I explore a series of historical moments when public polemical writing was highly visible and relatively unimpeded; typically moments such as these occur just at the breakup of periods of political censorship or repression. In this chapter I begin by using examples offered in tracts produced by Diggers and Levellers in the decade 1640–50 in England, a period widely acknowledged, since Christopher Hill's study *The World Turned Upside Down*, to be an era of diastolic public dissent, and one that marks a brief span of relative freedom in English print in an otherwise strictly censored era.[3] By focusing on the use of the manifesto's signature pronoun "we," I aim to suggest how the entity soon to be known as "we the people" developed in conjunction with the new genres of public declaration, and how the public performance of "we" in polemical tracts provided an edge of urgency that was sharply at odds with the gradualist agenda of political modernity. This path leads me to a discussion of the conflicting imperatives of universalism as they are played out in the manifesto form, and finally, at the other end of the modern period, to a few examples of the polemical refocusing of universalism that took place at the turn of the twentieth century by modernists who used the manifesto to ironize the overextended claims of "the modern." But before I turn to these more con-

---

[3] See Hill 1972, 17 and passim. Stephen Toulmin calls these the decades of the European "politics of certainty," when the issues of "certainty, rational consensus, and necessity, which the 16th-century skeptics had left as a challenge to philosophy," became the centerpiece of a general intellectual "Quest for Certainty" which was manifest in the "shift within philosophy, away from practical issues to an exclusive concern with the theoretical—by which local, particular, timely, and oral issues surrendered their centrality to issues that were ubiquitous, universal, timeless, and written" (69–70). It is tempting to see the development and increasing public use of a hybrid form like the manifesto at this time as part of an early rhetorical response to the paradigm shift from humanist skepticism to Enlightenment rationalism. For the form characteristically retains the humanist concern with individual cases—the situatedness of local, particular, historically nuanced events—while appealing to the (then) emergent categories of abstract political principles.

textualized analyses of the form's use, I want first to offer a formal overview of the manifesto.

## Locating the Manifesto

In characterizing the manifesto as a "genre," I wish to preserve the broadest possible sense of that term, which I take to be one that describes groups of texts whose similarities fluctuate into differences with changing historical pressures and reading practices. I have no wish to produce a definitive profile of "the manifesto," secured by taxonomies of conventions and modalities. Such an endeavor would be sharply limiting in any case, since in the first place it would obscure the particular historical conditions that make possible ideological readings of individual manifestoes, and in the second place the term "manifesto" has itself taken on wide valences in our culture. The category has included such disparate texts and acts as Wordsworth's Preface to *Lyrical Ballads,* Newt Gingrich's *To Renew America,* the Unabomber's forty thousand–word treatise, and Andre Agassi's tennis game.[4] In 1989 Tom Wolfe called his puffy essay on "the new social novel" a manifesto, but by contrast, a year later, the Asian and Pacific Students Association did not call their extraordinary manifesto by that name. The term is often used retroactively to identify a text's foundational status—the 1912 imagism tracts, for example, or Luther's Ninety-five Theses. "Manifesto" may be shorthand for a text's particular stridency of tone, as with polemical editorial writing or grandstanding letters to the editor; in these and many other instances the term refers both to the form and to the passional state (frustration, disappointment, aggressive resolve) that precedes or engenders the text. To call a text a manifesto is to announce ahead of time its ardent disregard for good manners and reasoned civility.[5] The term's vagueness extends even to the group of texts explicitly bearing the title "manifesto," which by itself does not distinguish among uses of the form that are utopian, political, or artistic.[6]

In spite of the remarkable range of practices signified by the term, it is nevertheless valuable, at least initially, to examine the manifesto form

[4]Robin Finn, *New York Times* September 11, 1995, B1: "With the sunshine blazing off his three earrings and his opponent in abject surrender to his three-set manifesto, Andre Agassi, unseeded but far from unsung, brought his remedial United States Open run to a crashing crescendo today by trouncing Michael Stich, 6–1, 7–6 (7–5), 7–5."

[5]One of the more pungent examples of this phenomenon in recent years comes from a senior scholar writing on the state of English studies, Cary Nelson's *Manifesto of a Tenured Radical.*

[6]See Meyer for a discussion of these three categories of manifestoes. I take up his thesis briefly in Chapter 5.

generically, though with the aim of finding a series of family resemblances rather than identifying a common set of fingerprints.[7] Bakhtin remarked that wherever there is a style there is a genre (66), and it is certainly the case that the manifesto is best known through its style—though it may also be the case that the only uniform convention among manifestoes is a particular hortatory rhetorical style. This it draws from its constitutive discourses, which include, among others, the discourses of religious prophecy and chiliasm (or millennialism); the martial language of war or siege; and the forensic mode of persuasive rhetoric. The history of the form helps to account for this eclecticism: in seventeenth-century Italy "manifesto" could refer to a document that publicized military intent or sovereign will, whereas a century earlier in that country "manifesto" named a document refuting anonymous character assaults in academic communities (Battaglia, 692). From the twelfth century forward the French word *manifestation* denoted the theological principle of divine revelation, and this concept was a driving force behind the influence of lay "prophets" in seventeenth-century England: to show "proofs" (also an *OED* definition) of Christ's manifest presence was to anchor idiosyncratic revelations in the new systematic rationalist style.[8] That theological use of "manifesto" can be found, for example, in a nineteenth-century American religious manifesto, which also attaches to the Reformation tradition of plain speech: "The following sheets have been written in great plainness and familiarity," begins the author of MANIFESTO, or A Declaration of the Doctrines and Practice of the Church of Christ, "as usefulness and information have been more studied than elegance of style or even systematic order" (Dunlavy, 1).[9] In fact, this particular manifesto's eschewal of rhetorical ornament is characteristic of a large number of manifestoes. Particularly after the form's emergence, early in the French Revolution, as the preeminent organ of counter-statist dissent, the manifesto's rhetorical mode of directness—

[7] I take the metaphor of "family resemblance" from Wittgenstein's discussion of language games in *Philosophical Investigations:* in examining what precisely constitutes a "game," says Wittgenstein, we are bound to find "a complicated network of similarities overlapping and criss-crossing." So it is with my exploration of the manifesto, insofar as I also want to characterize the similarities among various kinds of manifestoes as "family resemblances"; what Wittgenstein teaches us about the connections among games obtains as well for similarities among manifestoes: "the various resemblances between members of a family: build, features, colour of eyes, gait, temperament, etc. etc. overlap and criss-cross in the same way" (32).

[8] See Darko Suvin's discussion of this etymology (2–3). See also Hill 1972, chap. 6, "A Nation of Prophets."

[9] See Londa Schiebinger for an account of the post-Enlightenment rhetorical shift in English scientific discourse from ornamental rhetoric (associated with France and with "the feminine") to facticity, scientism, and plain language.

its deployment of a declarative, passionate voice—underscored the emphasis, in revolutionary discourse, on "transparent" communications between citizens. If truth was written on the human heart for all to read, as Danton and others averred, then rhetorical complexity could be and frequently was equated with forms of secretive counterrevolutionary sentiments. Sansculottes brooked no distinction between private and public forms of goodness; all corners of the good citizen's life should be available for mass republican approval. So a genre like the manifesto, which frames its declarations with assurances of unobstructed rhetorical clarity—Jefferson's "self-evident" truths, or the radical London Democratic Association's 1838 "oath of the patriot . . . not taken in secret upon a book—but engraven[ed] upon the heart and proclaimed in the face of heaven and before men" (8), or the Fourth International's resolve "to call things by their right names; to speak the truth to the masses, no matter how bitter it may be"[10]—such a genre functions for these and for other revolutionaries as a mouthpiece to channel self-adjudicating political truths.

Linked with the form's passion for truth-telling is its staging of fervid, even violent, rage. David Graham Burnett has offered the thesis that "manifesto" derives etymologically from a Latin composite of *manus* and *fectus*, or "hostile hand" (44), and this translation acknowledges the nascent fury embodied in the form: like a fist striking through the scrims of civic order, the manifesto aims to challenge false conciliation in the name of a truth that fills the hearts and minds of its putative constituents. And it seeks to assure its audience—both adherents and foes—that those constituents can and will be mobilized into the living incarnation of the unruly, furious expression implied in the text. The manifesto is, in other words, a genre that gives the appearance of being at once both word and deed, both threat and incipient action.

In challenging the dominant forces against which it arrays itself, the manifesto deploys several characteristic conventions. While many of these conventions depend on the local contexts that give rise to individual manifestoes, there are three argumentative gestures that appear frequently. First, the manifesto often fashions a foreshortened, impassioned, and highly selective history which chronicles the oppression leading to the present moment of crisis. Sometimes this narrative is explicit and detailed, as it is in the carefully plotted pages of the Communist Manifesto, or in the eloquent concluding chapter of *The Wretched of the Earth* by Frantz Fanon. At other

---

[10] Quoted on masthead of *1917: Journal of the International Bolshevik Tendency*, Toronto (1994–96); see also *Manifesto: International Committee of the Fourth International*.

times the historicizing narrative is accomplished in rapid shorthand, as in the opening sentence of the 1969 "Redstockings Manifesto": "After centuries of individual and preliminary political struggle, women are uniting to achieve their final liberation from male supremacy" (272). Another oft-employed convention involves the forceful enumeration of grievances or demands or declarations which cast a group's oppression as a struggle between the empowered and the disempowered, or between the corrupt and the sanctified, or between usurpers and rightful heirs. The numbered lists in which these demands are often presented convey a specific rhetorical force: the parataxis of a list—its refusal of mediated prose or synthesized transitions—enhances the manifesto's descanting imperative. The 1967 "NOW Bill of Rights," for example, moves relentlessly from one diverse demand to another—maternity rights, tax deductions, reproductive control, and so forth—until it accrues the force of an unconditional mandate. A third convention makes use of epigrammatic, declarative rhetoric which directly challenges the named oppressor—be it as vague as "the bourgeoisie" or as specific as "the king of England"—while uniting its audience in an exhortation to action. This is the mode in which a Commune manifesto urges the soldiers of Versailles to defect from the Thiers forces and join the cause of the Communards: "Let the aristocrats, the privileged, the hangmen of humanity defend themselves . . . Quit your ranks!" [11]

By alternating among the discourses of history, logic, and prophecy, the manifesto aims to legitimate its revised historical perspectives, its insistence on new hierarchies of power, and its newly invigorated metaphors that help to create new enunciative positions within ideology.[12] In shifting the cultural position of a marginalized group, the manifesto yields an alternative historical narrative, one that foregrounds the group's grievances and thereby struggles squarely within but also in opposition to a culture's foundational narratives. "Our history is the unthought chapter in your history," declares the typical manifesto to its opponents, "and now your history will be justly superseded by our unfolding future."

Indeed, the manifesto's "history" functions more like myth than like empirical historiography; as Claude Abastado puts it, the manifesto "undoes time and redoes history"(6).[13] In its impulse to mythography, it cre-

[11] "Commune de Paris: Le Peuple de Paris aux Soldats de Versailles," in Clarétie, 2:568.
[12] For a discussion of the use value of new metaphors, see W. J. T. Mitchell, chap. 6, on Marx's "camera obscura" and "fetish"; Berman on the Communist Manifesto's metaphors of nakedness and sorcery; and Suvin for a broad discussion of the role of metaphor in the Communist Manifesto.
[13] See Abastado for an account of the manifesto's temporal qualities. My formal understanding of the manifesto is generally indebted to this brief, concise essay.

ates a simulacrum of rupture in the dominant political order. By revising history in the manner of chiliastic prophecy, by placing a group's apocalyptic present tense at the fulcrum of a self-ordaining future, the manifesto breaks up statist versions of "progress" that justify modernity's historical narratives. What the dominant order calls "progress," the manifesto aims to expose as aberrancy or mythopoesis or hegemonic opportunism; to what the dominant order relies on as "the real," "the natural," "the thinkable," the manifesto counters with its own versions of "the possible," "the imaginable," and "the necessary." Thus the manifesto both generates and marks a break in history: it is both a trace and a tool of change. A 1922 manifesto by Mexican artists illustrates the subtlety of this double move: "We proclaim that this being the moment of social transition from a decrepit to a new order, the makers of beauty must invest their greatest efforts in the aim of materializing an art valuable to the people."[14] Laying their fingers on the pulse of the new world—"the moment of social transition"—the manifesto's revolutionary artisans mark the artistic praxis that will *create* that new world.

## Diggers and Levellers

The manifesto's conventions help a group to script its identity in opposition to a more loosely conceived and descriptively rendered "other" because the form offers a textual field for the selective declaration of beliefs and the formation of principles, be they individualist, sectional, or statist. Later in this chapter I have more to say about the production of identity in the manifesto; for now I want to touch briefly on statist and anti-statist uses of the form during the early years of the English Commonwealth.

Historically, manifestoes and related forms appear most often in clusters around those political crises that involve definitions of citizenship and political subjecthood. England in the 1640s and 1650s constitutes one of the earliest of these historical conjunctures. In G. E. Aylmer's words, "No where else before the 1760s or even perhaps before 1789 do we find the combination of radical journalism and pamphleteering, ideological zeal, political activism, and mass organization that prevail in England from 1646–49" (quoted in Dow, 32). The radical texts produced by the Levellers and Diggers in these years—the former group agitating for political reform, the latter for agrarian and economic reform—addressed centrally

---

[14] "Manifesto Issued by the Syndicate of Technical Workers, Painters, and Sculptors, Mexico City, 1922." In Chipp, 462.

the problem of sovereign authority, challenging implicitly and sometimes explicitly the tenet that sovereign authority could legitimately reside in a "body" other than that of the people. Henry Parker's radical assertion in 1642 that "power is originally inherent in the people" (quoted in Dow, 17) is echoed to some extent in virtually all of the Leveller and Digger writings. At the same time, however, writers of these dissenting tracts took care to position themselves squarely within the evolving contours of the new republic: they wrote, in other words, not as external critics but as potential participants in a nascent commonwealth, and all of their tracts bear the marks of their struggles to modulate between the voice of passive obedience and the demands of active citizenship.

The Digger movement of 1649–50 was a rural, radical, and short-lived response to the enclosure laws and the widespread poverty and starvation generated thereby. Shaped by the writings and teachings of Gerrard Winstanley, the Digger project envisioned poor commoners "as a national class, not a local group," and aimed to bring them together "in a non-hierarchical agrarian communal praxis," in the words of James Holstun (172). Winstanley asserted that the widespread rural destitution that prevailed after the failed harvest of 1648 could be alleviated only by the poor's cultivation of "waste" land and commons for their own use. His proposal amounted to a form of agrarian communism, one that drew its rhetorical strength from contemporary developments in natural rights ideology. The earth was a "common treasury"[15] bestowed by God for use by all men and women; Winstanley maintained that "the meaning of freedom [lay] in the unrestricted right to use the earth" (quoted in Hopton, 5). The considerable scope of the threats posed by the Digger movement to post-feudalist and early capitalist tenets of property ownership were quickly perceived by the ruling classes, and the movement was swiftly and brutally suppressed. Diggers were arrested, their houses pulled down, their property destroyed, and their communities dispersed; the government justified its actions with the argument that common lands were traditionally the property of nobility—although, Diggers argued, the king who had granted those lands was now deposed, and any aristocratic rights to

[15] Robert Coster's tract "A Mite Cast into the Common Treasury: or, Queries propounded (for all men to consider of) by him who desireth to advance the work of publick Community" (December 18, 1649; rpt. in Hopton, 11–13) takes the form of five questions, four answers, and two proposals concerning ownership and distribution of land. The answer to the first question—whether all men should not be free to "enjoy the earth"—describes Creation as "a common Treasury of Livelihood for all" (11–12). "Common" is used ingeniously to refer to three separate but imbricated entities in this tract: common people, common ground (literally, the earth), and "commons," the name describing land appropriated illegally by the nobility.

common property had been "cut off with the king's head," as Winstanley put it (quoted in Hill 1975, 27).

At the height of their production, Digger songs, poems, "queries," "requests," and declarations all maintain a qualified tone of humility and take pains to align the Digger community rhetorically with godliness. At the same time, however, they display the complex negotiations that the Diggers sought to undertake between a position of obedience to the new (and still unstable) republic and a critique of its deviance from holy law. A declaration by the Buckinghamshire Diggers is representative in this regard.[16] On one level, the declaration defers to the ostensibly progressive aims of the state in the wake of Charles I's execution four months earlier: "We have great encouragement from this present *Parliament*, by making of those two excellent Lawes, the one to cast out *Kingly Power*, and the other to make us all a free people" (Hopton, 32). This deference is continually offset, however, by the Diggers' scorn for the republic's continued tolerance of nobility, that is, "Lords of Mannors" who "will allow us none of the earth whilst we are alive, but onely when we are dead, they will afford us just as much as will make the length of our graves, because they cannot then keep it from us" (Hopton, 31). Such an intolerable contradiction at the heart of the republic leads the Diggers to impugn the Parliament along with the aristocracy, and to position themselves in their tracts, by contrast, as the purest representatives of God's voice on earth.[17]

The filiation of the voice of the people both to the will of God and to natural law's "deracinating power" (Holstun, 176) undergirds the revolutionary call that is repeated through "The Diggers Song," and indeed throughout subsequent historical moments of popular rebellion, especially the French Revolution: that is, the call to "stand up."[18]

> Your houses they pull down, stand up now, stand up now,
> Your houses they pull down, stand up now.
> Your houses they pull down to fright poor men in town,
> But the gentry must come down, and the poor shall wear the crown.
> Stand up now, Diggers all. (Hopton, 27)

[16] "A Declaration of the grounds and Reasons, why we the poor Inhabitants of the Parrish of *Iver* in *Buckinghamshire*, have begun to digge and mannure the common and wast Land belonging to the aforesaid Inhabitants, and there are many more that gives consent" (May 1, 1650). In Hopton, 31–34.

[17] This alignment of the people—especially poor people—with uncorrupted truth is amplified by the Diggers' use of a convention in English Protestant discourses of dissent that link the English monarchy and aristocracy with six hundred years of illegal Norman rule.

[18] Note, for example, the epigram for the radical *Révolutions de Paris* (1794): "The Great appear such only because we are on our knees: Let us stand up!" (Gilchrist and Murray, 14).

Even as this song concludes with the Diggers' promise to "conquer them by love," the image of the poor rising up to crown themselves reads somewhat more threateningly as an adumbration of mob action. By the 1650s the argument that "the origin of government lies in the consent of the people" had gained some ground; nevertheless, as F. D. Dow notes, "republicans of many hues still hesitated to concede that *active* political rights should be widely dispersed and preferred instead to uphold a distinction between the 'few' and the 'many' in the actual working of government" (10). Popular actions signaled a blurring of the hierarchy of the few and the many, but Diggers' tracts actually threatened to displace the distinction altogether, reflecting the tenets of the anti-hierarchical religious revolution that framed the creation of the Commonwealth, and hence implying that "the few" could never adequately represent the numberless poor. As if to underscore those infinite numbers, the imprimatur on Diggers' prose tracts includes not only the signatures of local inhabitants, but also inevitably a reference to the countless "many" who give their consent to the movement.[19]

Equally important, the tracts represent the Diggers *to themselves:* these are group-defining texts not addressed as petitions to a sovereign ruler but, rather, offered as dialogues and catechisms and songbooks by the poor to the poor. I will have more to say about this distinction—between petition on the one hand and self-proclamation or anthem, as it were, on the other—but for now I want to suggest that the distinction itself points to a turn in rhetorical forms at the time, one that is tied directly to the emergence of an organized popular voice. In Holstun's analysis, Digger texts (and specifically Winstanley's writings) principally aimed to "win over a rural proletariat (and other sympathetic groups) to a programme of mass political action" (186); if this is so, then we may well recognize in them a trait that characterizes the audience-forming manifestoes of the next century. Moreover it is helpful to notice that the "we" of the Diggers' tracts is less a textual entity than an organic one, and it is therefore less dependent on literacy than on class alliance. The Digger "we" expands as it circulates through the sites of Digger insurgency—Surrey, Wellingborough, Iver, Cox Hall, Enfield. Digger songs proclaim, in a characteristic voice of mani-

---

[19] A Northampton declaration, for example, bears the imprimatur of "those that have subscribed, and hundreds more that give Consent." ("A Declaration of the Grounds and Reasons why we the Poor Inhabitants of the Town of *Wellinborrow,* in the County of *Northampton,* have begun and give consent to dig up, manure and sow Corn upon the Common, and waste ground, called *Bareshanke* belonging to the Inhabitants of *Wellinborrow*" [March 12, 1650; rpt. in Hopton, 29–30].)

festic immediacy, that "we must be bold / now for to claim our right," for "the time, I say, it is now come."[20]

Diggers also went by the name "True Levellers," a moniker reflecting Winstanley's belief that "natural rights"—for which Levellers agitated in their petitions and proclamations—were rooted fundamentally in agrarian rights. In contrast to the rural poor who constituted the main body of Diggers, the Levellers were, in the words of Nigel Smith, "a literate and skilled urban group, the most socially mobile part of the early modern population"; theirs was "the world of the 'middling sort,' which bridged the gentry and the labouring poor" (144). Under the unofficial leadership of John Lilburne, Levellers produced textual polemics that spoke even more explicitly (and more explicitly theoretically) than those of the Diggers for "the people," in the political cause of republican representation. Like the Diggers (and like many antecedent groups participating in the long tradition of religiously grounded agitation), the Levellers articulated their cause to divine authority; but unlike the Diggers, they mounted arguments that moved them closer to a secular, rationalist formulation of individual rights.[21]

In the Levellers' most famous manifesto, "Englands New Chains Discovered" (February 1649, in Haller and Davies, 156–70), Lilburne surveys the broken promises of Parliament, details the stifling control of its aristocratic and conservative factions, and enumerates proposals for parliamentary reform. In the words of William Haller and Godfrey Davies, the force of this manifesto—indeed, of all the Levellers' tracts—derived not just from their collective status as the expression "of a party rather than the expression of any single mind" (19), but especially from the political dilemma into which it forced Parliament: "The Levellers set themselves up to 'give a rule' to the Long Parliament, and that body had either to concede their right to do so—which is to say to grant to their kind of organized opposition and complaint a place and function in the state—or to repress them" (36). I would add that the forms in which the Levellers presented their critical commentary—forms that were by turns legalistic, vatic, analytical, and imperative—amounted to radical transformations of previous, more ameliorated forms of popular political dissent which had drawn as a matter of course on the rhetoric of passive obedience.

The example of the petition, mentioned earlier, was perhaps the most prominent of these traditionally sanctioned forms. The typical petition of-

---

[20] From "A hint of that FREEDOM which shall come, When the Father shal Reign alone in his Son" (Surrey Diggers, 1650; rpt. in Hopton, 25–26).

[21] See Dow, chap. 4.

ten included a self-abasing request addressed to an authoritative figure or body; it made use of a distinct set of pronouns referring to its own authors as "they" (*not* "we") and the royal or parliamentary addressee as "you," or "your most excellent majesty," as demonstrated in the concluding lines of what is perhaps the most famous seventeenth-century petition, the "Petition of Right": "They [the authors] most humbly pray of your most excellent Majesty . . . their rights and liberties according to the laws and statutes of this realm" (84). Even by the year of this petition's publication, 1628, the rhetorical burden borne by the petition form had begun to shift, as evidenced by J. P. Kenyon's note that "there was some doubt at the time, and there still is doubt, precisely what the Petition [of Right] was, and whether it was equivalent to a statute or superior to it" (60). But when the Levellers made use of the form in 1648, they did so in a way that exceeded all of its customary conventions. Their ironically titled "Humble Petition" to Parliament reads like a prelude to the last straw: "The truth is," begins the headnote to a list of twenty-seven criticisms, "we have long expected things of another nature from you" (151). At the close of the list comes a veiled threat: "If all this availeth nothing, God be our Guide, for men sheweth us not a way for our preservation" (155). Gone is the deference and humility so legible in previous uses of the genre; in their place stands the confident "we" of a new civic voice making demands. In this and in other tracts, the Levellers' form of complaint envisions a new kind of political subject—a "citizen"—precisely insofar as it creates an unprecedented *performative* verbal medium in which such subjects could recognize themselves.

The question of genre—the question of how an unrecognized group striving for legitimation frames its dissent within a broader interpretative political context—is of special importance during these years. Although in 1648 "the people" were not yet acknowledged as a distinct and active political force, nor yet had legal status been granted to groups organized to speak on behalf of the people, the fact was that dissenters were assembling and publishing tracts under the presumption of freedom of expression in the new republic. Smith characterizes the Levellers as self-described descendants of "earlier transgressive exploiters of print" (141), and Haller and Davies note that "the Levellers' right to speak for that abstraction, the *populus* of timeworn political theory, could be questioned, but not their ability to speak to and for the multitude which under their leadership now believed itself to be the people" (37).[22]

---

[22] Ann Marie McEntee outlines the case of women Levellers who petitioned with increasing zeal in these years. She suggests that the right to petition, granted irrevocably in Magna Carta,

It would seem, however, that whether or not "the people" had a voice, they had begun to emerge as the animated subjects in new rhetorical forms: a genre like the manifesto accorded them a discursive voice that drew its power from the force of "the many" for which it claimed to speak, as well as from its dependence on the emergent languages of the republic itself, that is, the languages of contestation, debate, and liberal freedoms. Indeed, the *form* of the Levellers' written dissent appears to have been a matter of considerable concern for the Parliament to which it was addressed. The parliamentary body that responded to Lilburne's charge, in "The Humble Petition," that Levellers had been denied the right of petition quarreled with what seemed to them to be his misuse of the term: "A Petition is to set forth your grievances," it observed, "and not to give a rule to the Legislative Power; if you meane it shall be an *Edict*, which you must compose, and the Parliament must verifie, call it no more a *Petition*" (quoted in Haller and Davies, 36). This statement is as much a repudiation of the Levellers' rhetorical *forms*—neither petitions nor edicts—as it is a remonstration against their impertinence. The Levellers may or may not have intended to "give a rule" to Parliament; but it is clear that the forms they crafted gave a shape to dissent and discussion and criticism while legitimating their speakers as representative members of an active *populus*.

Thus Parliament's nervous insistence on the formal distinctions between a petition and an edict can be understood, from our perspective, as the index of an important shift in public discourse. The genre that Parliament refuses to recognize, but that we may identify as a precursor of the emergent modern form of the manifesto, provides a speaking position for the evolving voice of the people as political participants in republican discourse. The genre's desultory appearance in this revolutionary period, and its more refined and widespread use in the subsequent revolutionary period of the 1780s and 1790s, coincides temporally with the slow development in England and the more rapid consolidation in France of the institutions of a deliberative bourgeois public sphere. Indeed it may be the case that the public sphere was pioneered by tracts such as the Levellers' manifestoes, which marked the "momentous" and acutely public turn in English history to "political theory based on natural rights" (Hill 1961, 179). Levellers' tracts were connected to the dissent issuing from Cromwell's New

gradually evolved, in public perception, into a right to make demands. "It was perhaps Parliament's failure to deal with disaffection," she writes, "that solidified the petitioners' self-perception as a politically powerful collective which had the right to admonish its legislative representatives" (108).

Model Army; just as crucially, they provoked discussion and won support from the petit bourgeois classes of apprentices and small masters in London (Hill 1961, 128). Jürgen Habermas has shown that the public spheres in Europe were animated by just these class members, "private people" from nascent bourgeois strata "coming together as a public" (1989, 27); when debating matters of public authority, they used a polemically charged form of "reason" to challenge the variegated force of unbridled sovereign domination. Such an institutionalized mediating zone between, on the one hand, the private spheres of civil society and family and, on the other hand, the zone of state authority would depend for its coherence on a core of participants versed in ideological challenges to absolute authority. In short, it might be said that the deliberative public sphere that marked the early proliferations of political modernity created new speaking positions and points of articulation for the writers and readers of dissenting manifestoes previously developed by groups such as the Levellers. The manifesto as we know it from the French Revolution forward, then, might be said to be both cause and effect of the maturation of the public sphere.

## The Public "We"

Especially significant in this regard is the way the manifesto as a form legitimates the polemical popular voice by propping it retroactively on republican principles: vox populi is held out in the manifesto as the lowest common denominator of power, and a government that denies its own power base by ignoring or repressing the criticism and challenges of this, its most fundamental constituency, risks delegitimation (at least within the script of the manifesto) on its own terms. On this reading, republican government becomes oxymoronic the moment that it misrecognizes its potential citizens and shades into antidemocratic elitism. Whether in the form of an edict or a petition, then, the Levellers' dissent developed a self-sustaining (because rhetorically self-evident) discourse of human emancipation: natural rights, once conceptualized, are nearly impossible to call back; the democratic lessons of the republic, once taught, cannot be unlearned.

The power of the people's voice—what will become, in the French Revolution, the absolute domain of "popular opinion"—is produced and deployed in the manifesto's use of the pronoun "we." Indeed, especially as manifesto-like forms gain wide intelligibility during the French Revolution, "we" becomes not only the nomenclature of a speaking group, but also a rhetorical device to *evoke* audiences, and to mark the distance in ideological ground between those created audiences and their scripted oppressor. With the proliferating discourses of radicalism in the eighteenth century, the discursive terrain in the manifesto between "we" and "you" or between "we" and "they" becomes increasingly uninhabitable: "we" (i.e., the signatories of or consenters to the manifesto) occupy a public position of high moral ground (even if only in the subjunctive mood), in part by being rhetorically and semantically opposed in a Manichaean fashion to "they," the blind opponents, who act as a textual repository for corruption or vice. The manifesto's creation of new audiences occurs, in other words, around an identification with virtue (in one or another of its many encryptions) and its oppression by hegemonic forces. As we shall see in Chapter 2, the rhetorical grid of virtue grounds the absolute character of revolutionary discourse after 1789.

I do not intend to imply that the manifesto magically creates new subjects and new subject positions simply by exploiting the elasticity of the word "we." The manifesto is not always—indeed, not often—to be understood as a causal agent in history, and though it assumes the voice of vatic authority, it does not create new social conditions by fiat. My claim for the genre is considerably more modest: the manifesto occupies a distinct generic space in the arena of public discourse, and thereby aspires to a concrete form of cultural work even if it only rarely performs that work. More specifically, the manifesto provides a foothold in a culture's dominant ideology by creating generic speaking positions; the nascent audience interpellated by "we" is then held together as a provisional constituency through a linguistic contract. The potential audience of this contractual "we" occupies the position of either supporting or rejecting the manifesto as a representative text.[23] That part of the potential audience withholding support ceases to be hailed in the "we" of an audience, and in effect takes up the position of the antagonistic "you" against whom the manifesto's charges are pressed. The part of the potential audience that assents becomes the "true" audience and forms an affective identification with the manifesto's "we."[24]

[23] This "we" works like Lyotard's denotative utterance, which is to say the "we" in the manifesto occupies the position of "knower" in a speech act (see Lyotard, 13). See also Seyla Benhabib's critique of Lyotard's "pragmatics" of language (112–16), wherein she reminds us that Lyotard's understanding of performative utterances ignores J. L. Austin's distinction between illocutionary and perlocutionary speech acts. I would argue that the manifesto's "we" makes use of a perlocutionary mode insofar as it achieves its effects *by* saying something.

[24] This may seem familiar enough as a conventional polemical configuration; cf. A. J. Greimas and J. Courtés's description of the nature of most narrative as "polemical" insofar as it frequently "set[s] forth together a subject and an anti-subject," and always presents "the figure of the opponent (animate or inanimate) . . . as a metonymic manifestation of the anti-subject" (239). In the

The use of "we" in forms that claim to speak for a constituency is per-haps more controversial now than ever before: control of the pronoun "we" lies at the heart of the debates that have surrounded identity politics and interpretive theory in the past several decades. Feminist and postcolo-nialist theorists in the late 1980s, for example, entered into an arduous round of discussions about the habitual misappropriations of "we," asking who is empowered and disempowered by various strategic deployments of the word. Of course, well before the politics of identity (which demand an accounting of who "we" are) met the Foucauldian injunction not to com-mit the indignity of speaking for others (thus demanding an accounting of what "speaking" is) in the late 1980s, the debates about the pronoun defined much of second-wave feminism from the 1960s onward, particu-larly with regard to pan-feminist tracts in which "we" is assumed to signify all women. Extrapolating and deconstructing the radical democratic promise of the phrase "we the people," groups long excluded from the *pop-ulus* promised by republican dispensations mounted campaigns for forms of civil rights and cultural recognition; in their efforts they simultaneously affirmed and challenged the idea that "we" could be given a specific con-tent. Thus, along with the mainstream civil rights movement's demand to be included in a national "we"—I, too, sing America—came varieties of identity politics that challenged the national "we" by asserting particularist senses of collectivity that could not be subsumed by civic nationalism. Within these identitarian movements, ethnic, feminist, and gay/lesbian, the internal logic of interrogating the status of the "we" quickly issued in a series of challenges to all notions of group identification: Who has the au-thority to designate membership in the group? Why should inclusion in the group—say, "woman"—take precedence over other possible identities and locations? If group identity is always a collective fiction, an imagined community, then on what grounds are some collective fictions better (and for what purposes) than others? Although these questions are both unan-swered and unanswerable, one thing seems clear from the past few decades of debate: the pronouns of public declaration are particularly elusive con-structions.

Émile Benveniste, for example, has shown how "we" cannot be simply a "multiplication of identical objects" as its structure implies, since such a

---

discursive space between "us" and "other," meaning is, to borrow Michel Pecheux's phrase, "logi-cally stabilized" (639)—that is, unambiguous, resisting interpretation, proceeding according to the logic that if something is X, it cannot be Y. The resultant binarism in discourses so structured produces an evaluative system that privileges those characteristics claimed by "us."

formulation implies an impossible duplication of "I"s. Rather, "we" is "a *junction* between 'I' and the 'non-I,' no matter what the content of this 'non-I' might be. This junction forms a new totality which is of a very special type whose components are not equivalent: *in 'we' it is always 'I' which predominates since there cannot be 'we' except by starting with 'I' and this 'I'* dominates the 'non-I' quality by means of its transcendent quality. The presence of 'I' is constitutive of 'we' "(202; second emphasis added). "We," as it appears in the manifesto, therefore, suggests the consensus of a group, but this consensus is in fact largely the product of a pronominal sleight of hand, whereby "we" disguises the metonymic function of the small group of composite "I"s who claim to speak for a whole.

This is, of course, to imply that the "we" of a manifesto is an inherently colonizing construction. Manifestoes that lay claim to multivocality may in fact be primarily the work of one or two persons, or may speak with unearned authority for the many, and there are obvious advantages to a speaking position that is at best a shaky amalgamation. As we have seen, a "we" signed by the few but putatively supported by the many is empowered largely by its indeterminacy. An unspecified "we" denotes and affords participation, on the part of its interpellated subject(s), in a provisional community whose power is located in a potentially infinite constituency. "We" resonates with the suggestive power of the limitless, volatile masses; it is the secular version of the Christian "we" that levels hierarchy; it is a pronominal gesture toward both a limitless kinship and indomitable mass resolve.

## Now, Not Later

If the "we" of the manifesto derives power from indeterminacy, its political effects are unambiguously potent for federations and republics alike. In her meditation on revolution, Hannah Arendt discusses what is perhaps the central tenet of developing republics in the late eighteenth century: "A republic granted to every citizen the right to become 'a participator in the government of affairs,' the right to be seen in action. . . . [T]he principle out of which the [American] republic eventually was founded was present . . . in the 'mutual pledge' of life, fortune, and sacred honour, all of which, in a monarchy, the subjects would not 'mutually pledge to each other' but to the crown, representing the realm as a whole" (130). Arendt celebrates the American Declaration of Independence as an iconographic depiction of the republic's "mutual pledge": that document's "grandeur," she writes, consisted "not so much in its being 'an argument in support of an action' as in its being the perfect way for an action to appear in words" (130).

Arendt's figuration is provocative: the Declaration, which in many respects performs like a manifesto, is the textual image of a public body in action. The document encrypts the founding gesture of the republic—its mutual pledge—in a way that puts the pledge into perpetual motion, which is to say that by virtue of its particular textual code, the Declaration functions as a self-renewing performative speech act. In this respect the Declaration may be understood as a manifesto-like text, since manifestoes aim for just this kind of figural projection of action. Arendt puts a concrete cast to the figuration by avowing that "the power of the action [of pledging to the republic] is great enough to erect its own monument" (130). In the broader context of Arendt's argument, the Declaration marks irrevocably the triumph of republican consensus over monarchy's tyranny, but more particularly Arendt's enthusiasm for the "monumental" status of the Declaration of Independence stems from her belief that the American Revolution was unique in its aim *permanently* to transform political structures (as opposed to merely producing affective shifts in a projected revolutionary national character or persona). The document's value, on her reading, lies in the way in which its focus on institutional change downplays—and perhaps even deflates—revolution's volatility.

But this emphasis on the concrete transformation of institutions is not a characteristic shared by most manifestoes—quite the contrary, since manifestoes frequently operate as textual equivalents of violence, retort, and even political or aesthetic brinkmanship, all of which signal an inevitable and cumulative explosion of impatience in the face of repeated or long-standing abuses and broken promises. Far more often the rhetoric of the manifesto runs along lines that celebrate the randomness and unpredictability of change: let the flowers of revolution bloom, it urges; the old must be pulled down before the unimaginable new can take shape. Thus the very concept of an institutionalized manifesto may be in some sense oxymoronic.

Yet we need only to look at documents like the Communist Manifesto to see how easily the manifesto can slip between iconoclasm and iconography. Indeed, there are several ways in which the Declaration of Independence demonstrates the deceptive qualities of manifesto-like forms: although the document declares the righteous intent of its American constituency to found a republic, the fact remains that the Declaration's early constituency probably *already* occupies the hegemonic position the text proposes to secure. In other words, the Declaration may be the voice not of a harmed minority but rather of a consolidated and empowered majority, perhaps even the voice of hegemony. Jacques Derrida's discussion of the document's performativity in "Declarations of Independence" focuses this causal impasse from a different direction by asking whether the Declaration *states* or whether it *produces* independence—that is, whether the Declaration marks the fact that "the good people have already freed themselves in fact and are only stating the fact of this emancipation . . . [or whether] they free themselves at the instant of and by [*par*] the signature of this Declaration" (9). Derrida's attention to the indeterminacy of performativity (an issue that implicitly broaches the problem of solidarity between writers and readers) does not settle for us the question of the Declaration's rhetorical status, but it does bring us around to a proposition I offered earlier: like the Declaration, all manifestoes aim to *invoke* even as they *address* charged audiences. It must be noted, however, that the manifesto's creation of a radical audience frequently occurs with an urgency unremarked in Derrida's discussion: the manifesto is, after all, a text of radicalism which forges an audience through its efforts at affective and experiential intelligibility. That is, an audience crystallizes as the manifesto formulates and performs a future audience's experience of and response to oppression.

As an illustration of this performative capacity I offer the famous final lines from the Communist Manifesto: "Let the ruling classes tremble at a Communistic revolution. The proletarians have nothing to lose but their chains. They have a world to win. Working Men of All Countries, Unite!" Here Marx posits several simultaneous audiences (ruling class, proletarians, working men) *and* radicalizes the coalescent identity of its primary audience in one stroke.[25] The passage is performative in at least two of that term's contemporary theoretical senses: in J. L. Austin's sense, by implying a priori assent, it forecasts the unified class that it invokes; and in Judith Butler's sense, it produces a flexibly scripted *faux* identity for workers and non-workers uniting under hortatory radicalism.[26]

The iterability of the Communist Manifesto—itself an iteration of earlier manifestoes and revolutionary political tracts—is easily demonstrated in other manifestoes. For example, the "manifesto" of the London Democratic Association, which predates Marx's by a decade, concludes with the following lines: "Democrats of the North—**Organise! Organise!! Organise!!!** THE TOCSIN SOUNDS! STRIKE FOR UNIVERSAL SUFFRAGE!!!" Seventy years later the echo is heard in a 1909 Suffragette manifesto: "**The time for argument is past!** The time for action is come. THE WORKING WOMEN OF

---

[25] While it is impossible to say exactly who constitutes that primary audience, we may surmise that it is amalgamated around descriptions of experience or affect contained in the manifesto.
[26] See Austin, Lecture 1, and Butler, 128–141.

LONDON ARE AROUSED. The end of the long struggle for political existence is in view." In the 1912 avant-garde "Manifesto of the Futurist Woman," hortatory revolutionary discourse resonates similarly albeit in a different direction: "WOMEN, FOR TOO LONG YOU HAVE LOST YOUR WAY BETWEEN MORALS AND PREJUDICES. RETURN TO YOUR SUBLIME INSTINCT; RETURN TO VIOLENCE AND CRUELTY." A final example is Fanon's more somber and explicitly Marxian manifesto at the end of *The Wretched of the Earth:* "Come, then, comrades, it would be as well to decide at once to change our ways. We must shake off the heavy darkness in which we were plunged, and leave it behind. The new day which is already at hand must find us firm, prudent, and resolute."[27]

The repeating structure and locutions of these manifestoes—the generic components of the form's iterability—return us to the claim with which I opened this chapter: that to write a manifesto is to echo a history of struggle against dominant forces; it is to link one's voice to the countless voices of previous perpetual struggles. This participation is made possible by the form's capacity to serve as an ideological sign, in V. N. Volosinov's sense of that term. As a form of discourse aiming to speak for a group that has somehow been excluded from or unrepresented in the putatively inclusive deliberations of the public sphere, the manifesto takes up the function of a sign of sectional political strife. It is an *ideological* sign because it can be evoked in any number of struggles, on any number of sides; such "multiaccentuality" paradoxically contributes to a sign's stability, according to Volosinov (23), and in this case to the manifesto's stability as a sign of political combat, for the very term itself resonates on some level with past passional uses of the form.[28]

The very fact that the manifesto form has distinctive rhetorical and formal features dating from prior to the development of the bourgeois public sphere means that the form can be identified as a genre and as an ideologi-

[27] See "The London Democratic Association, To the Masses of Yorkshire About to Assemble En Masse to Demand their Rights," *The Northern Star,* October 13, 1838, 8; Women's Social and Political Union, "Votes for Women, New Movement: Manifesto," ca. 1909; Valentine de Saint-Point, "Manifesto of the Futurist Woman"; Fanon, 311.

[28] Peter Stallybrass takes up Volosinov's description of the sign's multiaccentuality in his analysis of the story cycle of Robin Hood—an analysis that bears on our own understanding of the manifesto's multiaccentuality. For Stallybrass, the meaning of the Robin Hood figure, which has been used by different classes at different historical moments (spanning seven centuries) for a variety of political objectives, "is not given at one originary moment; on the contrary, his meaning is produced and reproduced within the hegemonic process" (63). So, too, the manifesto, intersected by "differently oriented social interests" (Volosinov, 23), cannot be understood in any originary moment; but the variability of produced manifestoes is determined in part by the publicly constituted significance of its name ("the manifesto"), and especially by its characteristic discursive atavism.

cal sign—one that is stable, paradoxically, throughout its generic and passional variations. In the eighteenth century, however, the manifesto's prevalence and importance in bourgeois and radical discourses indicate that once the social conditions arose in which manifestoes could actually *reach* the putatively limitless, volatile public, then for our purposes the form had achieved the critical mass of historicity that allows us to see it retrospectively as the distinctive genre of modern social agonism. We may view the manifesto, in other words, as a touchstone in the history of political conflict in the modern period. The promises held out by the developmental narratives of modernity—promises of universal freedom, autonomy, equality, and inclusion—are reiterated and recast in political manifestoes of the eighteenth and nineteenth centuries as the broken promises of modernity. Each new manifesto in effect embellishes a long-standing diachronic narrative of exclusion and oppression; the cumulative narrative wrought by successive manifestoes serves as a rebuke to modernity's narratives of progress.

If we return for a moment to my examples of the manifesto's iterable structures and locutions, we may notice that they share a striking rhetorical characteristic that will help to expand an understanding of the manifesto's intimate relation to the narratives of modernity. In each example the manifesto closes with a resounding invocation of an apocalyptic present tense. *Now* is the time for action; *now* is the moment when history begins anew. Workers of the world must unite now; women of England must seize the reigns of their destiny now; the colonized peoples of Algeria must now begin to turn back the European tide. The past has been barbarically deforming, but it has led at long last to this millennial present; the inevitable violence that must attend the present moment of action is part of the painful but necessary parturition that issues in the birth of a utopian future of political equality. Faintheartedness therefore cannot be tolerated at this moment: the present conflict must be rigorously embraced.

This dramatic emphasis on *now* as a coherent moment in a well-defined political telos is intelligible from a variety of perspectives. As the linguistic mark that signals inevitability, it is a rhetorical trope associated with chiliastic discourse, wherein the advent of religio-political struggle catalyzes a preordained chain of events that will deliver the sublunary world to the divine realm of God. According to Stephen Toulmin, the advent of rhetorical chiliasm is coincident with the seventeenth-century installation of rationalist proofs and predictions and the decline of tolerant humanist skepticism. The secularization of this discourse in manifesto-like tracts involves the translation of transcendent inevitability into a naturalized narrative of political liberation leading to final, irrevocable, universal emancipation. Moreover, the emphasis on "now" in the manifesto is connected to the developing public spheres of modernity that form the contextual basis for the manifesto form. "Now," argues Homi Bhabha, marks both the continuous present tense of Western ideological regimes and the "lag-time" experienced by the colonial and postcolonial worlds for whom "the new" comes too late and only in ineffectual fragments.[29] If, as I have been suggesting, the manifesto is the genre of the broken promise—the genre that narrates the incongruous experiences of modernity by those whose needs are ignored or excluded in a political culture that promises equality and autonomy—then it must also be understood in relation to the public spheres where those promises are tendered.

Habermas argues that the bourgeois public sphere's employment of the language of deliberation and debate, drawn in part from the world of letters and cultural criticism, shaped its own discursive imperatives. The bourgeois character of the public sphere determined the manner and the rhetoric of its debates, so that a shared sense of liberal freedoms—equality, common interests in consensual law, a respect for formal and informal modes of expression stemming from the ideals of individual autonomy and unimpeded commerce, and so forth—helped to create the sense that public interchange resembled an organic nexus wherein the many came together out of a shared concern for the common good. In these languages of contestation and discussion, derived as they were from intellectual sources, a premium was placed on the maieutic movement of ideas and the critique of ideas; the "coffeehouse discussion," made familiar to us by Habermas as a representative site of the emergent bourgeois public sphere, is widely understood to be a discussion moving toward change rather than a form of absolutist demand for change. Therefore, while the manifesto may be understood as a form with deep ties to the bourgeois public sphere, it should also be stressed that the form's capacity for unyielding aggression marks its difference from (and its excess in relation to) the public sphere.[30]

For the manifesto eschews just this gradualist language of debate and reform. The insistence of manifesto rhetoric signifies an impatience with deliberative modes: "The time for argument is past," declares the typical manifesto; "no more talk: now it is time for action." In rejecting the model

[29] See Bhabha 1994, esp. chap. 12, "Conclusion: 'Race,' Time, and the Revision of Modernity."
[30] Habermas (1989) notes that "people's public use of their reason" in the public sphere encompassed the subtle German nuances of the term "reason" (*Rasonnement*): "simultaneously the invocation of reason and its disdainful disparagement as merely malcontent griping" (27).

of the coffeehouse argument—in challenging dialogue and deliberation by means of a "hostile hand"—the manifesto in effect rejects the neutralizing discursive forces of the public sphere, which always and everywhere move to subordinate a sectional group's specific demands to a shifting but nevertheless hegemonic formula of "universal good."[31] Universal good, the manifesto suggests, looks very different to those who have limited or ineffectual access to the coffeehouse and its class-marked discourses.[32] The "universal," moreover, is subject to revision.

The manifesto's critique of the limited scope of "the universal" and the form's impatience with the language of deliberation may be seen even more broadly as a challenge to the operative forms of universalism by which the bourgeois public sphere justifies its dominion. The discourses of the bourgeois public sphere assume as the hypothetical agent in their debates a universal subject, a citizen possessed of both rights and well-oiled critical faculties, whose imagined well-being acts as a model for the blueprints of social and political change. I want to propose that when the conditions of possibility emerged for an ideology of a universal subject with universal rights and sensibilities—that is, when political and economic developments in post-Enlightenment Europe generated the modern concepts of equality and rational autonomy—at this moment the manifesto appeared as a public genre geared to contesting or recalibrating the assumptions underlying a "universal subject." To put this in formulaic terms, I might say that where the universal subject is, there the manifesto shall be; for since the mid-seventeenth century the manifesto has acted out both an affirmation of and a challenge to universalism. On the one hand, the manifesto always displayed—indeed, performed—its indebtedness to the political developments of modernity that made possible the ideal of citizenship; as we have seen, the form was of a piece with the appearance of democratic cultural formations. On the other hand, the genre's whole raison d'être was to critique the uneven implementations of universalism—failures linked to what Habermas has characterized as bourgeois ideology's

[31] Chantal Mouffe's description of hegemonic sublations of sectional interests is relevant for an understanding of the manifesto's negotiation of hegemonic forces: "If hegemony is defined as the ability of one class to articulate the interest of other social groups to its own," it can occur when "the interests of these groups [are] articulated so as to neutralise them and hence to prevent the development of their own specific demands" (183), from the introduction to *Gramsci and Marxist Theory*.

[32] This topic has formed the center of many influential feminist discussions about Habermas's view of the bourgeois public sphere. I will have occasion to review several of these texts in Chapter 2. See, for example, Fraser, Landes, Eley, Schor, and Joan Wallach Scott 1992, 1995.

"overshooting of the mark,"[33] whereby bourgeois culture makes broad universalizing promises that it cannot possibly keep.

Neil Lazarus and his co-authors discuss this constitutive facet of bourgeois culture, this "overshooting," in their effort to demonstrate Habermas's insight that bourgeois ideology's failures are autotelic, insofar as those failures help to map out the unrealized normative ideals for "universalizing emancipation" (107). They quote from *Theory of Communicative Action* to demonstrate the line of Habermas's argument: the "normative contents" of bourgeois culture's "abstract and ahistorical ideas, overshooting as they do existing social realities, not only support a critically transforming practice by providing some initial guidelines, but also support an affirming and endorsing practice by providing a measure of idealistic transfiguration" (104). Thus bourgeois culture is necessarily inconsistent, offering more than it can possibly deliver—and, I might add, offering to the many what it can deliver to only the few. But however "normative" and ultimately therapeutic these excessive promises may be, they still provoke angry responses from forms such as the manifesto, which registers a group's impatience with a paper credit system of democratic ideals and demands instead that its audience be paid immediately in the coin of the realm.

Habermas's claim that the bourgeois public sphere is, in the words of Lazarus and his co-authors, "a site in which the exchange, not of commodities, but of arguments[,] produces universality as an immanent criterion and regulative norm" (102) may be pursued even further in connection with the manifesto form. For according to Habermas, there grows up within modernity a *critique* of modernity and its attendant structural ideals of universalism and reason: this critique he casts as a "200-year-old counterdiscourse inherent in modernity itself" which "set out from Kantian philosophy as an unconscious expression of the modern age and pursued the goal of enlightening the Enlightenment about its own narrow-mindedness" (1995, 302). If this is indeed the case—if modernity's hallmark absence of oligarchic authority leaves a void filled from the beginning by self-criticism—then it might shed further light on the function of the manifesto in the emergent bourgeois public sphere. I would argue that the concept of "counterdiscourse" of which Habermas speaks is immediately apposite to the manifesto form: the manifesto, with its chal-

[33] Lazarus et al. reiterate this term in their probing discussion, though I am tempted to recast the image as an *under*shooting of the mark: that is to say, modernity makes a target of grand promises, and its arrows consistently fall short.

lenges and threats and impatience, may be a persistent mode of modernity's inevitable counterdiscourse; but it may also be the form that *exceeds* and thereby challenges the neat bicameralism of discourse and counterdiscourse theorized by Habermas. In either case, it is accurate to say that the manifesto is a *constitutive* discourse of modernity, and I mean "constitutive" here in a very particular sense. On the one hand, the manifesto circulates through and is intelligible via the discourses of modernity; it is neither outside of nor excluded from the universalism by which "progress" is measured. But on the other hand, it is more than merely a "discourse" in the post-Marxist sense of that term: it carries an incipient threat of action against the democratic state by groups who do not have much to lose from the state's disruption and even dissolution.

That the manifesto may issue in violent action is axiomatic. The manifestoes that fueled the Commune rebellions, for example, or the manifestoes associated with the string of anarchist bombings in the early twentieth century can leave little historical doubt that the manifesto exceeds the usual roles of "discourse" in the public sphere. Its refusal to be absorbed or recuperated into the public sphere's communicative ideal places it in a unique critical position: the manifesto makes legible the recidivist failures of the Enlightenment, and in so doing seems to rededicate the as yet incomplete projects of modernity. At the same time, however, it constitutes a repudiation of modernity, whose contradictions it bares. Without the *idea* of the manifesto, the dialectic of enlightenment stands still; but the very *fact* of the manifesto—the fact that it refers to the historical continuity of bodies in struggle rather than simply ideas in contention—turns the axis of modernity to expose the abiding ideological flaws in its democratic conceit.

## Identity in Motion

To say that the manifesto is a discursive mode of challenge in bourgeois ideology is not to say that its origins and effects are confined to the bourgeois public sphere. On the contrary, the very fact that manifestoes, over the course of their history, increasingly became documents of demand rather than of "reason," the works of anonymous collectives rather than named citizens, the products of univocal imperative rather than measured cultural criticism—all this is evidence not only of the elasticity of the public body in the bourgeois public sphere, but also of the manifesto's simultaneous participation in spheres beyond those bounded by bourgeois social institutions. In his preface to *The Structural Transformation of the Public Sphere,* Habermas refers briefly to another kind of public sphere, a "variant" on the liberal model of the bourgeois public sphere. This is the "plebeian public sphere," which "in a sense was suppressed in the historical process. In the stage of the French Revolution associated with Robespierre, for just one moment, a public sphere stripped of its literary garb began to function—its subject was no longer the 'educated strata' but the uneducated 'people.' Yet even this plebeian public sphere, whose continued but submerged existence manifested itself in the Chartist Movement and especially in the anarchist traditions of the workers' movement on the continent, remains oriented toward the intentions of the bourgeois public sphere" (xviii).[34] It seems clear that the manifesto is an important genre of this plebeian public sphere, given the sheer numbers of manifestoes produced during the French Revolution, the Chartist movement, the Commune, the European anarchist actions, and the American labor movement of the 1920s. For Habermas to construe the plebeian public sphere as a political satellite of the bourgeois public sphere, however, is to guarantee in advance the plebeian public sphere's "orientation" toward a social sphere and a mode of discourse that the manifesto often explicitly repudiates.

Nonetheless, this concept of a plebeian public sphere has been widely discussed and theorized in recent years, in particular by those who aim to posit an alternative discursive dimension of social consciousness that is tied not to the discourses of the "educated strata" but rather to the *experience* of oppression or exclusion in modernity.[35] As Stanley Aronowitz explains it, the plebeian public sphere should be distinguished from the bourgeois public sphere precisely as a radically different form of "cultural literacy" to which literacy (in the narrow sense) is irrelevant: "The criteria for citizenship in a situation of popular participation are shared histories of oppression and shared modes of life, not high cultural formation or literacy" (1993, 89).[36] Moreover, he suggests, the expressions of the subaltern groups bound by nonintellectual criteria for citizenship partake of "a form

[34] Nancy Fraser points to this passage as indicative of the blind spot in Habermas's thesis: "Although Habermas acknowledges that there were alternative public spheres, he assumes that it is possible to understand the character of the bourgeois public by looking at it alone, in isolation from its relations to other, competing publics. . . . In fact . . . an examination of the bourgeois public's relation to alternative counterpublics challenges the bourgeois conception of the pubic sphere" (78 n. 9). Lazarus et al. call this formulation of Habermas's argument a "straw-Habermas"; Habermas, they counter, "has recognized from the outset that the bourgeois public sphere . . . was 'persistently contradicted by the realities of bourgeois life and shown to be a *bourgeois ideology*'" (107).

[35] See, for example, Negt and Kluge's *Public Sphere and Experience;* Fredric Jameson's discussion of that text, "On Negt and Kluge," in Robbins; see also Fraser, Bhabha, and Fanon.

[36] It should be noted that Aronowitz conceives a plebeian public sphere as an explicitly proletarian public sphere. Compare this understanding of citizenship as negatively defined with Balibar's discussion of "ideal universalism," also negatively defined (65–66).

of speech that requires no formal educational preconditions" (89). What is interesting about Aronowitz's formulation is its emphasis on speech (in contrast to Habermas's more diffuse understanding of "discourse"), for it is this kind of speaking voice, I would argue, that is inscribed in the manifesto form. In the following chapters I will examine Habermas's formulation of a plebeian public sphere in greater detail; here I want to remark on the *synaptic* role that a speech-like genre such as the manifesto can play between, on the one hand, the counter-publics "stripped of their literary garb" and made up of proletariat classes, and, on the other hand, the political culture of the bourgeois public sphere that is bound in principle (though not in practice) to honor historicized claims to equality.

If the manifesto is indeed a genre that can provide a segue between the bourgeois and the plebeian public spheres, it is capable of doing so partly because of the indeterminacy of its constituency: as I have argued, the "we" of the manifesto is highly unstable, inflectable, expansive, and mobile. Such mobility allows its constituency to locate itself in the shifting gap between the promise of universal rights and the harmful withholding of rights. From this position, the group for which a manifesto speaks may project itself as not so much an essential identity as a *negative* entity, a group for whom emancipation does not yet exist, a group pulled into a provisional identity because it has been denied a viable rights-bearing identity.

The formation of this kind of negative identity has been discussed by the historian Jacques Rancière in the context of universalism and identity politics. Rancière maintains that when an oppressed group comes together around claims to equality, that group participates in the process of what he calls "political subjectification." Subjectification, he writes, "is the formation of a one that is not a self but is the relation of a self to an other. . . . [A] subject is an outsider, or more, an *in-between*. . . . Political subjectification is the enactment of equality—or the handling of a wrong—by people who are together to the extent that they are between. It is a crossing of identities, relying on a crossing of names: names that link . . . a being to a nonbeing or a not-yet-being" (60 – 61). Using "proletarians" as an example of people who are "between"—that is, people who are "denied an identity in a given order of policy" (61)—Rancière wants to show how the concept of universal equality is not a property available to particular groups of people, nor a coherent ideal, but rather a *logic* to be used in arguments that test the viability of the distribution of equality. Of the proletariat class one may ask, " 'Do [they] or do [they] not belong to the category of men or citizens or human beings, and what follows from this?' The universality is not enclosed in *citizen* or *human being*; it is involved in the 'what follows,' in its discursive and practical enactment" (60).

Rancière's discussion of the "in-betweenness" of universalism, and of the people who lay claim to universalism, may be helpful in understanding how the manifesto stages the transitional identity of its group: the manifesto presents a kind of political dramaturgy through which "universal" ideals are tested, and also through which political identity is shown to be relational. As an example of this dramaturgy let us return to the Lesbian Avengers' Dyke Manifesto with which I began this chapter. Although it is impossible to translate the stunning visual force of this paratactic manifesto into tidy quoted passages, I nevertheless transcribe a section of the broadside that begins about halfway down the front side of the page:

The majority of American voters think our lives are immoral and wrong.
FUCK LESBIAN CHIC.
NO ONE IS SAFE.
**We have to respond—not on their terms but on ours.**

Butch, femme and androgynous dykes, leather queers, drag kings and queens, transsexuals and trans-genders will not be thrown to the wolves so that straight-acting "gay people" can beg for acceptance at our expense.

Lesbian and gay people of color will not be forced into partial identities that deny the complexity of our lives.

Lesbian and gay youth, people with AIDS and low-income QUEERS WILL NOT BE DENIED FULL ACCESS, support and participation in our struggles for justice.

We have no desire to win a battle if it means losing the war.

The Dyke Manifesto lays open the ostensibly static category of "lesbian" and reveals within it an extraordinary motion of bodies, partial identities, public struggles, class-based oppressions, and political passions. The manifesto vehemently rejects any attempts from within or outside homosexual communities to shape a coherent identity in the tradition of liberal reform: in the best of circumstances, such identities are easily edentated and repackaged into majoritarian versions of a "universal" subject. And since, according to the manifesto, "the majority of American voters" already reject prima facie the "lives" of dykes as "immoral and wrong," the reformist politics championed by "straight-acting 'gay people'" amount to the worst kind of collaborationism. So it is with "lesbian chic" as well, which, in this context, forsakes activism for an apolitical aesthetic that can be absorbed into the dominant homophobic culture under the sign of fashion. Against the begging and posturing identities of assimilationists, the dyke subjects of the manifesto reverberate with a fierce dynamic energy; the manifesto's graphics frame that energy with a close-up photo of dykes in Lewiston, Maine, punching hostile hands in the air during their rally against that city's Proposition XXX.

In this manifesto, "dyke" amasses an aura of meaning far exceeding that of "lesbian": a "dyke" is a lesbian subject pushed to action and shaped by an array of alliances; "dykes" shout from the gap between oblivion and entitlement; "dyke" is a political identity brought to life by the kiss of righteous rage. And when that political identity comes to life, it sheds its skin again and again: dykes move between classes, between genders, between sexualities and races. The opening line of the broadside hails a whole array of potential dykes with the names by which they are known epithetically, they claim, to the Christian Right: "**Hey you** pervert, freak, bulldagger, unfit, sicko, lesbian, bitch!" By the broadside's final line, those epithets have been resignified and amalgamated into an enraged group of new political subjects uniting provisionally but forcefully under the banner of dissent: "1000'S OF ANGRY DYKES CAN'T BE WRONG—AND WON'T GIVE IN. EVER." These dykes are legible not as members of a discrete and accountable social or political group—not as "identities," in Rancière's understanding of that term—but rather through their alliances with others (leather queers, drag kings and queens, low-income queers, and so on). The dykes of this manifesto aim to give a voice to "people who are together to the extent that they are between," as Rancière has it; and the subjectivization that takes place in this manifesto illustrates the "crossing of identities, relying on a crossing of names."

Moreover, the amalgamated subjects of the Dyke Manifesto represent something quite different from a choral voice seeking access to the rights and privileges of the liberal bourgeois public sphere. They reject the discourses of that public sphere out of hand: "We have to respond," they insist, "not on their terms but on ours." The demand for "full access" in this manifesto means nothing less than a dramatic exposure and upending of the implicit universal standards by which the control of access is regulated; and this project, shared by virtually all manifestoes, necessarily involves an interrogation of the forms of universalism that are operative in the liberal bourgeois public sphere. In the analysis undertaken by the Dyke Manifesto, that universalism presumes conformity to an extremely narrow model of a Christian, conservative, heterosexual, white, middle-class, vanilla, family-valuing capitalist—a model so tightly defined by its exclusions that it appears to be oxymoronically *anti*-universal. As with other manifestoes, the Dyke Manifesto operates by lighting up a polemical field scorched by the failed promises of an incomplete or incompetent political order, and by challenging the status of the "universal subject" on which that order is implicitly based.

Within the terms of the broader discussions of universalism that have dominated the theoretical landscape of late, the universalism projected in this and many other manifestoes is critiqued as a form of false universalism; what is offered implicitly here and explicitly in other manifestoes is an attempt to fashion a new or rehabilitated universal ideal. To put this more baldly: all manifestoes pose both a challenge to and an affirmation of universalism. The Communist Manifesto challenges the authority of bourgeois universalism even as it asserts the ideal of a universal working class; the Symbolist Manifesto of 1886 mocks the universalism of art criticism while at the same time arguing for the aesthetic as a category of the universal; the 1969 Redstockings Manifesto challenges the universalist assumptions of male supremacy while holding up gender identity as the universal common denominator among women. However paratactic or irreverent or systematic a manifesto may be, it always makes itself intelligible by putting the case of a particular group into a context that honors the *idea* of a universal political subject. If, as David Palumbo-Liu has argued, "the particular and the universal are not mutually exclusive, but rather mutually inclusive, and, in fact, constitutive" (199), the genre of the manifesto roundly illustrates the point.

## Moderns Negotiating Universalism

Precisely because it calls into question the subject of a putatively universal, revolutionary "we," the manifesto form is helpful in tracking the vexed efforts of feminist women to enter, occupy, and reconstruct the public spheres of modernity by means of manifestoes and related polemical tracts. That task constitutes a primary focus for the remainder of this book. Much can be learned about the successes and failures of modernity's political agendas by keeping an eye on the successes and failures of women in the public sphere (as Engels and others first argued in the nineteenth century), and the use by women of the manifesto form helps us to see how revolutionary movements—in the arts, in politics, in cultural spheres—themselves often reproduce assumptions about an ideal universal subject. In Chapter 2 I will discuss polemical material produced by feminists during the French Revolution and in its sequelae. By way of closing the present chapter, however, and in order to adumbrate the direction in which that discussion will take me, I sketch out here an introductory problematic of the modernist period to which I will return in later chapters. For that period represents a historical conjuncture of extraordinary intersections, between political and aesthetic avant-gardes, for example, and between women's political and artistic struggles, between anarchist violence and widespread statist attempts to recuperate fracturing empires, between an alienated work force and newly consolidated and technically proficient management. This is the time when the self-styled avant-gardes of the nineteenth century give rise to a new dispensation of twentieth-century, media-driven public discourses of cultural dissidence, which involve explicit critiques of modernity—mainly in the form of countless revisions of universalism in the name of individualism.[37]

As I have already noted, the modernist period is characterized by the production of an unprecedented number of manifestoes, many of which simultaneously challenge and instantiate the premises of the modernity with which they are linked. Two groups of manifestoes from this time are especially famous, and both were produced by dissenting groups that contested bourgeois "progress" as partial, ideologically driven, and outdated (i.e., not "new"). One group is the "modern women"—a contextual identity if ever there was one—whose manifestoes attempted to negotiate a place for "woman" within the theoretical creation of "new" subjects in the fin de siècle. I am thinking not only of Suffragettes here, but also of some of the women active in birth control movements, labor movements, and artistic movements at the turn of the century. The other group may be thought of as the "anti-modern" modernists who practiced a semi-parodic resignification of the manifesto form. By "anti-modern" I mean those modernists who were self-proclaimed enemies of bourgeois rationalism and what they took to be the instrumentality of modernization.[38] In En-

[37] For valuable discussions of modernist critiques of modernity, see Felski 1995, Aronowitz 1993, Jameson 1981, Stevenson, Williams 1988, 1989, and the collection of essays edited by Giles, especially Sheppard.

[38] The reactions of anti-moderns to the failures of modernity vary from country to country, of course. Richard Sheppard writes that in Germany "the process of modernity was exceptionally rapid; and the liberal democratic, humanist ideal had a comparatively weak hold in the public domain. Consequently, many German modernists experienced the conflict particularly intensely." By contrast, in England, where "the Arnoldian ideal was more robustly ethical than its German coun-

gland, Ezra Pound and Wyndham Lewis are the obvious players in this group, but perhaps even more conspicuous are the continental dadaists and surrealists whose manifestoes attest to a wholesale repudiation of the logic of universalism, even as they make shrewd use of the genre's proclamatory powers in an age of furious competition for cultural shelf-space among artistic movements. As an example of a manifesto from this latter group, I offer a passage from "Dada Manifesto 1918" by Tristan Tzara, written at the end of the catastrophic war that dadaists took to represent the telos of modern progress:

> To put out a manifesto you must want: ABC
> to fulminate against 1,2,3,
> to fly into a rage and sharpen your wings to conquer and disseminate little abcs and big abcs, to sign, shout, swear, to organize prose into a form of absolute and irrefutable evidence, to prove your non plus ultra and maintain that novelty resembles life just as the latest appearance of some whore proves the essence of God. His existence was previously proved by the accordion, the landscape, the wheedling word. (76)

This is the best exfoliation of the manifesto form that I know: Tzara turns his epigrammatic wizardry to piercing caricature, embellishing and demolishing most of the rhetorical traits by which we know the form. The manifesto is a pedagogical vehicle, he implies: it teaches us fundamentals, little abcs and big abcs. It is a form marking the contours of rage, and it deploys the verbal accoutrements of rage—shouting and swearing and fulminating. It is a testament of "proofs," marshaling arguments and conquering disbelief in the name of truth. With wry disdain Tzara observes that the manifesto is often small, petty, and absurdly self-important, announcing nothing more than some new fashionable trick of modernity; its centripetal formality may threaten to engulf diverse constituencies. But in spite of the rhetorical traps that Tzara detects, he also grasps its potential for an avant-garde critique of bourgeois rationality and of the contradictory valorizations of individualism and universalism that cut across the currents of modernity. Tzara continues: "I write a manifesto and I want nothing, yet I say certain things, and in principle I am against manifestoes, as I am also against principles . . . . I write this manifesto to show that people can perform contrary actions together while taking one fresh gulp

---

terpart," and where "the Great War did not produce the same social upheaval as it did on the Continent," it "generated much smaller, less radical and less threatening avant-gardes (i.e. the Georgians, Imagists and Vorticists) than was the case on the Continent" (7).

of air; I am against action; for continuous contradiction, for affirmation too, I am neither for nor against and I do not explain because I hate common sense" (76).

Here Tzara stakes out the form ironically, not to forge a group identity but to flush out a radical individualism—by which I mean, in this context, an individualism existing outside the deterministic rationalism of bourgeois ideology and above the mass conformity entailed in liberal democracy. In the same move he offers this individualism as the grounds for the vaguest possible universal ideal: a freedom that allows the taking of "one fresh gulp of air" by many individuals. Tzara uses the manifesto form, in other words, as we would expect him to, by pitting the individual's particular against an incomplete universalism. It is, in his hands, a tool with which to repudiate hegemonic values; a vehicle for complaint against the discourses of the public sphere that enforce the partial logic of universalism; and, most subtly, a textual effort to reconceive the universal as a site of continuous and nondeterministic cultural revisions.

Tzara's manifesto is also quite generically functional: it is a birth narrative of the dada movement, a declaration that celebrates the beginning— just now—of a new history of anti-bourgeois freedom. As he declares a bit later in the manifesto: "And so Dada was born of a need for independence, or a distrust toward unity. Those who are with us preserve their freedom. We recognize no theory" (77). Part of the intended irony of this nativity narrative, of course, comes from Tzara's announcement, in the passage quoted earlier, that "I want nothing." A manifesto without demands is a manifesto that changes the terms of political struggle, thus suggesting that struggle, too, is merely one more facet of the parliamentarian politics of the bourgeois public sphere.

The stance of casual remoteness taken up by dadaists is characteristic of many other avant-garde manifestoes. Curiously, however, it is not the stance adopted by a proto-dadaist—and a "new woman" into the bargain—who wrote her "Feminist Manifesto" just a few years earlier: that is, the poet Mina Loy. Loy's manifesto wants plenty, starting with the leveling of patriarchy, parental freedom for mothers, and a revolutionary "wrenching" of women's roles away from the limited choices of prostitution and "parasitism"—a word from the lexicon of first-wave feminists that described woman's position in marriage. Above all, Loy seeks to crystallize an audience of feminist avant-gardists who reject collectivism and retain the values of individualism. To this end she grapples with the incompatibility between modernist individualism and the universalism to which feminism tends. While the manifesto retains the flagrant anti-bourgeois flourishes of

Loy's avant-garde project—it calls for the surgical destruction of virginity as a cure for bride-price, for example, and rejects wholesale the reform feminism practiced by suffragists and political activists—it also engages directly the problems of modernity: the hollowness for women of the promises of equality, and the nearly farcical impossibility of autonomy for women. Above all it takes up, however obliquely, the questions of universality that bore down on those who occupied the juncture of feminism and the avant-garde in 1914. Rejecting the position that would lump women into the category of the universal male subject, she exhorts her female audience to reimagine an independent and unentailed category of the feminine: "Leave off looking to men to find out what you are *not*—seek within yourselves to find out what you *are*" (1996, 154). Even as she rejects the classical view that sees woman as an incomplete version of man, however, her disarticulation of "woman" from the figure of the universal male subject forces her to recognize the constrictions that subtend the position of "woman" within a universalist model of sexual relations: "The value of woman depends entirely on *chance,* her success or insuccess [sic] in manoeuvering a man into taking the life-long responsibility of her" (155).

Ultimately the conflicting challenges of universalism and feminism force Loy into a number of complex tasks in this manifesto. First, she faces the challenge of deploying the rhetoric of social action associated with the political avant-garde, while trying at the same time to preserve the uniqueness of the radical individual from the homogenizing social effects of bourgeois individualism. Loy works this out at times by donning a socially constituted identity, "Woman," while marking the gesture at every turn with detached ambivalence. Second, like other feminist avant-gardists, Loy tries to particularize a female subject who is neither set in opposition to nor subsumed by the political model of a universal rights-bearing male. This move involves the challenge of envisioning a radical universalism according to which gendered universal rights are positioned separately but equally, even as the capacity for unique creativity is accorded to both men and women. And third, she faces the task of forcibly separating a materially based concept of the universal from social or naturalist essentialism so that hierarchy does not reenter the new, radically revised universal through the back door of biology.

I will have more to say about the "Feminist Manifesto" in Chapter 4; here I simply want to observe that while Loy's particular engagement with feminism necessitated an engagement with modernity—and a subtly theorized one at that—her efforts to resignify the universal in this manifesto came to naught. The manifesto was never finished, and remained unpublished until 1982. The form may have offered her a way of averring, in the idiom of the avant-garde, that the oppressed state of women stemmed from "conditions as they are presently constituted" (154), as she puts it. But it did not resolve for her the experience of the conflicts between individualism and universalism, between feminism and modernity. Perhaps it never could. Notwithstanding Habermas's claim that a critique of universalism is "inherent in modernity itself," it is not at all clear that the counterdiscourses for that critique are equally available to all the putative subjects of modernity. In fact, Loy's manifesto stands as something of a limiting case for the manifesto form: although a manifesto may partake of many of the genre's most compelling conventions, although it may invoke and even participate in the iterable history of struggling subjects in public realms, there are no guarantees that a manifesto will reach—let alone transform—the publics, subaltern or otherwise, that it aims to address. The history of public speech acts is one marbled with failures and misfires; and when speech acts are explicitly political in aim and intent, their receptions are bound to be overdetermined by the context-bound exigencies of voice, space, and place.[39]

With this caveat in mind, I turn in the next chapter to some of the exigencies that formed the discursive matrix of the French Revolution, in order to bring into focus the role that gender has played in the dynamics of public dissent under the sign of modernity. The French Revolution offers a legible starting point for the study of the conditions of modern dissent, and it has been narrated—especially in the bicentennial boom of scholarship—as the story of "the people" first finding their voice, and then unwittingly introducing their own form of absolute authority in place of the absolute authority of feudal monarchy.[40] Against the backdrop of the ancien régime the drama of the developing republic unfolds: the bourgeoisie hammers out its platform as the remnants of aristocracy are vanquished; the script of democracy goes through rewrite after rewrite. This is the first true moment of the manifesto, when contestation and violent revision overhaul universalism in the image of freedom or equality (depending, minute by minute, on the reigning faction). It is also the moment of modernity, when a discursive public space is cleared for the circulation of the values of autonomy and individual agency across the bourgeois classes.

[39] See Ellen Willis's rich discussion of the constitutive differences between speech and action in the context of hate speech and censorship. Willis argues that the only speech acts that genuinely coerce human will are utterances like "Your money or your life."
[40] François Furet is generally credited with the development of this argument

And yet, against all logic, it is *not* the moment for women's freedom and equality, nor is it the moment for African emancipation in the French Caribbean colonies. In France, women play erratic supporting roles in the Revolution—generically representing "the family" and related forms of political dependency—and are violently ejected from the stage when their participation becomes explicitly feminist.

This paradox—that the promises of universal political inclusion, extended to all but granted to few, encode "natural rights" on an ideological template of exclusion—is illustrated in a preliminary way by the famous *Manifeste des Égaux* ("Manifesto of Equals"), written in 1794 to formalize the radical Bavouist principles of absolute equality during the second phase of the Revolution. On the one hand, this document carries all the markings of the political manifesto, including an urgent investment in the "now," and the avowed expression of the goal of "revolution for true equality" (Maréchal, 95). It declares: "The hour for decisive action has now struck. The people's suffering has reached its peak; it darkens the face of the earth. . . . Now the time has come to mend matters. . . . You who are oppressed, join us: come and partake of the feast which nature has provided for all her sons and daughters" (Maréchal, 94). Sons and daughters should all claim their "natural" birthright of equality, since "all men have the same needs, all are endowed with the same faculties, all are warmed by the same sun, and all breathe the same air." But at the same time, and without any self-consciousness, the manifesto qualifies its claims about "nature" with one major proviso: the assumption that "age and sex are the sole natural distinctions existing between men" (Maréchal, 92). The manifesto, in other words, gives with one hand what it takes away with the other: equality for everyone except those who are naturally unequal. This paradox is of course familiar as the paradox of Western universalism, a doctrine of liberation available to all but those who do not deserve it. Its foundational contradictions play out differently across categories of race, nationality, sexuality, and ethnicity in the modern period, but in the French Revolution, as we shall see, they are especially evident in the manifestoes and polemics that cast political virtue in gendered terms and, conversely, reframe the politics of gender as the politics of counterrevolution.

# 2 Manifestoes and Revolutionary Discourse

## Women in the Cross Fire

In September 1791 Olympe de Gouges, French revolutionary playwright and pamphleteer, responded to the new French constitution's Declaration of the Rights of Man and Citizen with her own feminist manifesto, the "Declaration of the Rights of Woman."[1] She prefaced her tract with a letter addressed to Marie Antoinette—a figure whose sexual and political reputation had been under attack in the pamphlet press for more than a decade—in which she implored the queen to silence popular calumny by assuming the "nobler function" of "lending weight to the progress of the Rights of Woman" (88). Using a conventional Enlightenment appeal to the laws of natural order, de Gouges's Declaration asks "man" to examine his oppression of women in view of the sexual equality and "harmonious togetherness" exhibited in the natural world, for, in stark contrast to the rest of nature, only man "has raised his exceptional circumstances to a principle. Bizarre, blind, bloated with science and degenerated—in a century of enlightenment and wisdom—into the crassest ignorance, he wants to command as a despot a sex which is in full possession of its intellectual faculties" (89). Seeing in patriarchal reaction the perversion of Enlightenment ideals, de Gouges offers her own Declaration as a correction, and boldly recommends it for decree by the liberal National Assembly.

In its Preamble, the Declaration speaks for "mothers, daughters, [and] sisters" who "demand to be constituted into a national assembly" (89). A

[1] I use the text of De Gouges's Declaration of the Rights of Woman as reprinted in Levy, Applewhite, and Johnson, 87–96. The Declaration of the Rights of Man and Citizen (1789) is reprinted in Stewart, 113–115.

group of seventeen articles, modeled directly on the 1791 Declaration of the Rights of Man, follows, detailing the putative guarantees of women's rights that should obtain under the republican-civic laws of the new French nation. A long postscript, couched as an apostrophe to French women ("Oh, women, women! When will you cease to be blind?" [92]), upbraids them for inhabiting the seductive gender roles of the aristocratic ancien régime—roles that are both unrepublican and self-defeating in their emphasis on artifice and coquetry. De Gouges rejects the institution of marriage, calling it "the tomb of trust and love" (94), and offers in its place (in an ironic echo of Rousseau) a "Social Contract Between Man and Woman" which will legally sanction—and protect the offspring of—all sexual relations between men and women. Finally, de Gouges closes her Declaration by condemning French colonists for their adamant resistance to the new National Assembly proposals for the abolition of slavery in the French colonies: though colonists may "make a claim to reign as despots over the men whose fathers and brothers they are," writes de Gouges, liberty "must be equal for all; liberty must hold the National Assembly to its decree dictated by prudence and justice" (96). In such a decree, presumably, rests de Gouges's hope for a social equality extending to *all* members of the Republic.[2]

De Gouges's tract appeared during a period marked out by Habermas as the time of the rapid emergence and imperfect consolidation of the French bourgeois public sphere. In his analysis, the early stages of the French Revolution effectively "created in France overnight, although with

[2] De Gouges's strong abolitionist position is overtly and systematically illustrated in her experimental "drama in prose," *L'Esclavages des noirs*, written in 1783 but first performed by the prestigious Comédie-Française (Théâtre de la Nation) in 1789. The play, a story of escaped slaves in Haiti who help to rescue a shipwrecked European couple and are then liberated by the governor-father of the European woman, builds its narrative around an investigation of "nature." In this play, as in de Gouges's Declaration, "nature" is a context, or perhaps more accurately a matrix, within which the twin yokes of liberty and equality differentiate and emerge as fundamental constituents of human nature. In *L'Esclavages*, however, human nature "is first revealed in that which distinguishes men from animals, not men from women, blacks from whites, or masters from slaves: in the same blood which flows in human veins" (Le Hir, 71). By contrast, in the Declaration, written eight years later in 1791 (before the Legislative Assembly replaced the disbanded National Assembly on October 1), animal nature is read as a template for human nature, which has been deformed by a perversely opportunistic brand of human rationalism.

The timing and language of de Gouges's call for the constitution of women into a national assembly are interesting. According to Conor Cruise O'Brien, the formation of a National Assembly to replace the Estates General represented something "wholly new," that is, the first and "most decisive" instance of formal nationalism in the Revolution. O'Brien argues that "the words 'National Assembly' are in fact a mandate for revolutionary change" (23). The 1791 Declaration of the Rights of Man first brings the locution of nationalism to a public institution; and de Gouges strategically presses the elastic concept of a new national institution into the service of her own vision of fully inclusive universalism.

less stability, what in Great Britain had taken more than a century of steady evolution: the institutions, which until then had been lacking, for critical public debate of political matters" (1989, 69–70).[3] Among the several new institutions of the French public sphere, Habermas's account emphasizes the particularly radical new constitutional guarantee that "free communication of ideas and opinions is one of the most precious rights of man" (rpt. in Stewart, 114). This guarantee was marked, in France, by a virtual explosion of public opinion and contestation; it was enacted in new media forms that included the unrestricted flow of pamphlets, the birth and death of hundreds of fledgling newspapers, and the widespread "placarding" of manifestoes, pamphlets, and broadsides onto public walls.[4] For the first time in France, the medium of print became, in Habermas's words, "an institution of the public itself," and a particularly resonant one at that: for the duration of the Revolution, and until the permanent institutionalization of the public sphere in the Second Republic, "the appearance of a political newspaper meant joining the struggle for freedom and public opinion, and thus for the public sphere as a principle," according to Habermas (1974, 53). And while it might be added that the "principle" of the public sphere was extremely elusive for many new *citoyens* and all *citoyennes,* in practice it produced an institutional discourse as finely self-differentiated by genre and rhetoric as any of the prominent discourses of modernity.

Hence, during France's rapid and revolutionary power shift from control by repression (characterized by full royal censorship and few sanctioned public media before 1789) to control by voluntaristic "consensus" (characterized by intense competition among a panoply of public media), the manifesto form's facilities and limitations came into especially sharp focus. Its earlier uses for statist interests—by the likes of Milton in the service of Cromwell, for example, or by the martial coordinators of Italian

[3] Keith Michael Baker argues that France's developing public sphere was probably more like England's than Habermas acknowledges: both countries had a significant tradition of literary public spheres that produced state-scrutinizing public opinion (see 191–95).

[4] See Jeremy Popkin, 141 and passim, for an account of the "birth" of the French newspaper after the deterioration of authorized censorship in June–July 1789. See Antoine de Baecque, 168 and passim, and Lynn Hunt 1996 for divergent but compelling accounts of the increasing importance of political and pornographic pamphlets during the Revolution. Simon Schama notes that in the decade before the Revolution, it was "unbound literature—almanacs and the posting of notices and placards—that would have increasingly connected the common people of the French towns with the world of public events" (181). It is important to recognize, however, that with the lifting of state censorship, the turn toward hortatory media accelerated, creating not only new readerships for new kinds of newspapers and periodicals, but also new conditions for a novitiate of occasional political authors. I would argue that these are the historical conditions under which the manifesto form flourishes.

city-states—were almost entirely supplanted by its use in this epoch as an instrument of revolution.[5] The one notable (and exemplary) exception to the shift was the "Brunswick Manifesto," produced by émigrés who had gathered outside France under the banner of the allied armies in 1792. The Brunswick Manifesto is essentially a threat directed against the revolutionaries in Paris who held Louis XVI under arrest. In a reversal of the roles being parceled out in the revolutionary manifestoes of Paris, the Brunswick Manifesto casts French *radicals* as usurpers of public will and émigrés as keepers of the national flame. Using the conventions of the form as I described them in Chapter 1, "Brunswick" reviews the Revolution's unlawful incursions against Prussia, condemns its anarchic threats to monarchy and church, and then presents a list of declarations, including the threat that "if the least violence, the least outrage be done Their Majesties . . . [i.e., of Prussia and France] they will exact an exemplary and ever-memorable vengeance" (310). In this telling, it is the monarchy that is menaced by the dominant rabble; truth and right reside with the marginalized but loyal émigrés, who represent the last line of defense against revolutionary tyranny. The Brunswick Manifesto, in other words, attempts to reclaim the manifesto as a statist form, and this attempt alone was enough to establish conclusively the émigrés' status as counterrevolutionaries. In fact, the rhetorical relations between power and insurgency set out in "Brunswick" helped to concretize an iconic figure of "Counterrevolution" against which militants could rally; this manifesto thus helped to establish its author and his supporters as a "we" of the ancien régime—that is, as a "them" to the revolutionaries of Paris—and undoubtedly hastened the death of the monarch five months later.[6]

[5] Milton's "Manifesto of the Lord Protector of the Commonwealth of England, Scotland, Ireland, &c.," written in Latin for Cromwell in 1655, follows many of the conventions I have outlined for the manifesto form, not the least of which are its rhetorical emphasis on the obviousness and inevitability of Cromwell's political rectitude and its thoroughgoing and revisionary foreshortening of historical narrative. It differs significantly, however, from the body of seventeenth-century agonistic manifestoes associated with the Commonwealth in the statist use to which it is put; in this it exemplifies the *OED*'s second definition of "manifesto" as "a public declaration or proclamation, usually issued by or with the sanction of a sovereign prince or state, or by an individual or body of individuals, whose proceedings are of public importance, for the purpose of making known past actions, and explaining the reasons or motives for actions announced as forthcoming." As it happens, Milton's manifesto staked out an official (and speciously justified) foreign policy against Spain with regard to Spanish trade in the New World.

[6] The Brunswick Manifesto also offers numerical demands, makes vague threats of violence, and speaks from a position of outraged morality. Its especially counterrevolutionary intent may be judged by a passage in which its putative author, the duke of Brunswick, vows "to terminate anarchy in the interior of France, to check attacks on the Throne and the Church, to re-establish legal power, to give the King the security and liberty of which he is deprived, and to enable him to exercise the legitimate authority which is his due" (308).

Generally speaking, however, the manifesto form became, like its contemporary radical newspapers and pamphlets, part of a specific mode of dissent in the discourse of the revolutionary public sphere. It drew on rhetorical conventions that functioned principally to align the demands of marginalized political groups with the "general will" of the nation, *la patrie*. Like other printed media in the early years of the Revolution, the revolutionary manifesto was brief enough to make production and reproduction relatively easy,[7] and it could afford a certain amount of protection to its authors through its potential for anonymity.[8] And, like placards and slogans, manifestoes could offer equal access, across a spectrum of political viewpoints, to new members of the culture of revolution.[9]

The spectrum of manifestoes that developed during the Revolution was especially important in two respects. In the first place, these manifestoes could act as textual vehicles for the narration of demands, with very little equivocation.[10] In the second place, as the institutional consolidation of "public opinion" increasingly threatened to exclude or preclude nonhegemonic sections of the public—that is, when the vehicle for public opinion shifted, in Habermas's words, from "a journalism of conviction to one of commerce" (1974, 53)—the manifesto could and often did provide an outlet and a register for those sectional voices.

Nevertheless, a form's potential function and its actual use are never the same thing, and in the distinction between function and use we find an illustration of the lacuna in Habermas's descriptions of the public sphere's communicative ideal. For this ideal relies on two very different conditions of possibility: first, the communicative potential inherent in

---

[7] Brevity also distinguished it from contemporary newspapers. Popkin provides an extensive account of the variety of formats adopted by the new revolutionary French newspapers: some used a smaller octavo size; others retained a more conservative and larger quarto size associated with the publications of the ancien régime. Both formats were unwieldy, and Popkin concludes that, "however radical their contents, the French papers of the revolutionary period remained resolutely conservative in appearance and demanded no revolution in reading habits from their readers" (154).

[8] Note, however, that anonymity was an explicit principle of anti-individualist *fraternité* (and perhaps a rather more covert mode of self-protection) for the militant sansculottes whose activities were prominent in 1792–95.

[9] It is important to acknowledge that some citizens had much wider access to revolutionary print media than others. Theoretically, anyone with access to rudimentary materials could plaster handwritten or printed notices on houses; less available to the public (and more subject to reprisals) were mass-distribution printing presses. Specific forms of political content also affected a tract's availability: as Dominique Godineau points out, printed texts that were explicitly feminist were frequently "vetted by revolutionary organizations before being circulated" (1993, 24).

[10] In this they must be distinguished from "petitions," which, as Joan Landes says, were "humble requests" (107), as we saw in Chapter 1.

all human language, without which no form of deliberative intersubjectivity (understanding, agreement, sympathy) would be possible; and second, an ideal speech *situation* in which participants, as discursive equals, suspend their prejudices and individual (social) interests.[11] What the example of the manifesto helps to illustrate, then, is the potential for disjunction between these two components of the communicative ideal. For the manifesto's use as a vehicle for public contestation and unilateral demands may, paradoxically, be so "successful" as to provide grounds for the exclusion of its authors from the public sphere; this exclusion, in turn, fractures the possibility of creating the social conditions necessary for the ideal speech situation. In this regard, Olympe de Gouges's fate is a case in point.

No manifesto can be understood outside the specific historical conditions of its production and reception; at the same time, however much we may generalize about the form's role as a link across avant-garde movements, no public polemical tract by a woman can stand as a representative "example" of a genre. These, then, are the conditions under which de Gouges herself was made an "example" of perverse feminist polemics by the legal machinery of the French Revolution: in July 1793, the forty-four-year-old de Gouges—a self-educated working-class advocate of a women's theater, and prolific *femme de lettres* with a reputation for public zeal—was arrested in Paris for violating a new censorship law. One of the first acts of the Terror, the law forbade the composition or printing of "works or writings which provoke the dissolution of the national representation, the reestablishment of royalty, or of any other power attacking the sovereignty of the people" (rpt. in Levy, Applewhite, and Johnson, 259). In fact, de Gouges's numerous published pamphlets and posters had long questioned the alleged unanimity of the "expressed desire of the entire nation" (255); during her trial, prosecutors found her most recent manifesto, "Les Trois urnes, ou le Salut de la patrie" ("The Three Urns"), to have "openly provoked civil war and sought to arm citizens against one another by proposing the meeting of primary assemblies to deliberate and express their desire concerning either monarchical government, [or] . . . the one and indivisible republican [form], . . . [or] the federative [form], which would be the source of incalculable evils and which would destroy liberty infallibly" (255). De Gouges represented herself, since the court refused to appoint a replacement for the assigned lawyer who failed to show up. Dur-

[11] See Anderson 1998, 2–5, for a succinct summary and critique of Habermas's theory.

ing the trial, according to the narrative of the hostile court reporter, she "never stopped . . . smirking" (258); at its close she was found guilty and was beheaded a day later, on November 3.[12]

The verdict against de Gouges did not issue solely from the tribunal's interpretation of the laws of censorship or sedition, however, for de Gouges's polemical feminism, though not explicitly addressed during the trial, was a clear subtext in the Jacobin case against her. Two days before her execution, the Committee of General Security recommended to the Convention the general suppression of women's political activity, with the result that the Convention banned the existence of all the numerous women's societies and popular clubs in Paris; thence began the Revolution's systematic backlash against women's organized participation in public revolutionary spheres.[13] A fortnight later, protests against the ban were brought by the Society of Revolutionary Republican Women to the General Council; the language of the council's response conveys something of the panic surrounding the obvious disjunction between the revolutionary principle of egalitarianism and the gender inequity enforced by the newly constituted revolutionary government—a government that had officially suspended the constitution in early October 1793 and inaugurated the Terror. It was a "horrible" thing, the speaker Chaumette decreed, and "contrary to all the laws of nature for a woman to want to make herself a man." "Moral law" binds woman to "the details of the household, the sweet anxieties of maternity." Those women who forget this law—women like "the impudent Olympe de Gouges, who was the first to set up women's societies, who abandoned the cares of her household to get mixed up in the re-

[12] Indeed, before the king's execution, de Gouges had written a public letter to the Convention in which she offered to defend the king in court on the grounds that his only real sin was to have been born into a monarchy just before its historical downfall: "I believe Louis guilty *as King;* but once shorn of this forbidden title, he ceases to be guilty in the eyes of the Republic. His ancestors had filled to overflowing the cup of the sufferings of France; unhappily the cup broke in his hands and all its fragments rebounded upon his head" (rpt. in Stephens, 169). This interesting position was ignored during the trial; see Michael Walzer for transcripts of speeches during the trial of Louis XVI.

[13] This crucial moment—October 30, 1793—is discussed by nearly all feminist historians of the Revolution. To cite a very few: Levy, Applewhite, and Johnson, 221–71; Hufton, 1–50; Godineau 1993; Sledziewski; Soboul, 158–67; Landes, 93ff.; Rose; and both essays by Levy and Applewhite. In a long oration the speaker for the Committee of General Security asked: "Do women have the moral and physical strength which the exercise of one and the other of these rights calls for? Universal opinion rejects this idea. . . . [I]t is not possible for women to exercise political rights. [Therefore you ought to] destroy these alleged popular societies of women which the aristocracy would want to set up to put them [women] at odds with men, to divide the latter by forcing them to take sides in these quarrels, and to stir up disorder" (rpt. in Levy, Applewhite, and Johnson, 215–17).

public, and whose head fell beneath the avenging knife of the laws"—constitute grave threats to the virtue and stability of the Republic.[14]

De Gouges's stated crime of incendiary agitation was compounded, in other words, by her feminism, the form of which exposed an unaccountable lacuna in revolutionary practice. Her appeal to public opinion and referendum—which after all implied, in Girondist fashion, that there were multiple positions to be taken on the issue of governmental structure, that popular consensus was not self-evident, that hybrid forms of government might replace absolutist forms—could hardly be read as a stance unconnected to her prominent feminist 1791 tract. For de Gouges's Declaration, though it has been called "not very original" (Sledziewski, 44) is in fact a wickedly ironic exercise in diagnosis, one that auscultates the hollowness of the Declaration of the Rights of Man and Citizen. Systematically sampling from and reinflecting the ideological authority of the Rights of Man, the Rights of Woman may even be thought of as an early instance of *détournement*. Each article of her Declaration echoes and slightly revises the articles in the Rights of Man; each revision lights up the original document's shortsightedness, with the cumulative effect of making the Gougesean ectype appear to be a thoroughly republican corrective.[15] For example, where the original Declaration asserts that "every society in which the guarantee of rights is not assured or the separation of powers not determined has no constitution at all" (rpt. in Stewart, 115), de Gouges's Declaration makes a significant addition: "No society has a constitution without the guarantee of rights and the separation of powers; the constitution is null if the majority of individuals comprising the nation have not cooperated in drafting it" (92). A majority, in other words, must participate in the legal codes that guarantee the rights of the new nation; without the inclusion of women in this process, the new nation is in violation of its own principles. Not only does de Gouges's emendation challenge the "self-evidence" of the rights of citizens (indeed, the self-evidence of "citizens"), but

[14] The repudiation of the protest proceeds by way of delegitimating the very grounds for protest: "Is it the place of women to propose motions?" Levy, Applewhite, and Johnson have translated and reprinted this transcript in its entirety, as well as the transcript of the National Convention meeting outlawing clubs and popular societies for women (212–20).

[15] The technique of revision through parody is of course quite common in history, but no less effective for its wide usage. The French Declaration of the Rights of Man and Citizen is itself based on the American state constitutions' bills of rights. For especially powerful revisions of the American Declaration of Independence, see "Declaration of Sentiments and Resolutions" (Women's Rights Convention, 1848), "Declaration of Independence" (Workingman's Party of Illinois, 1876), "Declaration of Interdependence" (Socialist Labor Party, 1895), and "Black Declaration of Independence" (National Committee of Black Churchmen, 1970), all in Foner.

also it posits feminism as the crucial but missing integer of the Revolution. Moreover, it introduces an unusually *textual* feminism that is of a piece with Enlightenment textuality,[16] and above reproach in its adherence— even its homage—to republican rhetorical codes. But precisely because it intimates a false homeostasis between the intent of the Rights of Man and Citizen and the will of the people it speaks for, de Gouges's tract functions at an entirely different generic level: I would argue that the presence of the Rights of Woman reframes the Rights of Man as a despotic foundational text, and that move, in turn, casts Rights of Woman as a radically new (though paradoxically derivative) manifesto, in every sense in which I have discussed the form so far.

The case of Olympe de Gouges helps to situate the problem of women's public discourse—or, more accurately, the appropriation of public discourse by women—within the historical moment of the circulation in the public sphere of important new forms of public discourse such as the manifesto. And certain features of a conceptual public sphere will help to frame an inquiry about emergent discourses of dissent and the problems they pose for women. Whether one takes "public sphere" to mean, as Habermas elaborates it, a common, public, discursive space within which citizens bracket their socioeconomic differences in order to deliberate about their common concerns, or whether one follows Jon Klancher in understanding that sphere as an ephemeral "textual society" which unified readers through the medium of new lettered periodicals (15), or adheres to Keith Michael Baker's analysis of the public sphere as an institution of a paradoxically *private* realm of civil society (188), or to Nancy Fraser's counterformulation of multiple public spheres,[17] one may nevertheless discern in all of these formulations the difficulties entailed in public feminist dissent in this period. These difficulties I wish to illuminate by way of an understanding of the manifesto and related forms.

Fraser famously offers a relatively early critique of Habermas's formulation of the public sphere by outlining the crucial yet problematic position

[16] See Toulmin, chap. 1.

[17] There are many more: see Aronowitz 1987–88, Negt and Kluge, and Robbins, for example. Also, for an interesting contrast, compare, on the one hand, Baker's stark contention that a public/private dichotomy simply does not obtain for an analysis of the development in the French Revolution of increasingly gendered spheres with, on the other, Arendt's proto-discussion of public spheres. Arendt writes: "Since the revolution had opened the gates of the political realm to the poor, this realm had indeed become 'social.' It was overwhelmed by the cares and worries which actually belonged in the sphere of the household and which, even if they were permitted to enter the public realm, could not be solved by political means, since they were matters of administration, to be put into the hands of experts, rather than issues which could be settled by the twofold process of decision and persuasion" (90–91).

that his concept holds for critical social theory. She probes his idealized formulation of public discussion—made possible by bourgeois society's new guarantees of free speech—which, Habermas argues, was meant to be (although it never fully became) "open and accessible to all[:] merely private interests were to be inadmissible; inequalities of status were to be bracketed; and discussants were to deliberate as peers. The result of such discussion would be 'public opinion' in the strong sense of a consensus about the common good" (Fraser, 59). Fraser acknowledges that even in Habermas's version of the public sphere, such a utopian ideal of unimpeded exchange was ephemeral at best and never achieved any degree of completion; her critique, however, challenges the presumption that such an exchange could have been "utopian" on its own terms, since the concept of "the public" was gendered as masculine.

Citing the work of Joan Landes on the French Revolution, Fraser argues that the very construction of a "public sphere" was in fact constitutively exclusive:

> For Landes, the key axis of exclusion [in the new "public sphere"] is gender; she argues that the ethos of the new republican public sphere in France was constructed in deliberate opposition to that of a more woman-friendly salon culture [of the eighteenth century] that the republicans stigmatized as "artificial," "effeminate," and "aristocratic." Consequently, a new, austere style of public speech and behavior was promoted, a style deemed "rational," "virtuous," and "manly." In this way, masculinist gender constructs were built into the very conception of the republican public sphere, as was a logic that led, at the height of Jacobin rule, to the formal exclusion from political life of women. (59)

This exclusion of women became axiomatic, as Landes and a host of historians—Dominique Godineau, Olwen Hufton, Dorinda Outram—have argued; and it was reinforced by the Republic's explicitly gendered symbol system, as Lynn Hunt and others have shown.[18] And although there have been useful modifications made to this stark reading of the Revolution as a historical conjuncture propped on gender axioms, it is nevertheless worth pursing here Fraser's skepticism about the degree to which "inequalities of status" in such a methodically gendered sphere could ever fully or effec-

[18] Lynn Hunt (1984) has demonstrated the extent to which the festivals created during and for the Revolution depended on the remaking of feminine allegorical figures; Joan Landes provides an extensive analysis of the symbolic figures of women and domesticity in David's paintings; Dorinda Outram gives a historical reconstruction of the Revolution's symbolic equations between the figure of Brutus and the revolutionary construction of virtue.

tively be "bracketed off" in the interest of deliberative consensus.[19] Even the liberal public spheres of Germany and England (and, before and after the Terror, France) functioned as "training grounds" for "a stratum of bourgeois men, who were coming to see themselves as a 'universal class' and preparing to assert their fitness to govern," according to Geoff Eley (quoted in Fraser, 60). Fraser therefore reaches what she calls the "ironic conclusion" that the "discourse of publicity touting accessibility, rationality, and the suspension of hierarchy [had itself been] deployed as a strategy of distinction" (60).

Fraser's aim, here and elsewhere, is to open up the question of the public sphere's role in actually existing democracy by showing how Habermas's formulation of a single bourgeois public sphere fails to take into account other coexisting public spheres, especially those of what she calls "subaltern counterpublics." Habermas's conception of the public sphere must be always already exclusionary, in part because the institutions of this public sphere mark and hierarchize social and cultural differences while implicitly claiming to ignore those differences, but also because Habermas's formulation itself leaves no room for the theorization of plural, competing public spheres. The focus of Fraser's argument—and it has been a tremendously influential one—therefore rests elsewhere than on the "discourses of publicity" that characterize and, in some sense, produce the bourgeois public sphere. But it is my aim here to take up and examine these discourses that purportedly "tout[ed] accessibility," to use Fraser's words. While they seemed to offer speaking positions and subject positions that transcended gender, such discourses in fact inscribed and enforced gender lines, and thus proved paradoxically inaccessible to the women who

[19] In some important recent work a handful of Marxist historians have questioned the trend of declaring the French Revolution a failure for women, since this is a position so easily assimilated by the neoconservative reading of the Revolution as a retardant of modernity and an abortion of Western social history. To take one example, Barrie Rose points to the sustained lower birthrate after the Revolution as a sign of its progressive legacy for women; Rose also argues that the reactive repression of women after 1795 did not necessarily issue from the successes of the bourgeoisie but was more likely a reassertion of the patriarchal values of the ancien régime. See also Sledziewski, Levy and Applewhite (1992), and Soboul for good discussions of the statistical evidence of militant women's dissent up until Thermidor.

In 1922 Winifred Stephens offered a balanced assessment of the Revolution's historical value for women: "The Revolution had conferred on women two new social rights: the right to divorce and the right to equality of inheritance. . . . [But] politically, women at the close of the revolution were worse off than at the beginning. In none of its aims had the Revolution failed more signally than in the establishment of equality. . . . Inequality between the sexes, despite the two reforms we have mentioned, it left more strongly accentuated than it had ever been; for relations between men and women, which before the Revolution had been regulated by vague custom, were now clearly defined by law and generally to the disadvantage of the woman" (272–75).

attempted to use them as passkeys into the developing liberal and republican public spheres.[20]

The use of manifesto-like forms by French women such as Olympe de Gouges, members of the Society of Revolutionary Republican Women, and members of the Cercle Social coincides roughly with the publication in England of a few feminist tracts, most notably Mary Wollstonecraft's *Vindication of the Rights of Women* (1792), as many feminist historians have observed. It is Joan Kelly's argument that this period beginning in 1789 marks the end of the so-called *querelle des femmes,* a nearly four-hundred-year-old tradition of feminist polemic in which women critiqued the ideology of cultural misogyny; in 1789, for the first time, Western European feminists linked their polemics with contemporary social movements that promised progressive, constructive social change.[21] *A Vindication,* for example, interpellates an audience emancipated by reason and principles of social equality, and invokes the condition of women as an index of broader political and social realities in England, while de Gouges's Declaration explicitly twins the emancipation of women with the successful consolidation of a representative French polity.[22] Enlightenment feminist tracts, exhibiting a new offensive (rather than defensive) form of argumentation and debate, concern themselves not so much with the reformation of consciousness, as had the writings of the *querelle,* as with agendas for social change, particularly agendas addressing the education of women. They make use of the newly available public discourses that afford them putative participation in public deliberation, and, especially in the case of the French feminists, access to the vehemence of revolutionary discourse.

[20] A brief review of the critically contested relation between the liberal and republican public spheres may be useful here. According to Habermas, both are subsets of the bourgeois public sphere that emerged in Europe in the latter half of the eighteenth century in response to the gradual (or, in the case of France, sudden) disappearance of forms of economic and political absolutism. The liberal public sphere is predicated on a model of private individuals *debating* public authority, usually on matters of labor and commodity exchange (Habermas 1974, 52), whereas the republican public sphere holds to a Rousseauian model in which public opinion dominates without benefit of (or interference by) debate (Habermas 1989, 99). Keith Michael Baker shifts the axis slightly in his analysis of "public opinion" in the French public sphere, wherein he distinguishes the rationalist conception of public opinion—practiced by the likes of Condorcet and based in physiocratic theories of modern reason—from a "voluntaristic conception of general will" (193) based in the theories of Rousseau and practiced with a mania for the political consensus of an entire body of citizens.

[21] See Kelly, esp. 79–80.

[22] See Elissa Guralnick for a discussion of the shared radical assumptions of Wollstonecraft's targeted audience. See also discussions of Wollstonecraft by Landes, Sledziewski, and Baker.

The enormous influence of revolutionary discourse in the French public sphere has been analyzed at length by, among others, François Furet, who characterizes such discourse as a kind of "maximalist language," impervious to political nuance and framed instead by conceptual polarities: us/them, virtue/evil, the people/the despot, masculine/feminine. The implication, of course, is that access to such a discourse will require a speaker's and an audience's repeated self-alignment with the valorized terms of these polarities. It must be said that Furet's analysis dilates the power of this "maximalist" quality to the point where "discourse" becomes synonymous with and even displaces "ideology." This unsatisfactory elision and this collapse are especially noticeable where Furet's disparagement of the Revolution is most urgent: for Furet, revolutionaries *are* their discourse, and ideology issues from the rigidity of this identification (rather than, say, material conditions or a group's imaginary relation to them). Be that as it may, it is certainly the case that revolutionary discourse possesses an impermeable quality that does not admit of much nuance or ambiguity; it is, for example, in evidence in many of the manifestoes discussed in Chapter 1. Because of this galvanized nature, revolutionary discourse is, Dorinda Outram observes, "useless for the negotiation of . . . sectional interests" (122), even though excluded groups with sectional interests may be eager "to use the discourse of dominant groups in demanding change, in order to gain the attention of such groups and to validate their own utterances" (130). Access to revolutionary discourse, in other words, may be no less difficult than the effective control of its unwieldy rhetorical mechanisms.[23]

Emerging manifesto-like tracts of this period employed revolutionary discourse, but of course were not solely constituted by such discourse; as I have noted, these new tracts could function both in the service of and in opposition to dominant political formations. Furthermore, while "revolution" became an increasingly hegemonic and finally an absolutist political ideology in France, manifestoes themselves sometimes acted as discursive struts for a broader, more radical, and less strictly nationalistic construction of the concept of revolution. According to Hannah Arendt, the political term "revolution" began at this time to include the notion that the course of history suddenly begins anew, "that an entirely new story is about to unfold" (41). Her postulate is well illustrated by the 1793 Marat-Mauger declaration that "all the revolutions which history has conserved

[23] Furet understands revolutionary discourse not as a language of revolutionaries speaking out against oppressive authority but rather as a weapon wielded by bourgeois politicians in class warfare.

for memory as well as those that have been attempted in our time have failed because people wanted to square new laws with old customs and rules, new institutions with old men. . . . REVOLUTIONARY means outside of all forms and all rules" (qtd. in Hunt 1984, 27). Proudhon completed this thought in 1851, and his brand of anarchism led to the doctrines of permanent revolution that undergird Trotsky's oeuvre: "A revolution is a force against which no other force, be it human or divine, can prevail. . . . [R]evolution advances with inevitable and menacing tread on the flowers strewn before it by its devotees, through the blood of its defenders and over the corpses of its enemies" (159).[24]

Revolution both enforces its own laws and defies law, and may be served in these reflexes by the manifesto. Furthermore, as Lynn Hunt argues, since French history offered no earlier epochs of dissent or political equanimity on which the Revolution might draw for its own stock of nationalizing myths, revolutionaries were forced to invent and invoke what Hunt calls "a 'mythic present,' the instant of creation of the new community, the sacred moment of the new consensus," which was "inherently undatable" (1984, 27). It is clear that the manifestoes of the French Revolution also helped to enact such a mythic present. They record the moment of collective respon siveness to a national event—in this case the birth of a republic—even as they foreground that response as the signal for a utopian new beginning, as a departure into an alternative version of national historical events. In this way the manifesto participated in the conceptual evolution of the French Revolution, for, says Arendt, this was the historical moment during which the term "revolution" was uncoupled from the lawfulness of a rotating, cyclical movement such as a planet or moon, and came to signify the "irresistibility" (47) and inevitability of that movement. The language of political inevitability deployed in the manifesto reflects and sustains this new eighteenth-century concept of revolution and helps to stamp the language of dissent in the nineteenth century with a specific narrative seal, as we shall see.[25]

## Radical Esperanto

In order to understand further the connection between the public sphere, the manifesto, and what Arendt calls the modern conception of

[24] From *General Idea of Revolution in the Nineteenth Century (Idée générale de la Révolution au XIXe siècle)*, see Proudhon, 159–61.

[25] Arendt maintains that "those who went into the school of revolution [in nineteenth-century Europe] learned and knew beforehand the course a revolution must take" (57).

revolution, and before we can return to the problematic relation of women to the discourse of publicness, it is necessary to elaborate a bit on the morphology of the manifesto form that I began in Chapter 1. There I suggested that the indeterminate "we" of the manifesto's revolutionary discourse occupies a position from which it can control etiology and teleology. When the "we" of the Communist Manifesto, for instance, declares that "the history of all hitherto existing society is the history of class struggles" (Marx and Engels, 335), or when the "we" of the Declaration of Independence declares that "the history of the present King of Great Britain is a history of repeated injuries and usurpation, all having in direct object the establishment of an absolute Tyranny over these States," its implicit control of first causes sets the trajectory for final outcomes. For Marx and Engels, telos is determined by categories of class struggle; for Jefferson (as for French revolutionaries a decade later), telos is constituted by the overthrow of tyrants.

The manifesto's revolutionary speaking position constructs political certainty, in other words, not just by reinforcing polemical fields, but also by assuming control of the language of history, the conditions of plot. And as we have seen, the invocation of history presented a problem for French revolutionaries, who undertook to repudiate all of French history, tainted as it was by monarchy and "unnatural" inequity. The task of creating the "mythic present," which underlay the Republic's obsessive production of new symbols, allegories, slogans, and festivals (the last of which, in Lynn Hunt's words, all "had in common the purpose of re-creating the moment of the new consensus" [1984, 28]) was for this reason also well served by the manifesto form. For if, as I argued in Chapter 1, the "history" textualized in the manifesto functions like a myth, then French revolutionary manifestic tracts could (and did) perform part of the work of securing mythic connections between the ancient republic of Rome and immediate efforts to install a republic in Europe. Moreover, for subsequent revolutionaries in the nineteenth and twentieth centuries, the manifesto's capacity for mythic connection could be renovated to include the concatenated episodes of the "permanent revolution," Proudhon's 1848 shorthand for revolution as a phenomenon occurring continuously in uneven development and at different historical junctures—or, in his words, the belief that in history, "strictly speaking, there have not been several revolutions, but only one and the same permanent revolution" (158). This propensity for continuity is a feature of the form's iterability: the manifesto bridges the episodes of the "permanent revolution" by acting as a kind of radical Esperanto across decades and nations and cultures.[26]

The manifesto also asserts its rhetorical certainty, inevitability, and "irresistibility" (to recall Arendt's term) through the use of the discourse of passionate, righteous anger: *Since* events have transpired in the perfidious way they have, the *inevitable* consequences of retaliation *must* follow. Supported as it is by a list of grievances, the manifesto's rhetorical construction of anger affords it the power of a threat of implicit or impending revolutionary violence. In conventional usage, the term "manifesto" signifies both the form and the passional state that precedes or engenders the manifesto text, as I have shown; and that state can be further illuminated by A. J. Greimas's lexical study of the emotional constellation of anger, which shows how "injured honor," "justice," "disappointment," and "hostility" are linked together by the sequence "frustration → discontent → aggressiveness" (149). In Greimas's formulation, righteous anger—the kind we associate with the manifesto—behaves as if, "as a consequence of an unfulfilled expectation, the *benevolence* that characterized the trusting, intersubjective relation gave way to *malevolence,* which will regulate the new relations; it is as if *contractual relations* had been replaced by *polemical relations*" (156). This latter point is particularly germane to the manifesto form, since one of its discursive functions in the public sphere is to register frustration and discontent at breaches or failures in presumed (or promised) contractual relations.

But this rhetorical violence is at the same time bound up in the public sphere's language of argumentation and debate. For if the manifesto seeks to provide a rationale for its figuratively violent repudiation of hegemony, it must make itself intelligible to dominant ideology. This proposition presents an especially tricky problem for subjects to whom dominant ideology already ascribes the characteristics of unintelligibility, irrationality, and immorality. The paradoxes of the manifesto form—its conflicts between participation and political marginalization, anger and restraint, threat and argument, mythic time and urgent agendas—can easily be projected onto the subjects who use the manifesto form. Magnified by the fish-eye lens of universalist normativity, such tensions may be read as

[26] Indeed, Trotsky's understanding that the permanent revolution would pass from national to international in scope seems to take for granted the existence of a reliable discursive form for that passage—which, in my thesis, is the manifesto: Whereas the teachings of Marx help to conceptualize alienated labor and means of production, it is the ringing phrases of manifestoes that help to narrativize the political unconscious.

symptoms of an inherent irrationality that threatens the stability of democratic ideals. This leaves several pressing questions concerning the manifesto's normative inflectibility: What rhetorical strategies are available to the angry disenfranchised woman, the angry colonized native, the angry racially proscribed non-citizen, the angry untouchable? For my purposes here, what are the available strategies and the implicit restraints on the angry *citoyenne* who wishes to join the dissent of the *citoyen?* Or, more specifically, the *citoyenne* who wishes to present her own demands for rights to the republic of *citoyens?* What are her "contractual relations" with the state and with the Revolution, unwritten as they are? How effectively can she mark the breach of those unspecified relations?

## Wollstonecraft and Virtue Transparent

Much recent work by cultural and literary historians has sought to disclose or to analyze the gendered terms of the developing bourgeois sphere, especially where those terms have controlled deliberation about feminist issues.[27] It has been argued in a hundred different ways—though not conclusively—that rationalist developments of the late seventeenth century served both to engender and to undercut feminist arguments issuing from Enlightenment tenets. Eighteenth-century polemicists such as Mary Astell drew on epistemologies of empiricism, individualism, new science, and rationalism in making a universalist case for the equality of women; Moira Ferguson argues that these same epistemologies were also fundamentally responsible for producing a post-Enlightenment society wherein "newly domesticated women accommodated the emerging capital-based economy [as] the individualist stance and ethic tended to become a male prerogative" (15–16). Universal individualism posed obvious difficulties for political women who, like de Gouges, were attempting to argue for woman's equality with—indeed her equivalence to—abstract, unmarked individualism, while at the same time embodying and asserting the rights of marked femininity. As Joan Wallach Scott puts it, "asserting equality led to asserting difference" (1992, 108). This paradox, which underlies the gender contradictions in revolutionary discourse, frequently derailed feminists' efforts to challenge republican representations of a unified and monolithic public.

[27] See, for example, the anthologies edited by Ferguson, by Henderson and McManus, and by Levy, Applewhite, and Johnson; see also the important historical work by Godineau, Hunt, Kelly, and Outram.

Wollstonecraft's *Vindication of the Rights of Woman,* for example, met with mostly favorable reviews from English periodicals of radical inclination (conservatives and their journals tended merely to overlook the Paine-inspired tract), but according to R. M. Janes, "most [liberal] reviewers took it to be a sensible treatise on female education and ignored those recommendations in the work that might unsettle the relations between the sexes" (298). In taking up the cause of educational reform for middle-class women, Wollstonecraft was widening a path already broken by others. The respected historian Catherine Macaulay's *Letters on Education* (1790) served as Wollstonecraft's model for equating education with virtue and arguing to uncouple learning from masculinity.[28] And the conservative Bluestockings had already begun to serve as a contemporary model for the intellectual women of the 1780s, "through combining piety, seriousness, and learning"—though, as Moira Ferguson and Janet Todd wryly observe, "they wanted this position neither improved for themselves nor extended to others" (318).

But Wollstonecraft's treatise is also distinctive for its appeals to radical language and radical styles of argumentation, though it stops well short of demanding political rights for women.[29] Anna Wilson has argued that Wollstonecraft's tract could interpellate no audience of radical women, for none existed (and none was plausible);[30] and Janes goes so far as to say that such demands would have been incomprehensible to her liberal readers in any case, for had she demanded "the franchise, equal access to professions, equal treatment under the law, abolition of discrimination on the basis of sex ... her readers might justly have thought her mad. Such recommendations would have borne no useful relation to the actual condition of women and the opportunities available to them" (307).

Janes's stubborn pessimism notwithstanding, Wollstonecraft's tract does indeed navigate a course between the expectations of a radical reading audience and the risks involved in advancing a feminist program. As Jon Klancher has shown, radical English texts at the end of the eighteenth century differed from contemporary mass journals insofar as the latter ensured that "no one speaks but everyone is spoken for" (100). Such radical

[28] See Poston, 204–12 and 319–20.

[29] See Guralnick for a useful analysis of Wollstonecraft's radical language.

[30] In Wilson's analysis, "Wollstonecraft is in the position of writing a polemic that is apparently addressed to an audience of middle-class women which has no collective sense of itself nor any capacity for political action" (94); she "has been unable to imagine ... a female audience capable of responding to a rational discourse, while her remaining audience, radical or otherwise ... threatens to rewrite her text" (97).

texts "confront[ed] their readers as collectives and representatives of collectives," aiming "not to form a singular bond between reader and writer, but to bind one reader to another as audience" (100). This binding of a radical reading audience in the 1790s usually occurred around the "Revolution debate" and those issues pertaining to republicanism generally.

*A Vindication,* published by the radical Joseph Johnson and addressed to the English radical circle, sought to introduce a feminist-reformist agenda to its audience. But the tract's reformism involves counterposing the image of the enlightened and reformed republican woman to that of the *un*-reformed woman—that is, the woman of frivolity, spectacle, and excess associated with the feminine (and feminized) aristocracy of the French ancien régime. The latter figure of "woman" (and the chain of pejorative metaphors that it forges across Wollstonecraft's text) functions as a prominent emblem of reaction, leaving Wollstonecraft with the unenviable (albeit self-imposed) task of negotiating the loaded image of woman-as-corrupt-spectacle even as she wields the conventions of the spectacular radical text in an argument *for* women's rights. The result is *A Vindication's* curious tone of reflexive self-effacement, contestatory principally insofar as it sarcastically exposes the uselessness of the bourgeois woman. In foregrounding a circumspect call for educational reform, *A Vindication* in effect subordinates woman's change to larger (and, implicitly, more important) social change.

Wollstonecraft's ambivalence toward her doubled task illuminates another facet of the problem faced by radical feminist polemicists: to write as a woman, for the cause of women, is to risk alienating one's putative audience, which in this case is an audience for whom "woman" is associated with specific contemporary political categories of divisiveness and even reaction. Wollstonecraft is understandably at pains to disassociate herself from such categories; according to Joan Landes, she "fears being mistaken by her own readers for a masquerading woman" (134), and so "orients herself almost exclusively toward the male logos . . . [celebrating] the virtues of reason and utility over feeling and flowery diction, and of writing over conversation" (135). She turns, in other words, toward what she takes to be *unmarked* writing, the writing of universalist neutrality. This is not so much an orientation toward "male logos" as toward the ideological ideal of unmarked masculinity—unadorned, a-rhetorical, impossibly "neutral." Wollstonecraft's participation in this paradox issues in her repeated insistence on the connection between virtue and an absolutely transparent writing style, for if artifice and rhetorical elegance are associated with feminine corruption, then her own stylistic transparency marks the emergence of a new, "reformed" ("unmarked") woman—the product, Wollstonecraft would seem to say, of a new order of masculine political virtue.[31]

The troubled relation of women to virtue which shadows *A Vindication* is much more palpable in the evolving republicanism of revolutionary France, where "virtue" functions as a particularly multivalent and contested sign. Dorinda Outram argues that the term "virtue" "bisected the apparently universalistic terminology of *le sovereign* into two distinct political destinies, one male and the other female" (125), and although this assertion may seem an excessively schematic characterization of the fungible codes of gender in the Revolution, it is nevertheless possible to see where the Revolution's widespread and multivalent uses of the concept of virtue helped to sort "the people" into gendered symbiotic domains.[32] Male virtue was frequently associated with an unyielding commitment to the Republic—a commitment personified (and made iconic) by Brutus, who sacrificed his (domestic) family for Rome. Female virtue, by contrast, was frequently represented in republican discourse as domestic, natural, and *un*-public, thereby differing sharply from the political corruption widely associated, both in popular media and in political theory, with the woman-centered salon culture of the ancien régime—a culture that was from the beginning conflated, in revolutionary discourse, with prostitution and sexual corruption. In two very different studies, Lynn Hunt and Antoine de Baecque have shown how revolutionary political pamphlets codified the image-laden contrast between a feminized, sexually profligate aristocracy of old and a masculinized, healthy, sexually vigorous new republic.[33] Fashioning a new form of "virtue" for the Republic, then, ulti-

[31] The question of what "transparent" (or for that matter "masculine") constitutes is entirely relativistic. Whereas Landes, reading Wollstonecraft, assumes a definitive equation between revolutionary rhetoric and stripped-down syntax, Gary Farnell reminds us that Edmund Burke contrasts "the simple, Adamic language of the English Establishment with the fallen, avant-garde discourse of Revolutionary France [and] defends defiantly the comparative anarchism of the former: [Burke remarks that] 'We . . . have learned to speak only the primitive language of the law, and not the confused jargon of [its] Babylonian pulpits'" (45).

[32] The fluctuations of class categories with the rise and fall of different political factions, for example, make it impossible to ascertain what might be a "male" political destiny or where "female" spheres began and ended. But even Albert Soboul, who is not particularly interested in making a special case for the paradoxical status of the *citoyennes,* nevertheless suggests the lability of the class and gender identifications of militant women during the antiterrorist repression of spring 1795: they were "characterized by two essential traits: a visceral egalitarianism and an intimate conviction that women, also, constituted the sovereign people" (166).

[33] Hunt's thesis centers on the "many bodies of Marie Antoinette" (1991, 108–30): she analyzes a multitude of pornographic pamphlets that were in circulation before the queen's execution in 1792, and concludes that if Marie Antoinette had "many bodies" (and certainly the pornographic press represented her homosexual body, her licentious body, her incestuous body, her maternal body, her foreign body, etc.), then as an aristocratic sovereign installed during the ancien régime, Marie Antoinette herself was multivalent and threatened the Republic with a kind of symbolic dis-

mately meant refitting it for double duty in a gender system embarking on new amplifications of masculinity. For if the activities of the political woman of the old regime—the powerful, class-marked woman of the salon—invisibly influenced official (public) policy, then the whole notion of the political woman still held out some symbolic threat to the republican concept of a virtuous, unmediated "people's will" that dictated government policy. The "new" man created by the Revolution would be impervious to the taint of femininity in any form.

The Revolution's discursive emphasis on the pairing of transparency and artifice has been analyzed by a number of commentators including Lynn Hunt, whose work on the symbolic codes of revolutionary allegories and festivals has particular resonance for the problems faced by feminists attempting to use revolutionary discourse. According to Hunt, "factional politics was synonymous with conspiracy, and 'interests' was a code word for betrayal of a nation united. Nothing particular (and all 'interests' were by definition particular) was supposed to divide the general will. Constant vigilance and the publicity of all politics were the ways to prevent the emergence of particular interests and factions. Behind these notions was the revolutionary belief in the possibility and desirability of 'transparency' between citizen and citizen, between citizens and their government, between the individual and the general will" (1984, 44).

Especially for the sansculottes, who developed what we might think of as a subculture around the sign of citizenship—complete with a code of dress to rival Freud's narcissism of minor differences—the concept of "transparency" accommodated a whole host of (quite artificial) political and aesthetic values: simple speech, the scorning of money, the public performance of friendship and *fraternité*, symbolic dress, moral opposition to irony, the commitment to visible collectivities.[34] The authenticity of "transparency" was always set in implicit contrast to counterrevolutionary "interests" masked by artifice, dissembling, privacy, and secrecy, and these

---

simulation. De Baecque argues that the pornographic political pamphlets of the late eighteenth century were instrumental in the creation of "a new political mythology, stamped by a strange frenetic Manicheanism that contrasts the degenerate aristocrat with the new revolutionary man of light" (168). The pamphlets repeatedly contrast debauched aristocratic homosexuality and impotence with the "controlled, hygienic, and virile" (169) practices of the republicans.

[34] The concept of transparency paradoxically helped to facilitate the divide between private and public spheres by offering ideological assurances of the utter permeability of that divide for the sansculottes: a good citizen was the same thing as a good husband or son or father; a man could not be one without also being the other. The rhetorical obliteration of distinctions between private and public goodness drew an ultimate equivalency of value between the two spheres. See the entry under "Sans-culottes" by Patrice Higonnet in Furet and Ozouf (1989a, 393–99).

were the very masks associated with the earlier tradition of "women's politics"—that is, the old regime salon politics of powerful aristocratic women—from which feminists again and again were forced to distinguish themselves.

Wollstonecraft's *Vindication* pointedly illustrates the stylistic implications of this task of self-differentiation, as we have seen. She vows in her introduction to be "concerned about things, not words" (10), since words (and especially words wound into "flowery diction") can be manipulated in the service of sectional interests. By this same token, Olympe de Gouges's *tout court* appropriation of the format of the new French constitution's Declaration of the Rights of Man and Citizen may also be understood as a tactic used to forestall doubts about rhetorical dissimulation (which, in her case, might be used to support the charges of royalism leveled against her, or the charge of aristocratic espionage leveled against most women's clubs). Joan Landes indicates, however, that in adopting revolutionary discourse for feminist purposes—a discourse modeled on Rousseau's notion of the virtuous self—such women also ironically adopted the gendered inflections of Rousseau's formulations. I am cautious about the applicability of this broad formulation to all women in all classes active in the Revolution, but evidence nevertheless suggests that revolutionary women were up against an instrumental contradiction between "an ideology of [universal] rights and a commitment to nature in which women are to be assigned a subordinate place" (Landes, 123).

Dorinda Outram paints the impasse in starker tones, naming more explicitly what she sees as an emergent separate spheres ideology: "For a woman to speak this . . . male language was in effect to endorse the destruction of her sphere, the home. . . . Such an inconsistency could do nothing but undermine the authority of any woman who tried to use this revolutionary discourse" (128). Building on (while challenging) the theses of François Furet, she maintains that authority in political discourse was available only to those who were capable of *personifying* its tenets. Robespierre's personification of the republican discourse of reason and passion, for instance, helped to consolidate public and private roles into a performance of patriotism. For women, however, such personification involved risking their credibility as stalwart revolutionaries of the domestic space while simultaneously risking suspicion in the active political sphere. The woman who refused to give up political activism faced a conundrum: either she had to conform to the political profile of the republican mother, or she had to risk censure as a selfish source of divisiveness for the Republic.[35] Still, as Outram points out, and as I will argue as well, revolutionary discourse could offer some distinct advantages to the feminist speaking subject. By assuming the voice of revolutionary discourse, a woman could evade the social trap that made femininity a cause for silence. Revolutionary discourse offered a performative link to republican universality and the advantages it held out, including the promise of authority to "the otherwise compromised position of the female speaker in a public arena" (Outram, 131). And to adopt a manifesto-like form in particular, with its minimalist oracular style, numbered and largely untheorized demands, and collective or anonymous authorship, is to adopt a form as free from apparent counterrevolutionary entailment as any available.

## Sectional Voices

Habermas dates the appearance of the plebeian public sphere to October 1793, from which we may surmise that he is referring to the Convention's official declaration of revolutionary government (and the concurrent suspension of the constitution "until peace" should be won between France and her enemies). When we recognize in his narrative the fact that the brief ascendancy of this French revolutionary "plebeian" public sphere occurs during the *signal moment* of women's institutionalized exclusion from political activity, we may feel the force of Joan Landes's thesis that "the Republic was constructed against women, not just without them" (171).[36] I shall return presently to Habermas's image of the plebeian public

[35] The records show that women spoke out publicly all the time during all phases of the Revolution before Thermidor (see, e.g., Soboul, 164–67; Godineau 1990; Farge). The conditions of their speech were quite specific, however: in the guise of being "mothers," "angry women," engineers of the domestic sphere, and demystifying voices of the Republic's conscience, women could and did speak "loudly" (a word seen frequently in transcripts of women's speeches). But, as I have argued elsewhere, a woman speaking as an allegory of the state secures a very different reception than a woman claiming to speak as a rights-bearing individual. It was these women who were at the greatest risk during the revolution. See Lyon 1994–95.

[36] Rose, Sledziewski, and Baker all challenge Landes's assertion that the Revolution was constructed against women. All of them point to the philosophy and influence of Condorcet's feminism, to revolutionary changes in marriage law, to the decreased hold of the Catholic Church on the French citizenry, and especially to the actual record of women's participation as active citizens in the Revolution. It is important, however, to pay attention to the kind and mode of discourse associated with the various factions that, on the one hand, agitated to produce progressive change for women or, on the other, programmatically obstructed the winning of individual rights for women. The former groups, using the rationalist discourse of human rights, tended to associate themselves with the physiocratic method of obtaining political consensus. The latter groups almost invariably traded in revolutionary discourse, which was used both by Jacobins (who were predominantly anti-feminist) and by sansculottes (who agitated for a standard of living set by women in their capacities as engineers of the domestic sphere). Baker accuses Landes of overlooking the contributions of Condorcet's feminism to the Revolution. While it may be the case that

sphere as a submerged but continuous entity (and the image's instructive resemblance to Proudhon's formulation of the permanent revolution). For the moment, however, I want to draw out the relation between the hypothetical appearance of this plebeian public sphere and the increasingly restrictive control of gender categories enacted in its discourse and its laws.

Between September 1791 and October 1793—or, roughly speaking, between the time that de Gouges published her Declaration and the time of her execution—the Revolution's symbolic construction of citizenship, accomplished through popular processions, speeches, and slogans, increasingly foregrounded the glorious spectacle of armed radicalism.[37] The representation of women in this construction was handled differently both by and within liberal and republican circles. On the one hand, a growing number of bourgeois liberal clubs established women's auxiliary wings and supported limited political rights for women, concentrating mainly on their entitlement to the vote, to education, and to indirect participation in the Legislative Assembly; but these clubs officially sidestepped the pressing question of whether women, as citizens, could claim the right to bear arms. At the same time, the liberal Legislative Assembly, following the lead of Prudhomme's editorials in *Révolutions des Paris,* refused to women the (male) constitutional right to bear arms or to carry the "Holy Pike,"—a weapon acknowledged as the national emblem of "independence, equality under arms, vigilance, and the recovery of liberty" (Levy and Applewhite 1992, 88). On the other hand, and in contrast to the liberal reformist attitude to women, the republican Paris Commune's General Council (which would condemn de Gouges a year later) honored militant *citoyennes* as patriots and leaders of the "national family *in arms*" (Levy and Applewhite 1992, 91; emphasis added), while laying aside the constitutional issue of whether the *citoyenne* should vote.

However considerable may have been these differences between the liberal emphasis on incremental reform and the republican emphasis on visible popular solidarity, they all but evaporated with the ascendancy of the Commune. When, in 1792, the Commune usurped the powers of the Legislative Assembly, it in effect replaced a site of factional debate with a mechanism for the universal proclamation of popular will. From this new

---

Landes conflates the physiocratic program with the Rousseauian program, one nevertheless feels the force of Landes's argument: Rousseau's program prevailed, after all. See Condorcet, "On the Admission of Women to the Rights of Citizenship" (1790) and "The Nature and Purpose of Public Instruction" (1791), esp. pt. III, C (97–142).

[37] For a measure of this trend, see the documents collected and translated by Levy, Applewhite, and Johnson, especially in Part III.

perspective the rights of women could be considered only insofar as they advanced the Commune's monolithic notion of the public good. And since that notion came increasingly to depend on "the well-ordered family as the foundation of the well-ordered state" (Scott 1988, 47), the Commune moved to stabilize the emblem of the national family by securely linking the domestic empowerment of women to the law of public good. In the waning months of 1792, after the king's arrest and the "Second Revolution" (in which, as Levy and Applewhite have shown, women played key roles), discursive avenues of liberal debate about the rights of women were further blocked by a narrowing of the free press, which, with the elimination of the royalist press in 1792, became polarized along the lines of Girondin and Jacobin debate.[38] Political clubs became the primary sites of broader and more participatory discussion; but clubs—both Girondin and Jacobin—began to ban women from membership or attendance in late 1792, as both militant republican women and reformist liberal women came to be viewed in their respective camps with mounting suspicion.

By the time the National Convention outlawed women's clubs and popular societies in October 1793, the newly reconstituted "we" of the Republic could declare that "the private functions for which women are destined by their very nature are related to the general order of society; this social order results from the differences between man and woman." Since it was "not possible for women to exercise political rights," the Convention moved to "destroy these alleged popular societies of women which the aristocracy would want to set up to put them [women] at odds with men, to divide the latter by forcing them to take sides in these quarrels, and to stir up disorder."[39] In short, women's participation in the plebeian public sphere was never completely purged of the taint of aristocratic espionage and factional chaos. Women's political subjecthood lay beyond the political imaginary of the plebeian public sphere, unrecognized by the National Convention (and perhaps unthought even by Habermas in 1962).

It seems clear enough that the moment of the consolidation of this plebeian public sphere—that is, the moment when consensual assembly became associated with a unified public opinion of "citizens assembled for acclamation" rather than for "rational-critical public debate" (Habermas 1989, 99)—cannot be understood apart from the evacuation of women

[38] See Gilchrist and Murray, 10–12, for an account of this narrowing of the field.
[39] "The National Convention Outlaws Clubs and Popular Societies of Women," in Levy, Applewhite, and Johnson, 215, 217. "Man," the presiding officer goes on to inform us, "is strong, robust, born with great energy, audacity, and courage; he braves perils and the intemperance of the seasons because of his constitution . . . he alone seems to be fit for profound and serious thinking."

from sanctioned activity in that sphere. But by the same token, so complete an evacuation compels us to look for other forms of discourse taken up by women, once their participation in the production of public opinion had been conditionally constricted. In fact, certain modes of discourse did remain available to republican women, and took two main forms. First, women wrote petitions to the Commune on behalf of relatives arrested during the Terror; these were characterized by humble language, deferential forms of address, personal appeals, and repeated assurances of patriotic intent.[40] Such petitions rarely were collectively authored, and they were devoid of the language of demands that shaped the rancorous *cahiers de doléances* of the early Revolution;[41] for, despite the fact that women's petitions during the Terror retained the name of *cahiers,* they never denoted sanctioned participation in the formation of a common will.[42]

A second, more powerful form of public discourse, however, began to be used by militant women who had been excluded from political clubs (and even club galleries), and "who could not make themselves fully heard in section assemblies," especially in the months after the Thermidorian government displaced the Terror in July 1794. This was women's practice of "speaking out in the markets, on bread lines, in the street, in groups, and in front of the Convention . . . [which] amounted to a diffuse and scarcely structured 'organization,' to be sure . . . but one that offered the advantage of being harder to control and to dismantle" (Godineau 1990, 71). The political import of such a practice may be guessed from an ordinance passed by the Convention in 1795, which, remarkably, prohibited groups of more than five women from congregating in the street.

Thus, while the discourse of women was virtually eliminated from civil institutions of public opinion, and even as those forums were eroded by

[40] See Levy, Applewhite, and Johnson, 221–70, for a broad selection of these humble petitions by republican women. Compare my discussion of petitions in Chapter 1.

[41] One notable exception was Pauline Léon's petition to the National Assembly arguing for the right of women to bear arms. Presented by a delegation of *citoyennes* to the Assembly, it contained more than three hundred signatures and preceded by nearly a year the Jacobins' crackdown on women's public assembly. See Levy and Applewhite 1992, 89–90.

[42] According to Landes, the *cahiers de doléances* were the formal responses to Louis XVI's direction to the general public to draw up communal lists of demands and grievances. More than sixty thousand of these responses still exist. Landes notes, however, that women rarely participated in this "officially sanctioned grievance process" (107). Ironically, during the Revolution, women's petitions were called *cahiers,* and this suggests to Landes that there existed "a never-realized potential for women to have been included in the 'official' political process" (232 n. 10). The effective suppression of women's political demands and public political activity during the moment of the "people's" sphere followed by two years the Legislative Assembly's suppression of manifestoes and petitions from the *sections* of Paris, a suppression that fueled the fires of republicanism and fatally weakened the Assembly's constitutional authority. See Levy and Applewhite 1992 for an overview of events from June 1789 through October 1793.

the bourgeois regime of Thermidor, women's *un*authorized discourse became a prominent formation of resistance. Marginalized though it was, its influence was obvious in legitimate instruments of public opinion. As Dominique Godineau has demonstrated, newspaper reports began to evince the rhetorical traces of the power of women's sloganeering. Commentators observed that "'if [women] began to dance, men would follow'; 'Women will begin the movement . . . men will come to the support of the women'; 'We cannot kid ourselves; in the stormy moments which have troubled this city, women have played the role of firebrands'"(quoted in Godineau 1990, 74–75).[43]

The verbal discourse of militant women, much like the discourse deployed in the manifesto, functioned as a denotative speech act for, in this case, a broad but specifically republican audience: it effected revolutionary action through the "hostile hand" of threat, exhortation, rhetorical polarization, and the enumeration of demands. In Godineau's formulation, the words of women "retained their full meaning, as the incitement and support of action" (76); in fact, "the word of women, often a prelude to the act of insurrection . . . became one of the elements of action, a specifically feminine element. Numerous documents convince us that *the word as an element of action* was one of the original features of women's participation in the revolutionary process" (78; emphasis added). This spoken discourse of women is, I would argue, the most performative of revolutionary speech acts: their anonymous lists of demands instigate immediate insurrection on the part of the men berated and ridiculed by revolutionary women. It is precisely this kind of performativity that manifestoes seek to incorporate: the written word as an element of action, the written word that retains the trace of the shouted threat, the body agitating in the street, the insult, the impatient shove toward embroilment and danger.

Like manifestoes issued during and in the wake of the Revolution, the word of women in the street drove a wedge into the republican political system. It is important to note, however, that the demands voiced in this way were formulated as the needs of women as subjects of the *domestic* sphere; they were articulated as the needs of the "natural" inhabitants of a conceptually gendered and devalued political stratum. Food shortages and

[43] Using a long list of excerpts from police reports, Godineau illustrates the "singular monotony" (i.e., ubiquity) of the recording of women's activities, including: "'Women say that men are assholes [*des jean-foutre*] to let themselves be led in such a fashion' (24 Germinal [1795])"; "'women call men "assholes" for not going to the Convention to demand an account of grain (supplies)' (25 Germinal)"; "'women . . . harangue men, treating them as cowards . . . a great number of the women want to rise up in insurrection' (7 Floréal)"; women "'provoke men to rebellion and pillage by uttering insults' (22 Floréal)" (74).

inflation provoked women to "cry out against the Convention, saying that men are stuck pigs (*couillons*) to endure hunger" (quoted in Godineau 1990, 74). These were not demands for *women's* political rights per se: by July 1794 agitation for legal and social reforms for women had, by and large, ceased. According to one record, women now "initiated processions to the local and national authorities to demand bread and the rights of the people; they created disturbances in the bread lines and began operations of *taxation populaire;* they collaborated in conspiracies; and they poured invectives on the Thermidorian police, magistrates, and National Guards" (Levy, Applewhite, and Johnson, 272).[44]

I want especially to remark here a covert discursive formation issuing from the relation between the incendiary words of women in the street during the later stages of the Revolution and the manifesto form as it took its force from the discourse of the Revolution. Women's words in the street, free from the constraints of the printed page and untethered by generic conventions, attacked the failures of the Revolution from a position within revolutionary ideology: in the name of the Revolution women demanded bread for the people but not civil or social rights for themselves. Even those demands, however, registered increasingly as refractors of public opinion, coming as they did from *citoyennes* who could be neither citizens nor political subjects. The shouted demands of women represented something beyond revolutionary ideology: they were always already sectional; they had *prerevolutionary* origins and came into existence with the rise of France and the consolidation of central authority.[45] The violence they embodied challenged the sanctity of the Revolution's separate gender spheres, insofar as the demands constituted an extreme, unchartered voice of "the people." For a revolution that limited women's political involvement to service to "the people" in the capacity of domestic partners and providers, the angry dissidence of women resonated on several levels. First, it demonstrated beyond all doubt the permeability of the so-called

[44] *Taxation populaire* was the enviable practice, by women shoppers, of seizing overpriced merchandise, declaring their own fair price on it, and then paying that price instead of the inflated price demanded by the merchant. *Taxation populaire* was a form of crowd action, and it was accomplished through the threat of mob violence.

[45] See, for an example of the transhistorical force of the word of women in the street, a woman's "Exhortation to the French People" (1725) quoted in Farge: "Since the injustice of those who govern us has no bounds, it is up to us, the French people, to set bounds to their power. It is time to take up arms and abolish tyranny . . . the remedy I am proposing to you is extreme, but when evil is inveterate one must apply steel and fire. . . . There is no other way, since all the remonstrances made by the parlement have been in vain." Farge adds that although the violence was repressed, "the discourse of that time left its mark and went on developing, to be applied later to a new political situation" (116).

domestic sphere; second, it exposed fractures in the theoretically unified will of "the people"; and third, and perhaps most important, it was living proof of the Republic's failure to provide adequately for "the people" at the level of the most basic social unit. Dissenting mothers could hardly be accused of divisive interest—at least not if "the family" were to retain its symbolic status as a microcosm of the Republic and its actual status as economic base. Women's charge that all men were "cowards for letting themselves be led about" by the Thermidorians (quoted in Godineau 1990, 74) foregrounded the fact that women were *not* "led about," that their participation in the public sphere was spontaneous and idiosyncratic, that they were fundamentally unrepresented.[46]

After the suppression of the plebeian public sphere in 1795, such idiosyncratic voices were thoroughly suppressed. Revolutionary discourse, however, inherited something of this voice in the street, the voice of women beyond the institutional law and beyond representation. This voice was to be emulated in the prose of subsequent installments of the *révolution en permanence*. During the Revolution itself, however, the manifesto would necessarily need to avoid appearing as a threat to the unity of public opinion in the plebeian public sphere, since, as a speechmaker in the National Assembly put it, "it is only through public opinion that you can acquire any power to promote the good . . . it is only through public opinion that the cause of the people—for so long given up as hopeless—has prevailed. . . . [B]efore public opinion all authorities become silent, all prejudices disappear, all particular interests are effaced" (quoted in Habermas 1989, 99). An effective revolutionary manifesto would therefore need to honor a monolithic construction of public opinion and be as free as possible from all markers of "interest." But as we have seen, even the *shouted* word of women necessarily bore the markers of "special interest." A "disinterested" polemic, after all, would necessarily be something of a rhetorical oxymoron.

A utopian editorial manifesto published by the radical abbé Fauchet in 1793 in *Le Journal des Amis* provides an example of the impossibility of producing a party-line revolutionary document that does not carry the scent of "interest." Making use of the vaguest apocalyptic language of revolutionary inevitability, the manifesto opens with the paratactic proposition

[46] The condition of being unrepresented as it is characterized by Godineau (1990) bears an ironic resemblance to the category of the proletariat as it is used and defined by Jacques Rancière: both the French revolutionary women in the street and the hypothetical proletariat (Rancière's "in-between") can be said to occupy "a common place that is not a place for a dialogue or a search for a consensus in Habermasean fashion" (Rancière, 62).

that "the universe will be free; all the thrones will be overturned. . . . Social wisdom will raise itself on the remains of the tyrannical and servile passions that ruled the ignorance of nations." Its "we" is as broad as possible: "Delivered from all chains we shall be happy with all things. Fraternity will unite the human family, and equality of rights will finally make man king of the earth." But in his reworking of the narrative of origins and telos, the abbé champions Girondin philosophy over Jacobin "common sense": "At present we are in the most terrible crisis of humanity. I believed that philosophy, which laid the way for it, would be able to soften it, to make less painful this second travail of nature. But philosophy . . . has still no hold over the hearts of men."[47] This centralizing of a Girondin program—the core of "interestedness" in the abbé Fauchet's seemingly uninflected utopian manifesto—was perfectly legible to Fauchet's opponents; he would be executed four months later by the now dominant Jacobins for his moderation and for his espousal of the Girondin cause, a cause that would, in the eyes of his enemies, subordinate public will to sectional recognition.

From the beginning of the Revolution, discussions of the divisive effect of interests on public opinion dominated newspaper discourse: the prospectus for *Le Patriote français* (April 1789) declared, "It is known that *there is only one interest*. . . . What we need now is unity of opinion" (rpt. in Gilchrist and Murray, 46–47). Lynn Hunt has argued that the republic's suspicion of "interest" was inseparable from its obsessional and central use of the language of unmasking (1984, 38–45); and certainly recent histories of women's participation in the Revolution show that women's interests were repeatedly unmasked and taxonomized as chaotic, counterrevolutionary, or divisive. But the alternative strategy meant appealing to the ideals of a single interest and unified public opinion, which, inevitably, falsely subordinated concerns for women's conditions to the "universal" goals of the Republic. In this universalizing impulse of the Revolution, the revolutionary manifesto was complicit: if to produce a "we" was to recalibrate the rhetorical relations between particular subjects and revolutionary ideology, the restrictions entailed in the universalism of this "we" nevertheless outstripped its inclusivity. Women had to behave as republicans unmarked by gender if they were to be taken seriously as revolutionary subjects: their wants could never exceed their needs, and those needs had to be commensurate with the needs of the universal revolutionary subject, which was, of course, male.

[47] Abbé Fauchet, "The End of the Old World," rpt. in Gilchrist and Murray, 263.

## Gender in Aesthetics

I have noted the striking resemblance between Habermas's notion of a continuous but submerged plebeian public sphere and Proudhon's *révolution en permanence*—the "one and the same permanent revolution" (158) issuing from the French Revolution and manifesting itself periodically in the agonistic voice and the agitating bodies of the people. The manifesto, as a discursive mode of this plebeian "public sphere stripped of its literary garb," retains in its conventions the trace of struggle for each of the Revolution's subsequent phases, developments, and incarnations. It also retains the valuative gendering by which the Republic encoded the signs of its national vigor and differentiated its nationalist program from that of the aristocratic old regime. And if we hold for a moment to Proudhon's and Habermas's formulations of a political imaginary in which revolutions—or, more broadly, historical moments of plebeian ascendancy—link themselves back to 1789, then the editorial manifesto of the final number of the avowedly antifeminist *Révolutions de Paris* (February 13–28, 1794) resonates rather sharply for the politics of gender in the Revolution's subsequent episodes:

> You generations that will succeed us, more blessed than we, having learnt from our mistakes and become wise by our follies, it will doubtless be enough to have charted for you the main reefs. . . . For too long have we allowed women to leave their homes to be present at the deliberations of the legislators, at the debates of the popular societies. You will recall their true, their unique vocation, and not permit them to deviate from it any more. They will continue to adorn the national feasts, but they will no longer interfere in public affairs. . . . The motherland will be neither a vixen nor a stepmother. You will see in her only a good mother of her family. You will love her, you will adore her. . . . Every citizen must love the Republic as his mistress. (rpt. in Gilchrist and Murray, 301–2)

This clarion call to future revolutions invokes the Republic's female allegories in all of their glorious contradictions—Marianne the maternal, virtuous mistress—even as it identifies political women as meddlers and interferers, "the reefs" around which subsequent generations must chart their courses. Indeed, as I will argue in the brief overview that follows, subsequent manifestoes of the political avant-garde reiterated this concern with republican roles and with the gendering of discourse; even the Communist Manifesto denigrates French communism of the 1840s as "completely emasculated" (Marx and Engels, 356), and cultural critics who were contemporaries of Marx in the nineteenth-century artistic avant-garde made strategic and similar use of gender in their writings. It can be said that one of the least acknowledged legacies of the French Revolution for the nineteenth century is this: while its discourse may have provided a pivot for radicalism across aesthetic and political sectors, it also enforced a deeply conservative set of codes through which certain putatively "universal" ideals were reproduced.

It is hardly surprising, then, that the public discourse of many women of the nineteenth-century political avant-garde remained palpably circumspect with regard to gender roles. Joan Wallach Scott has argued in broad terms that the Chartist movement positioned itself within the contemporary popular debate on natural rights and labor by designating as "feminine" those strands of the debate from which it wished to distance itself, especially the populist strands (such as Owenism) that were utopian or religious. For the "masculine" Chartist movement, "masculine/feminine serves to define abstract qualities and characteristics through an opposition perceived as natural: strong/weak, public/private, rational/expressive, material/spiritual" (1988, 63). Although this set of dichotomies may blur the nuances of historical specificity, Scott is nevertheless correct to contend that the gender assumptions contributing to Chartist constructions of class and universal human rights left women of the movement with two possible positions from which to represent themselves in the discourse of rights. The first position was that of the universal member of the working class, unmarked by special interests. The second position was that of the "troubling exception, asserting particular needs and interests detrimental to class politics" (64). These, as we have seen, were approximately the two positions available to radical women active in the plebeian public sphere of the Revolution. Thus, according to Eileen Yeo, many Chartist women often "presented themselves mainly in a multi-faceted family role—as the primary tenders of the family . . . who demanded the vote for their male kinfolk in a bid to help the family as a whole."[48] Writing about women Chartists who agitated in the streets, Jutta Schwarzkopf quotes a women's tract which boasts to oppressors that "domesticated woman [is] leaving her homestead and battling for the rights of those that are dear to her" (97). In short, home-identified women forged an activist identity for themselves by exploiting the elasticity of the seemingly inflexible concep-

[48] Eilieen Yeo, "Some Practices and Problems of Chartist Democracy," in Epstein and Thompson, 345–80; quoted in Scott 1988, 65.

tual spheres of home and street: they justified public rioting as a way of securing domestic survival. In the nineteenth-century, and even into the
twentieth century in England, the spectacle of women in the streets carried
with it the distinct taint of Jacobinism. Burke's portrait of the maniacal female revolutionary had stuck, to such a degree that demonstrating
Chartist women were viewed not simply as "unnatural" but as un-English.
John Dinwiddy has shown in detail how a revisionary appreciation of the
Revolution was adopted in the 1830s by some radical Chartists, leading to
widespread suspicion in the establishment that foreign (i.e., French)
influence fueled the fires of dissidence everywhere in England. One Rev-
erend Francis Close, chastising female Chartists in 1839, is quoted by
Schwarzkopf in this connection: "Alas! in these evil days—these *foreign*
days on *British* soil . . . women now become politicians . . . and so desti-
tute are they of all sense of female decorum, of female modesty and
diffidence, that they become themselves political agitators—female dicta-
tors—female mobs—female Chartists!" (116).

In noting that women who organized politically did so overwhelmingly
in the name of the family, I do not mean to suggest that activist women
simply played into the program of republican motherhood.[49] My argument is not about degrees of "false consciousness" but about discursive
contingencies, and specifically about how the configurations of the "permanent revolution" frequently retain the Republic's gender directives and
represent for women the problem of differentiating themselves as individuals while laying claim to the rights underpinned by the doctrine of universal freedom and equality. The trained eye will see this encoding through
gender—indeed, the identification of active citizenship with masculinity—reemerging in many of the revolutionary aesthetic manifestoes that
appeared in Europe in the late nineteenth and early twentieth centuries,
particularly those produced in France and Italy.

Any reading of aesthetic manifestoes cannot overestimate the importance of the manifesto form's gender markings, especially since aesthetic
manifestoes and political manifestoes are so rarely read or theorized in relation to each other. To take a notable example, Marjorie Perloff has argued
that "the Futurist manifesto [of 1909] marks the transformation of what
had traditionally been a vehicle for political statement into a literary, one
might say, a quasi-poetic construct" (81–82). But no genre transformation
can ever be said to be a complete one; and in this case Perloff's formulation

[49] In fact, as Ellen DuBois points out, Chartist women were the first to struggle for female
suffrage; they failed famously, however, in their attempts to have it included in the People's Charter (see DuBois, 24). For an excellent history of the Charter's revision, see Gareth Stedman Jones.

occludes the ideological connections between the political and aesthetic programs that share a revolutionary discourse. Indeed, Perloff leaves aside the politicality of the aesthetic manifesto *as well as* the literary artistry of the political manifesto: in her brief formulation, political rhetoric as art disappears.[50] What the intersections between political avant-gardes and artistic avant-gardes show us, on the contrary, is that the revolutionary discourse that structures many aesthetic manifestoes cannot be understood solely by means of aesthetic codes.

According to Renato Poggioli, in the years between the revolutions of 1830 and 1848 in France, the term "avant-garde" shifted in use from its original military milieu to a metaphoric description of forward-looking political vigilance, even heroism. Representatives of this new avant-garde linked political and aesthetic realms through an ethos of political activism. In 1845 Gabriel-Désiré Laverdant published *De la mission de l'art et du role des artistes,* one of the first continental tracts to imagine art as an instrument of radical social agitation.[51] "To know whether the artist is truly of the avant-garde," writes Laverdant, "one must know where Humanity is going, know what the destiny of the human race is " (quoted in Poggioli, 9). For Laverdant the artist, *historical teleology* is necessary to any radical artistic production, just as it inheres in revolutionary discourse as a principle of utopian inevitability. Thirty years later, the European political avant-garde was forever welded to the idea of a permanent revolution by the bloody failures of the 1871 Commune insurrection. When the emerging artistic avant-garde of this time foregrounded its connection to revolutionary struggle, it did so on the level of rhetorical and anti-institutional practices, from Zola's "revolution" of the "experimental method" to Strindberg's fantasy of artists growing "strong as the pioneers of the French Revolution."[52]

This alignment of political and artistic avant-gardes was always asymptotic, however, and when after the 1880s a burgeoning number of artistic circles claimed the term "avant-garde" for themselves, that term eventually came to be synonymous with artistic, rather than political, vanguardism.[53]

[50] That said, Perloff's discussion of the manifesto's transformation at the hands of F. T. Marinetti and others is carefully honed and extremely useful. See Perloff, 74–84, and chap. 3, passim. For an important analysis of the relation of the Communist Manifesto to early (French) literary modernism, for example, see Berman, 87–129.

[51] Shelley is one of the early figures in England to amalgamate aesthetic and populist polemic. For an account of his artistic and political response to Peterloo, see Rowland, chap. 4.

[52] Émile Zola, "The Experimental Novel," quoted in Ellmann and Feidelson, 285; August Strindberg, Preface to *Miss Julie,* quoted in Ellman and Feidelson, 290.

[53] See Poggioli, 12. For an interesting discussion of the difficult and magnetized relationship between avant-garde art and avant-garde politics, see Wollen, esp. chap. 4.

Certainly, for that matter, the aesthetic manifestoes that appeared in the years following the publication of Jean Moréas's Symbolist Manifesto (1886) increasingly distanced themselves from what Habermas calls the "literary garb" that had previously clothed public discourse about art. Likewise, as artistic manifestoes became terser and more oblique, parodic and paratactic, they challenged the post-Kantian autonomous category of the aesthetic, and engaged with a revolutionary discourse that putatively took as its subject an audience of artist-revolutionaries. In the words of the French historian Eugen Weber, "Revolution had always gone with rhetoric; now [in the 1880s] it was increasingly consigned *to* rhetoric" (171). Nowhere is this clearer than in the Symbolist Manifesto, where Moréas relates the history of art in the language of revolutionary cycles and employs metaphors of deposed monarchs and inevitable upheaval.[54] He declares, in phrasing reminiscent of Laverdant and the abbé Fauchet, that "a new manifestation of art was expected, necessary, inevitable. This manifestation, which has long been desired, is blossoming" (rpt. in B. Mitchell, 27).

This is not to say that aesthetic manifestoes, with all their talk of blossoming flowers, worked to vitiate the form's political charge. On the contrary, the manifesto's appearance in its aesthetic form was precisely of a piece with the revolutionary—though perhaps entirely textual—attempt to repoliticize art in the face of its instrumental commodification in the late nineteenth century. The work of Peter Bürger is crucial to an understanding of the cultural formation in which the aesthetic manifesto operates and of which it is a constitutive part. Bürger's central argument in *The Theory of the Avant-Garde* is that the very concept of an artistic avant-garde cannot be understood or theorized except as a repudiation of and an attack on the bourgeois institution of art—that is, on art as an apolitical discourse, quarantined from praxis by the conditions of modern alienation masquerading as "autonomous" aesthetic value.[55] In light of this understanding of the revolution consigned to the text, the manifesto may be seen not as a paper tiger but as an intervention in the organization of cultural practices.

Given this commitment on the part of groups in the historical avant-garde to reintegrate political and artistic programs in the service of an anti-bourgeois ideal, it is all the more remarkable that the avant-garde's at-

[54] For example, "From the honorable and miserable attempt of the Parnassiens, Romanticism hoped for illusory renewals, until finally, as a monarch fallen in its infancy, it allowed itself to be deposed by Naturalism" (B. Mitchell, 27). All translations from this manifesto are mine.

[55] See esp. chaps. 2 and 3.

tack on art-as-institution rejects the deliberative discourse of the bourgeois public sphere and yet at the same time retains the gendered and often
racialized markings that structured bourgeois *aesthetic* discourse. Especially in the periods during and after the fin de siècle, strains of avant-
garde discourse display a kind of potentiated gendering and racializing
that results from the intersection of aesthetic and revolutionary codes of
valuation. That is, whereas aesthetic discourse had evaluated institutional
art by using the language codes of "masculine" and "feminine," revolutionary avant-garde discourse, using the same language codes, rejects nearly all
institutional art as "feminine." The "masculine," in this new layered formulation, emerges as the valorized term of revolutionary struggle in a super-
saturated field of "feminine" aesthetic inferiority.[56]

It goes without saying that, historically, aesthetic commentary and
criticism relied on (admittedly fluid) gender codes long before the
French Revolution. But my argument here concerns a specific discourse—the discourse of aesthetic evaluation—as it assumes a polemical pitch in discrete postrevolutionary moments. Even in Wordsworth's
1802 Preface to *Lyrical Ballads* (a preface that owes not a little to the
French revolutionary valuation of transparency and the unadorned language of common men),[57] one finds an explicit repudiation of the "fran-
tic novels" and "sickly and stupid German tragedies" (161) associated
with a feminized reading audience. Some famous derogations of critics
date from this period as well. Théophile Gautier's Preface to *Mademoiselle du Maupin* (1834), described by some as the "principal manifesto" of

---

[56] Compare also the fluctuating use of the terms "savage" and "primitive" as refutations of the
"civilized" bourgeois institutions of art. I am not suggesting that primitivism and misogyny were
the sole engines driving the attribution of aesthetic value in avant-garde art, however. In England
the distribution of aesthetic value across gendered terms occurred as much in response to two
other gendered phenomena. The first was the post–fin-de-siècle cultural anxiety about aesthetics
and masculinity, which relationship had been seriously challenged and revised via the English
schools of aestheticism led by Pater, Wilde, Synge, and other avatars of a homoerotically inflected
aesthetics of masculinity. (See Tim Dean for a compelling account of homosexual-aesthetic codes
in Joyce, and compare the connection made in Dean's argument between homosexuality and
artistic insight with the avant-garde code of Wyndham Lewis and Ezra Pound, which identified
the "extreme" masculinity of heterosexuality as the "new spine" of art.) The second gendered phenomenon was the widespread web of connections between mass culture and femininity, for which
Andreas Huyssen gives ample evidence.

[57] Compare, for instance, Robespierre's numerous maxims about virtue shining through "the
eloquence of the heart," since "virtues are simple, modest, poor, often ignorant, sometimes coarse;
they are the attribute of the unfortunate, the patrimony of the people" (quoted in Hunt 1984, 45,
73), with Wordsworth's assertions that in "low and rustic life . . . the essential passions of the heart
find a better soil in which they can attain their maturity, are less under restraint, and speak a
plainer and more emphatic language" which operates apart from "social vanity" and therefore
gives rise to "simple and unelaborated expressions" (165). The common denominator is of course
Rousseau.

*l'art pour l'art* (Burnett, 38), imagines literary critics as eunuchs who impotently look on while virile poets deflower the poetic muse.[58] A generation later, Swinburne casts the critic as "a dowager of somewhat dubious antecedents" (30) and calls for an "adult art" that is "noble and chaste in the wider masculine sense, not truncated and curtailed, but outspoken and full-grown" (32). To these may be added countless oft-discussed examples, but my point is this: however conventional the gendering of aesthetic genres, subjects, techniques, and enterprises had been before the dissemination of French revolutionary discourse, that gendering takes on extreme colorations once the rhetoric of the political avant-garde is rearticulated to the artistic avant-garde. The deepening inflections of gender in nineteenth-century aesthetic discourse work increasingly to contrast the past to the future: new activist art movements are valorized over older, traditional artistic schools;[59] the product without precedent is privileged over all forms of market mediation.

The manifestoes produced by the Italian futurists in the first decades of the twentieth century dramatize more explicitly the dependence of some strands of the artistic avant-garde on the discourse of the plebeian public sphere, as I shall show in the next two chapters. Lauren Shumway has described the discourse of this later phase of the historical avant-garde as a form of "stylistic terrorism," which "should inform our understanding of the fundamental topos of the avant-garde manifesto—the topos of the absolute necessity of a given form of cultural production as the *only* possible form for culture to take in the present period for such-and-such reasons, and the absolutely negative character of all other forms of cultural production in the same period" (57–58).

As we have seen, the rhetorical perimeters of this either/or discursive field is also the operative perimeter of revolutionary discourse, as it has been analyzed by Furet and, later, Outram. Here, for Shumway, "stylistic terrorism" explicitly serves the aesthetic and the economic aims of an avant-garde group. Initially rooted in revolutionary discourse, stylistic terrorism creates an intertextual field within which revolutionary semiotics are made widely intelligible. At the same time, such a widespread intelligibility threatens the cultural survival of the avant-garde group that thrives

[58] See Burnett for a fuller account of the sexual metaphors used by Gautier in his Preface.

[59] Poggioli differentiates between schools and movements in this way: "The passing beyond the limits of art, the aspiration toward what the Germans call *Weltanschauung*, is perhaps the principal characteristic by which to separate what we call movements from what we call schools" (18). In *The Gender of Modernity*, Rita Felski (1995) has forcefully analyzed the influence of gender in nineteenth-century evaluative schematics produced in the arts and social sciences; esp. chaps. 1 and 2.

on an economy of scarcity. A conflict occurs because, in the words of Shumway, "while esthetic value can only benefit from the greatest possible extension of the intertextual field . . . the economic value of the avant-garde text decreases as it becomes more and more popular" (58–59).[60]

In discussing this conflict, Shumway seems to have in mind the Wyndham Lewis–Ezra Pound axis of the European historical avant-garde; certainly Lewis's and Pound's embarrassingly obvious ambivalence toward "the popular" and "the commercial" forced their manifestoes into some bizarre and at times hopelessly knotted arguments. By contrast, however, neither F. T. Marinetti and the Italian futurists, nor the 1913 Armory Show exhibitors, nor the dance schools established by Isadora Duncan, nor the 1922 dadaists can be similarly charged with protecting the "aura" of the avant-garde work of art; as Peter Nicholls (1989) has shown, Marinetti (for one) aimed positively to saturate the economic market of the avant-garde with the products of futurism.

There were, in other words, several strains of an avant-garde coexisting in different places throughout Europe and the United States (as well as in Latin America) at the turn of the century. Many of them had their eyes on the bourgeois market; most positioned themselves deliberately as avatars of what Rosiland Krauss calls "the cult of originality" (155),[61] and a majority of them, determined to circumvent the critical apparatus of the bourgeois public sphere, simulated a discursive agenda of radicalism.[62] This last characteristic held especially for avant-gardes of the Continent, including those located in Spain, Germany, Russia, and France, where recent waves of anarchism and then syndicalism had effected a renewed mobilization of the working classes. In England, by contrast, French anarchism and syndicalism triggered a Burkean reaction of horror in the popular and established presses, and there was very little in the way of radical discourse to be seen in the late nineteenth-century writings of British

[60] This is the famous commodity conundrum of the historical avant-garde, which has been theorized extensively by Bürger following the Frankfurt school, and by Paul Mann, among others, following Bürger.

[61] In referring to an avant-garde "cult of originality," Krauss means "more than just the kind of revolt against tradition that echoes in Ezra Pound's 'Make it new!' or sounds in the futurists' promise to destroy the museums that cover Italy as though 'with countless cemeteries.' More than a rejection or dissolution of the past, avant-garde originality is conceived as a literal origin, a beginning from ground zero, a birth . . . without ancestors" (157).

[62] These are members the group that Arendt refers to disdainfully as "coffee-house revolutionaries," the artists and writers who joined "professional revolutionaries": "It is well known that the French Revolution had given rise to an entirely new figure on the political scene, the professional revolutionist, and his life was spent not in revolutionary agitation, for which there existed but few opportunities, but in study and thought, in theory and debate, whose sole object was revolution" (258–59).

artistic schools or movements.[63] When, in the years just before World War I, elements of the newly formed British avant-garde did adopt radical discourse (a phenomenon that occurred only after such discourse had been taken up by militant suffragists, striking miners, and Home Rule protesters), the British media responded with especial horror and vitriol, as we shall see in the next chapter.

## New Women, New Aesthetics

The imagined audience for European radical artistic avant-garde discourse (as it appeared first on the Continent and then in England) bore little resemblance to the participants of the eighteenth-century plebeian public sphere imagined by Habermas. Some avant-garde groups were as suspicious of "the uneducated people" as they were of the bourgeois intelligentsia and its critical organs, while others made a show of addressing their discourse explicitly to "the people" or to some imaginary public sphere "stripped of its literary garb."[64] Groups such as the Italian and Russian futurists interpellated an audience that participated in new forms of public deliberation such as radio, circulating postcards, and advertising, as well as popular newspapers and magazines linked more explicitly to literacy. By the fin de siècle, "the people" of the hypothetical plebeian public sphere were inseparable from "the reading public" and "the masses" associated with expanding popular culture. Granted, earlier constituencies of the plebeian public sphere, such as anarchist French workers, the Parisian Communards, and the English Chartists, were all figured by their opponents as "masses," too, but not with this republican spin. For by the end of the nineteenth century, and especially in England, "people," "public," "reading public," "mobs," and "masses" were all nearly interchangeable terms, each one subject to contestation.

[63] One of a few notable exceptions to this trend may be found in the early socialist writings of G. B. Shaw. As Raymond Williams has made clear, however, Shaw's polemical brand of socialism gave with one hand what his cynicism took away with the other. Williams quotes from Shaw's 1889 *Fabian Essays:* "The right is so clear, the wrong so intolerable, the gospel so convincing, that it seems to them [i.e., Fabian reformists] that it *must* be possible to enlist the whole body of workers—soldiers, policemen and all—under the banner of brotherhood and equality; and at one great stroke to set Justice on her rightful throne. Unfortunately, such an army of light is no more to be gathered from the human product of nineteenth-century civilization than grapes are to be gathered from thistles" (Williams 1989, 182). Shaw, in other words, treats revolutionary discourse as high-wattage figurativeness even as he uses it as a light to shine on the regressive tracks of the recent past.

[64] For example, the Italian political publication *Lacerba,* increasingly influenced by futurism during the 1910s, had at one point a working-class circulation that exceeded twenty thousand.

A strategic conceptual elision of "the people" with "the masses," for example, had been occurring in the discourse of the bourgeois public sphere ever since the consolidation of "the people" into a category of political subjecthood. "The people" belonged to a utopian sign system within which political agency was to be distributed equitably (as in the Diggers' resourceful recourse to the quasi-religious body of "the people," or de Gouges's crime of "attacking the sovereignty of the people"); "the masses," by contrast, signified an entity for which such a distribution would be perceived not only as a monstrous miscarriage of judgment but as a virtual and practical impossibility.[65] This connection between innumerability and the masses reached a new pitch in England when, in the wake of the 1870 Education Act, burgeoning literacy (and the concomitant increase in the production of goods for reading consumption) threatened forever the ability of gatekeepers to regulate the means by which British society had constituted its "reading public." The archconservative critic Elizabeth Linton voiced such a concern in 1890 when she wrote: "The democratic wave which has spread over all society—and washed down some things which had better have been left standing—has swept through the whole province of literature. The spread of education among the people demands literature cheap enough to at once suit their pockets and meet their wants" (quoted in Ardis, 41). Such bitter regret on Linton's part discloses not only a fearful reaction to the shrinking influence of critical deliberation on literary production, but also a fear that the bourgeois public sphere has been supplanted—or irrevocably contaminated—by an autonomous and unmediated plebeian circuit of literary production and consumption. The plebeian public sphere, which in Habermas's formulation was always "oriented toward the intentions of the bourgeois public sphere" (1989, xviii) in spite of itself, seems for Linton to have come unmoored from that orientation as the result of a democratic tidal wave.

[65] This conceptual elision of "the people" of the revolutionary public sphere and "the masses" of the industrial revolution was especially complex in early nineteenth-century England, where the newly emergent entity "the reading public" tended to absorb and displace the ideal of a deliberative bourgeois public sphere. Indeed, for this reason Habermas cautions us against framing the bourgeois public sphere as an ahistorical entity: as a category, it cannot be "transferred, idealtypically generalized, to any number of historical situations that represent formally similar constellations" (1989, xvii). And again (this time with a disturbingly negative inflection): "After the rise of Chartism, the February revolution, and the slow spread of literacy, the public body expanded beyond the bounds of the bourgeoisie. The public body lost not only its social exclusivity; it lost in addition the coherence created by bourgeois social institutions and a relatively high standard of education" (1974, 54). William Rowland has shown how early nineteenth-century poets such as (the early) Wordsworth and, later, Shelley attempted to connect their own radical innovations in verse to the spirit of political revolution, while at the same time forcefully staking out market space for themselves within the burgeoning new profession of letters.

According to Ann Ardis, Linton's indignation in the face of the expansion of literacy and literature was an explicit response to the large number of New Woman novels produced mainly by women between 1885 and 1895 and New Woman plays produced in the aftermath of Ibsen's theater revolution. By and large these were novels and dramas about female independence and sexual self-determination. Ardis shows how Linton connects the liberated New Woman of this literature with all manner of apocalyptic signifiers, from French anarchists of the previous decade to destructive plagues in which women "[swarm] out at all doors, running hither and thither among the men" (quoted, 22).[66] Such familiar images associating the expansion of popular culture with chaotic and unrestrained women came not only from conservative cultural gatekeepers such as Linton, but also from artistic camps that valorized experimental and nontraditional literature, as well as from a stratum of self-styled socio-medical writers including Havelock Ellis and Otto Weininger, for whom female sexuality was synonymous with a complex pathology.[67]

The New Woman came into being simultaneously as a force of social change and as a figure of fiction and drama. In her role as the literary protagonist of a large number of English works, the New Woman was an "idealistic, frequently neurotic and explicitly sexual non-conform[ist]" (Tickner, 184), that is, a bourgeois psychological subject available for contemplation rather than an embodiment of a Victorian "type" of woman. As aspiring political subjects, both in and out of literature, New Women acted as stimuli for the political revision of an increasingly obsolete model of universalism. If women's consignment to passive citizenship hinged solely on technicalities of the franchise—indeed, if modernity itself was increasingly understood not as the domain of universal man but instead through

[66] See also Ardis, 118–26. Rosemary Hennessy is critical of New Woman scholarship, which, she maintains, reinforces the heteronormativity that New Woman novels claimed to challenge (but, on her reading, did not): in her words the New Woman phenomenon is "a classic instance of a counterdiscourse, one that merely re-arranges the prevailing paradigm without really challenging its terms" (110). In this case, however, I would argue that the New Woman counterdiscourse is classically overdetermined, in Althusser's sense of the word, insofar as the "prevailing paradigm" it re-arranges has different effects for different subjects across classes and through degrees of patriarchal differentiation. See Hennessy, chap. 4.

[67] Andreas Huyssen was one of the first to mark out a thesis describing the role of "woman" in the contested relation between a "masculine" high art and the "feminized" consuming masses of modern culture. Rita Felski (1995) has more recently reworked these arguments with an eye toward incorporating the contradictions offered in fin-de-siècle works of sociology and cultural commentary. In Felski's analysis, "woman" represented to theorists of modernity both a force that threatened the progress of the modern (through excess consumption, through market forces issuing in mass commodification, and through an inherent inability to produce "the new") and as a way of figuring the past cultural coherence that had been lost in the atomization of the modern. She calls this latter formulation "the nostalgia paradigm" (see chap. 2).

the trope of unfettered womanhood—then politically active women were bound to represent a new form of universal ideal, one rooted in the rejection of bourgeois parliamentarianism and the embrace of a noninstrumental conception of human community.

To put it more succinctly, the New Woman enacted and emblematized the rupture of domestic space and its leakage into bourgeois public space: employed outside the home and for the most part unallied with any political or reformist programs, she was both a product and an inventor of the experience of modernization. The appearance of the New Woman broke up the nineteenth-century category of female fallenness, in part by reintroducing agency into the figure of the sexually active woman[68]—although, paradoxically, it was also usually the case that at the hands of male playwrights and novelists, New Women were caricatured as indecisive or confused. In the words of Jill Davis, "progressive/socialist men" of this period—even those writing the so-called "New Drama"—reacted to feminism either by "retreat[ing] from materialist into essentialist ways of thinking when faced with the 'Woman Question'" or by recuperating and ironizing the claims of feminism (22). Actresses and women managers eventually began taking matters into their own hands, writing and producing explicitly feminist plays.[69] New Women novelists, for their part, helped further to confuse the gender codes of aesthetic evaluation by introducing into English literary culture an explicitly sexualized genre, as Ardis argues: "On the one hand, the fact that this fiction sold so well offered proof to its most hostile reviewers that it was a commodity. It did not have value as Art; it was simply faddishly up to date in its portrayal of women rebelling against the traditional code of 'womanliness.' On the other hand, this fiction was gaining pace on high culture; its advocates described it as *the* new fiction, the wave of the future—which only made its unconventional content seem more 'dangerous'" (42).

The latter point—that in its overhauling of the nineteenth-century novelistic conventions of autonomous realism the New Woman novel placed itself at the forefront of literary innovation—suggests that the

---

[68] See Anderson 1993 for a thorough account of the epistemological role played by "fallenness" on the representation of culture in the Victorian novel.

[69] See Fitzsimmons and Gardner: "Whilst there is little evidence that many actresses began their careers with a radical view of the repertoire, it is clear that some were radicalized by the frustrations of playing parts that were not only far from presenting their—or any other woman's—experience of life but also presented images of women that ran counter to their personal politics" (ix). For a selection of New Women plays by women, see Fitzsimmons and Gardner. For examples of New Women plays by men, see Pinero, Jones, and Shaw, especially *The Second Mrs. Tanqueray*, *The Case of Rebellious Susan*, and *Mrs. Warren's Profession*, respectively.

genre acted as a sort of literary proto–avant-garde in a country where there had been little evidence of *any* artistic avant-garde throughout the nineteenth century. Or, to put it another way, it is surely no accident that the radical voices of the English avant-garde—the voices sounding in the years of the avant-guerre—were heard well *after* this influx of unconventional women into the literary marketplace. If, as Ardis contends, women writers had advanced the cause of experimentalism, not only in novelistic technique but also in the sexual and social lives of women, then they were de facto participants in and contributors to the artistic and social critique characteristic of the nascent avant-garde. One might go so far as to see the plain, "hygienic" dress of the typically represented New Woman (Gardner, 4) as an adumbration of Adolf Loos's avant-garde proclamation that "the evolution of culture is synonymous with the removal of ornament from utilitarian objects" (quoted in Wollen, 14).[70] Of course, women's participation in this critique was problematic: by becoming active agents therein, women troubled the iconographic codes of gender by which social and aesthetic criticism made itself intelligible. On the one hand, the model of deeply subjective feminine sexuality that emerged in the avant-garde literature and subculture of the New Women profoundly challenged one critical pole of "the feminine" grounded in an old regime model of debauched and corrupting feminine sexuality. On the other hand, in the face of the New Woman's radical revision of what it meant to be a "public woman"—neither an inert fallen woman nor a proxy citizen but, rather, sexually and economically independent, bristling with agency—another critical pole of "the feminine" could no longer easily hypostatize femininity as domestic, quotidian, dyssexual, and unintellectual.

The increasing participation of women in the avant-garde projects of the century's opening years exerted a double pressure on the institutional discourse of criticism, and on the revolutionary discourse with which factions of the English avant-garde subsequently announced themselves. Marinetti's futurist manifestoes were the impetus for the polemical discourse adopted by the English vorticists; and Marinetti deliberately staked out gender as one—perhaps even *the*—prominent code of aesthetic and social value. His reactivation of republican gender directives in his revolutionary manifestoes—manifestoes directed, at least putatively, to "the

[70] Wollen elaborates: "Peering into the future, Adolf Loos and Thorstein Veblen gave one exemplary prognosis for modernism: utility will supplant ornament, the engineer will supplant the leisure class, production will supplant consumption" (18). Both men were ideological and aesthetic supporters of the Women's Dress Reform movement, which had, of course, been spearheaded by New Women.

masses" excluded from the literary public sphere—unmistakably was meant to invoke a plebeian public revolt against "the old" and to herald a new public sphere unmediated by the corrupt traditions of a literary and artistic old regime. In Marinetti's manifestoes, women are addicted to the passion of *amore* and therefore threaten the revolutionary purity and integrity of the "new man" advocated by his movement; Venice, city of museums and self-veneration, is a diseased old whore; liberal government itself—to which suffragist women appeal for the implementation of universal rights—is an ideological apparatus of intermediacy with which no new man or woman should involve herself or himself.

The polemics of the English avant-garde take up this republican gender code wholesale, as we will see later. Unlike the Italian futurist tracts, however, the English avant-garde polemics that I shall examine do not—indeed, cannot—propose a *tout court* repudiation of women, their artistic productions, or their political and social contributions to the avant-garde. On the contrary, Wyndham Lewis and Ezra Pound, his literary partner in vorticism, had a complex stake in sustaining alliances between men and women of the avant-garde. What the English polemics do retain from their Italian precursors is a subject position and an aesthetic that insists on the denaturing of femininity within the avant-garde semiotic. This strategy accomplishes at least two things: on the one hand, it admits into the avant-garde circle only those women who do not reproduce the "feminine" pole of either of the critical axes mentioned earlier; and on the other hand, it reinforces the epistemological utility of those axes so that they may continue to be used for evaluative purposes within an intertextual field of revolutionary discourse. An elaboration of this strategy and its consequences will form the starting point for the next two chapters.

I want to close here by broadly reframing the impact of revolutionary discourse on the polemics written by women seeking access to the English literary and political public spheres in the years before World War I. Peter Bürger, following in the Marxist tradition, has elaborated the argument that the historical avant-garde's anti-institutionalism aimed "to reintegrate art in the praxis of life" (87). The question of whether or not the Italian futurists and English vorticists are successful examples of this tenet (a question that has driven a whole branch of avant-garde criticism) is less germane here than the fact that, in their particular uses of revolutionary discourse, these groups literalize Bürger's argument. For in reanimating revolutionary semiotics of purity, chastity, action, and violence, they fashion an aesthetic of *hygiene* that traverses the personal, social, and nationalist/political. One need only recall the title of one of Marinetti's long artistic manifestoes, "War, the World's Only Hygiene," to understand how well revolutionary discourse may act as a conduit between aesthetic doctrines and identity politics.

Militant Suffragettes had staked a claim in revolutionary discourse well before the appearance in England of futurism or its offshoots; yet the rhetoric of hygiene (literally, vital health) assumed a sharpened polemical focus in militant Suffragette literature shortly after Marinetti, Lewis, Pound, C. R. W. Nevinson, and others connected "hygiene" with the idea of purging from aesthetic and cultural productions any feminine (unhealthy) influence. Only then did Christabel Pankhurst turn the guns of her militant suffrage discourse against the unhealthiness of syphilitic male sexuality; only then did the rhetoric of women's civil rights intersect with revolutionary approximations between the health of the polity and the sexual vitality and purity of art and of individuals—resulting in a temporary shifting of the field of gender in the revolutionary tradition.

The semiotics of revolutionary discourse determined the form and the shape of other feminist polemics as well. During the period of first-wave feminism, women such as Mina Loy and Valentine de Saint Point who took up the futurist manifesto form ended up uncharacteristically calling for purity in the reproduction of the race; feminists such as Dora Marsden who were active in the avant-garde and yet eschewed revolutionary discourse talked almost exclusively about individuals and individualism, thereby effacing all political categories and ironically enacting the "passéism" against which Marinetti's polemics were launched. And as recently as the 1960s, when revolutionary discourse again emerged as a prominent discursive formation connecting aesthetics, civil rights, and institutional iconoclasm, second-wave feminist polemicists found themselves (as their first-wave forebears had done) making choices between forms of political identification that undermined the "interestedness" of their political claims and "idiosyncratic" identity politics that threatened their alliances with the revolutionary left. First- and second-wave feminists alike ended up in league with a form of anti-bourgeois utopianism that invited their support even as it discounted the possibility of their equality as political subjects.

The cultural and political alliances of radical groups in prewar London, to which I turn in the next chapter, provide us with an especially vivid example of the ways in which socio-aesthetic critiques of modernity enacted the contradictions of modernity. Suffragettes strove to enforce the systematic political coherence promised by the rationalism underpinning modern government, but instead discovered that government was constituted more by erratic partiality than by theoretical consistency. Avant-garde artists aimed to harness the energy of the ever-developing, ever-differentiating heterogeneity promised by modern "progress," but found that the modern commodification of art made the negotiation of commodification the central act. The strange (and strained) alliances thus forged in the name of resistance, though ephemeral, attest to the ease with which revolutionary discourse synthesized a whole ideological range of critiques mounted against the universalizing liberal state.

# 3 Militant Allies, Strange Bedfellows

## Suffragettes and Vorticists before the War

I want to begin this examination of the discourses of prewar London in the literary archives, since that is where most feminist revisions of literary modernism have mounted their challenges to prevailing configurations of the literary-historical record. Such revisions tend to be more or less polemical, depending on where and to what extent they locate textual sites where oppositional voices have been muted. Sandra M. Gilbert and Susan Gubar's *War of the Words,* an encyclopedic study written in the 1980s, pitted feminist literary work against masculinist literary work, theme against theme, even character against character, and so recreated an epic version of literary modernism that followed the contours of the late Victorian "sex war." Later, books such as Shari Benstock's *Women of the Left Bank* and, more recently, Bridget Elliott and Jo-Ann Wallace's *Modernist (Im)positionings* aimed to challenge arbitrary geographic and disciplinary divisions of "the [male] Modernist facade" (Benstock, xi) in order to concentrate on the lives and cultural productions of specific communities, thereby marking out less a modernist sex war than sites of anthropological recovery.[1]

[1] In the 1990s a number of excellent works of feminist modernist criticism and theory were published under the sign of what we might call "modern studies feminism" (in contrast to the polemical "recovery" feminism that dominated the 1980s). These newer works emphasize modernist sociological theories of culture (e.g., Rita Felski's *Gender of Modernity*), modernist anthropological theories of identity (e.g., Alice Gambrell's *Women Intellectuals, Modernism, and Difference: Transatlantic Culture, 1919–1945*), the politics of modernist institutions of cultural production (e.g., Jayne E. Marek's *Women Editing Modernism: "Little" Magazines and Literary History*), and the implications for feminist criticism of continental/Marxist/Frankfurt school theories of modernism (e.g., Anne Friedberg's *Window Shopping: Cinema and the Postmodern*).

By contrast, my model for revision involves a broader treatment of the discourses produced in prewar England and is based on an understanding of the early phase of modernism as a congeries of proto-movements hammered out in polemical tracts, and especially in manifestoes. When read in concert with the numerous polemics produced by other radical groups in formation just before World War I—groups like the Suffragettes[2]—modernist manifestoes turn out to be more than just radical ripostes or lists of demands. As a form that textualizes the otherwise ephemeral moment of an avant-garde group's emergence, the manifesto was ideally suited to such early modernist polemicists as Wyndham Lewis, F. T. Marinetti, and Ezra Pound. These were founders of movements who sought in their didactic texts to narrate and thereby to secure their groups' originary moments, in order both to crystallize the groups' artistic critiques as formal doctrine and to foreground their own pointed contestations of cultural conventions. The founding manifestoes of the early modernists tended to slant contemporary cultural chronicles in such a way as to occlude the historical presence of competing radical groups and movements—among which the militant Suffragettes figured significantly—and to obliterate altogether a group's dependence on cultural agents who could not, strictly speaking, be invoked as avant-garde influences. Among such agents we may number the middle-class women who founded or financially supported the avant-garde literary and artistic organs, soirées, openings, and studios in and around which avant-garde groups took shape.

But for my purposes it is not enough to say that modernist manifestoes "obliterated" women and their role in the production of an avant-garde; it is even too reductive, too easy, to say that modernist manifestoes siphoned off the revolutionary energy of suffragism. After all, in a historical moment characterized by numerous well-publicized challenges to the hegemonic liberal state, "revolutionary energy" cannot be said to originate in one place or to develop in one direction. Any attempt to orchestrate a dialogue among the polemics produced by the radical men and women in the historical conjuncture of prewar England, then, will require a more fluid understanding of interaction among oppositional groups in order to frame the polemics of modernism and suffragism within the shifting terrain of modern culture.

My discussion will center on three key texts from the early London modernist period: *The Founding and Futurist Manifesto* by F. T. Marinetti,

[2] I follow historians of suffragism (and contemporary newspaper accounts) in using the term "Suffragette" to denote the post-1905 suffragist who was self-identified with militancy and who was law-breaking rather than law-abiding.

published in Paris in 1909, read by its author to the London Lyceum Club for Women in 1910, and republished in an English art review in 1912; *The Great Scourge and How to End It,* a 1913 collection of editorials by the militant Suffragette Christabel Pankhurst; and *BLAST,* the manifesto-journal first produced in 1914 by Wyndham Lewis, the self-appointed spokesman for the newly formed group of English artists that he called vorticists. Within the space of just a few years these three texts provoked uniform responses of scandalized astonishment from the London press, but histories of prewar England have nevertheless disjoined them along lines of gender or discipline, and have thereby obscured the interdependencies between the militant women's movement and the English avant-garde. My aim in realigning avant-garde discourse and militant suffrage discourse is to show how the rhetoric and tactics of the militant women's movement were enfolded into the foundations of English modernism, and how, conversely, the closely watched public activities of futurists and vorticists in England helped to produce the public identity of the militant suffrage movement. The form that this mutuality took cannot be understood apart from a shared sense of deep disappointment that the promises for radical change, brokered by the languages and institutions of modernity's progressivist telos, had in fact been co-opted by the modern instrumental status quo.

## Suffragettes and Vorticists

A brief review of the activities of militant suffragists and the prewar avant-garde in the years before World War I will help to map out their historical relatedness. The women's suffrage movement had been active throughout the second half of the nineteenth century, but in 1905 the Women's Social and Political Union (WSPU), a small organization of Manchester suffragists, adopted for the first time the militant strategy of civil disobedience. On October 13 a twenty-five-year-old law student named Christabel Pankhurst and her millworker friend Annie Kenny, aiming to expose what they considered to be pseudo-democratic posturings on the part of the Liberal Party, disrupted a meeting at the Manchester Free Trade Hall by shouting from the gallery, "Will the Liberal Party give votes for women?" [3] The women were evicted from the meeting, arrested

---

[3] There are numerous detailed accounts of the militant suffrage campaign. See, for example, MacKenzie, Morrell, Raeburn, Rosen, and Tickner. Christabel Pankhurst's suffrage activism began in childhood. Her father, Richard, was a lawyer and a political activist for radical Liberal and then Labour causes, including women's suffrage. Her mother, Emmeline, was active in poor law and suffrage work, particularly after Richard's death in 1898, and formed the WSPU in 1903; she was a

for assault, and then jailed when they refused to pay a nominal fine. This widely reported event catapulted the English suffrage movement into the headlines, where it stayed for the next nine years. Pankhurst and her mother, Emmeline Pankhurst, moved the WSPU to London, where it soon became the most militant and best funded of the many suffrage groups then in formation. Under the editorship of Frederick and Emmeline Pethick-Lawrence, the WSPU issued *Votes for Women,* one of many suffrage newspapers with circulations exceeding 20,000. The WSPU's meticulously organized membership gave speeches, heckled parliamentary speakers, and, in conjunction with other suffrage organizations, produced enormous demonstrations: one featured a pageant with 30,000 marching suffragists, and, according to *The Times*'s estimates, drew up to 500,000 spectators.[4] But as the WSPU's strategies grew more militant, the crowd-pleasing pageants were gradually replaced by less glamorous though no less theatrical operations involving marches on Parliament and disruptions of political meetings; correspondingly, press coverage of "the Cause" began to treat it as a form of social pathology.[5] Physical attacks on individual WSPU members increased, and the police themselves frequently roughed up the implacable suffrage deputations to Parliament.[6] When

---

compelling public speaker whose repeated imprisonments and forced feedings made her the acknowledged leader of the militant fight for the vote. Of Christabel's three younger siblings, two became known for their activism: Sylvia, allied with the Labour Party, edited two suffrage newspapers and organized working-class women in London's East End, and Adela migrated to Australia, where she agitated both for the vote and for labor issues. See MacKenzie, David Mitchell, Raeburn, and Romero for various accounts of the Pankhursts' lives.

[4] A lead article in the first issue of *Votes for Women* (October 1907) announced to enlisting members that "if you have any pettiness or personal ambition you must leave that behind before you come into this movement. There must be no conspiracies, no double dealing in our ranks. Everyone must fill her part. The founders and leaders of the movement must lead, the non-commissioned officers must carry out their instructions, the rank and file must loyally share the burdens of the fight. For there is no compulsion to come into our ranks, but those who come must come as soldiers ready to march onwards in battle array" (quoted in Rosen, 93). Note the revolutionary convention deployed here, which twins transparency with loyalty to the movement. While this form of organization may indeed be deemed "strikingly undemocratic" (Rosen, 93), it is also clearly conventional within a republican tradition of activism.

[5] By 1914 the *Daily Mirror* was reporting that "any observant person can pick out a suffragette in a crowd of other women," and running captions like "Screaming with Impotent Rage" under photos of Suffragettes (May 25 and May 15; quoted in Tickner, 167, 207). Antonia Raeburn maintains that the press routinely suppressed photographs of Suffragettes under attack and instead portrayed them as violent aggressors (e.g., 110).

[6] The most famous confrontation between Suffragettes and police, known as "Black Friday," occurred on November 18, 1910, when a large deputation of women attempted to see Prime Minister Asquith in order to secure a promise that the suffrage bill would be brought up after the new elections. The women were met by hundreds of uniformed and plainclothes police apparently under orders to repel but not arrest the demonstrators; as a result, the women were tripped, kicked, thrown down, and, in a few cases, dragged down side alleys by police and hired toughs. See the accounts by Morrell and by Raeburn.

jailed, Suffragettes were classed as criminals rather than as first-division political prisoners, and were therefore subject to prison codes enforcing silence and hard labor. In 1908 an artist named Marion Wallace Dunlop, convicted of vandalism for painting part of the Bill of Rights on the wall of a Parliament building, began a hunger strike to protest her criminal status, and thereafter the hunger strike became the standard tactic by which Suffragettes secured early release from prison.

As acts of Suffragette militancy widened and rallies grew more strident in tone, the Home Secretary instituted a policy of forcible feeding, whereby hunger strikers—in the end, over a thousand of them—were held down by prison matrons and tube-fed by prison doctors several times a day.[7] Public outcry and sensational press coverage issued in more overt police intimidation of Suffragettes, calculated to decrease the number of suffrage-related arrests (and therefore the number of inmates who would inevitably hunger strike). To avoid intractable shoving matches with police, which were especially debilitating for the many middle-aged and elderly women involved, militants turned to crimes that would either go unsolved (anonymous letter-box bombings, arson, golf course vandalism) or result in immediate arrest (window-smashings, assaults on policemen and politicians). The height of the Suffragette window-smashing campaign—and the beginning of what would become the most intense phase of militancy—occurred on March 1, 1912, in London's fashionable West End. At 5:45 P.M., approximately 150 women posing as "women" (i.e., middle-class shoppers) produced hammers and rocks from handbags and broke £5,000 worth of plate glass shop windows in Regent and Oxford streets. Christabel Pankhurst escaped arrest for these "vitrifragist" outrages, as one peevish press account dubbed them (Kramerae and Treichler, 474), by going underground to Paris, where she lived in exile for two years. From an undisclosed Paris address, Pankhurst summarily dissolved her alliances

---

[7] Accounts of tube-feedings are numerous; Mrs. Mary Leigh's description is reprinted in MacKenzie: "The sensation is most painful—the drums of the ears seem to be bursting and there is a horrible pain in the throat and the breast. The tube is pushed down twenty inches. I have to lie on the bed, pinned down by wardresses, one doctor stands up on a chair, holding the funnel end at arm's length, so as to have the funnel end above the level, and then the other doctor, who is behind, forces the other end up the nostrils. . . . When the glass junction [in the rubber tubing] shows the fluid has gone down, a signal is given" (128–29). An October 10, 1909, letter to *The Times* from Suffragettes awaiting trial explains that they intend to hunger strike in order to present the government with "four alternatives: to release us in a few days; to inflict violence upon our bodies; to add death to the champions of our cause by leaving us to starve; or, and this is the best and only wise alternative, to give women the vote" (quoted in MacKenzie, 135). See Barbara Green's thick description and fascinating analysis of the spectacle of forcible feeding in chap. 2 of *Spectacular Confessions*.

with insufficiently militant supporters (including the Pethick-Lawrences and their *Votes for Women*), launched a more radical WSPU newspaper called *The Suffragette,* condensed the WSPU membership to a loyal core of about three thousand, oversaw an arson and vandalism campaign in London, and wrote dozens of editorials, a series of which she collected in 1913 in *The Great Scourge and How to End It.*

The WSPU arson campaign involved the destruction of public and private property, including empty churches, unused buildings, and train depots. By 1913, when forty-two major cases of arson were committed by Suffragettes in just six months, public opinion (catalyzed by press coverage) had turned emphatically against the militants. The WSPU was forced to protect its leaders by forming a division of bodyguards (known simply as "the Bodyguard"), and by developing a national underground. Condemnations by both anti-suffragists and non-WSPU suffragists alike appeared regularly throughout 1914, especially after an artist named Mary Richardson slashed the Rokeby Venus by Velázquez in the National Gallery, thereby inaugurating a series of painting slashings which closed museums and damaged nearly a dozen works of art. The militant activity of the WSPU—and the sputtering editorials it generated in the largely anti-suffrage popular press—ceased abruptly when England entered the war.

Meanwhile in these same years the London avant-garde community was taking shape.[8] Wyndham Lewis, Ezra Pound, and the handful of artists soon to be known as vorticists had already settled in London when Marinetti, visiting in 1910 to promote his new Italian futurist movement, electrified the nascent English avant-garde. In a speech to the Lyceum Club, he urged his audience, whom he addressed as "victims of . . . traditionalism and its medieval trappings," to throw off the "lymphatic ideology" of English Victorianism.[9] The renegade excitement that Marinetti's visit generated was galvanized six months later when Roger Fry mounted the first postimpressionist exhibition, the show that also gave the English public its first horrified glimpse of continental painters such as Gauguin and Cézanne. And in less than two years, a futurist exhibition at the Sackville Gallery (complete with translated manifesto-catalogues)[10] brought futurism squarely before the popular press—which, sensing futurism's growing

[8] For accounts of this community, see Cianci, Cork, Dasenbrock, Hansen, Levenson, Perloff, and Wees.

[9] Rpt. in Marinetti, *Selected Writings,* 60, 64. All Marinetti sources are reprinted in this volume and cited parenthetically by page number only.

[10] Later in 1912 Fry organized a second postimpressionist exhibition for the Grafton Galleries; and in 1913 the art critic Frank Rutter organized the popular "Post-Impressionist and Futurist Exhibition" at the Doré Gallery.

cultural capital, quickly appended the term "futurist" to all avant-garde art, and anything else that was quirky, trendy, or inscrutably modern.[11]

The unexpected ease with which futurism was articulated to popular culture precipitated a crisis of differentiation within the English avant-garde. By mid-1914, Wyndham Lewis—and most other early admirers of Italian futurism—had deserted Marinetti's ranks. Around the same time, and for only superficially different reasons, a conflict developed between future vorticists and members of the Omega Workshop in Bloomsbury. The latter, a collective of artists organized by Roger Fry in 1913, produced postimpressionist furniture and "decorative" designs in the style of Matisse and Kandinsky. The workshop briefly employed several future vorticists, including Lewis; within a few weeks of his participation in Omega, however, Lewis staged a walkout. His defection from Omega, he explained in a published letter, was triggered not only by Fry's somewhat arbitrary management but also—and more important for our purposes—by his disgust at the workshop's decorative aesthetic and its doctrines of anonymity and collectivism, which Lewis associated with an effeminately "pleasant tea-party."[12] Professing a deep commitment to what he called "an art of individuals" (*BLAST* 1:8), Lewis opened his own short-lived Rebel Art Centre in March 1914 by borrowing money and space from the painter Kate Lechmere, who was then excluded from the Centre's Saturday meetings because of her sex.[13] Three months later Lewis published yet another repudiation, this time of an English futurist manifesto coauthored by Marinetti (who spoke no English) and English futurism's one remaining adherent, the painter C. R. W. Nevinson. Their manifesto, it seems, had been printed on Rebel Art Centre stationery and distributed by the thousands in London galleries; worse than this, however, was the fact that it bore Lewis's unau-

[11] See William Wees, 108–9, for an account of the "futurist" trend.

[12] Lewis's "Round Robin" letter, signed by his supporters and submitted to *The Times* for publication, attacks Fry for his "meanness" and, more trenchantly, anathematizes the workshop as a "family of strayed and Dissenting Aesthetes . . . compelled to call in as much modern talent as they could find, to do the rough and masculine work without which they knew their efforts would not rise above the level of a pleasant tea party, or command more attention." See Lewis's *Letters*, 47–50, for the complete text. See Charles Harrison, 45–113, for an anti-Bloomsbury account of Fry, Clive Bell, and the various strands of English postimpressionism. See Christopher Reed for a compelling analysis of the homophobia embedded in Bloomsbury scholarship on this and other points.

[13] The women artists associated with Lewis and vorticism were characteristically marginalized by both the policies and the self-representations of the movement, as vorticist William Roberts's painting *The Vorticists at the Restaurant de la Tour Eiffel: Spring 1915* (reproduced in Wees, plate 6) illustrates: eight male Vorticist artists sprawl in a casual and intimate semicircle around a table; behind them, unnoticed, looking timid and chagrined, the painters Jessie Dismorr and Helen Saunders belatedly enter the restaurant.

thorized signature.[14] Lewis's by now characteristically vitriolic response to the threat of assimilation—this time as he rescued his endangered signature from the jaws of a competing movement—demonstrates yet again the struggle for self-representation that defined the desultory trajectory of vorticism's emergence.

By now Lewis, Pound, and artists such as Frederick Etchells, William Roberts, and Henri Gaudier-Brzeska had disavowed the futurist aesthetic of speed, movement, and incipiently interpenetrating forms; the futurist ethos of socially conscious art; and, most thoroughly, the Omega valorization of workshop collectivism. Lewis was at last ready to propose and elaborate a vorticist aesthetic. The vorticist multi-manifesto, *BLAST*—written almost entirely by Lewis, with additions by Pound—came out July 2, 1914, after many delays.[15] It contained several manifestoes, as well as the first installment of *The Good Soldier* by Ford Madox Ford, a story by Rebecca West, art reviews, poems, and drawings. In its pages Lewis identified vorticism as an individualistic, noncollectivist, racially coded, and decidedly English affair; meritocratic where Marinetti's futurism was at least putatively democratic; controlled and precise (in intent if not in practice) where the Latins "gushed"; inspired by an elite "northern genius" antithetical to popular continental "passion."

The vorticists, having been enabled by Fry's public relations work for postimpressionism and initially borne aloft by Marinetti's sensational headline grabbing, published *BLAST* as the culmination of four years of incremental self-differentiation from other flanks of the English avant-garde. The starting point of that process is the 1909 *Founding and Futurist Manifesto*, the "quasi-poetic construct" (Perloff, 82) that chartered the fragile English chapter of Marinetti's movement. After an opening narrative describing an exhilarating car wreck on an industrial road, Marinetti's manifesto offers eleven futurist resolves to embrace speed, war, machinery, and danger. Two of these resolves are of particular interest:

> 9) We will glorify war—the world's only hygiene—militarism, patriotism, the destructive gesture of freedom-bringers, beautiful ideas worth dying for, and scorn for women.

[14] The manifesto, "Vital English Art," was published in *The Observer*. It attacked all "passéism" in English art, including "the English notion that Art is a useless pastime, only fit for women and schoolgirls," as well as "the effeminacy" of English artists, in particular "their complete absorption towards a purely decorative sense." See C. R. W. Nevinson, 79–81, and Wees, 109–12. Lewis's attachment to the sanctity of his "signature" is of a piece with his investment in the peculiarly English early modernist obsession with individualism.

[15] *BLAST* was supposed to be issued serially, but only two numbers appeared. The second, "The War Number," came out in July 1915.

10) We will destroy the museums, libraries, academies of every kind, will fight moralism, feminism, every opportunistic or utilitarian cowardice. (42) [16]

Clearly "women" and "feminism," as Marinetti deploys those terms here, are associated with the cultural stasis and decay decried at length throughout the futurist program. In the revolutionary and aesthetic discourses that intersect in futurist manifestoes, "the feminine" constitutes an intensely pejorative field of meaning, which Marinetti uses to differentiate his masculinist program from bourgeois culture. To this end, his manifestoes consistently triangulate women, decay, and lechery.[17]

Yet it is striking—indeed, almost paradoxical—that however inadvertently, these passages from the Futurist Manifesto also valorize and reflect the nature of militant suffrage activity: Christabel Pankhurst's description of Suffragette militancy as "a surgical operation" and "a great blasting away of ugly things" echoes Marinetti's call for the destruction of museums and his glorification of war as hygiene, for example.[18] Indeed, Marinetti's audiences were composed of suffrage supporters as well as nascent avant-gardists: his very first Lyceum Club speech to Londoners was reviewed in

[16] This portion of the manifesto has always triggered much feminist commentary. More recent examples include discussions by Rachel Blau DuPlessis, Roger L. Conover (1982), Carolyn Burke (1996), and Cinzia Blum (1990, 1996); see also Nicholls 1995, 86–91.

[17] "The Futurist Program" was of course no more than a virtual set of interactive aesthetic and social dicta, extrapolated and reconstituted in innumerable manifestoes; but see, for an illustration of futurism's habitual triangulation of woman-lechery-decay, Marinetti's "We Abjure Our Symbolist Masters, the Last Lovers of the Moon," wherein he lists "the four intellectual poisons" that "one must at all costs combat": "1) the sickly, nostalgic poetry of distance and memory; 2) romantic sentimentality drenched with moonshine that looks up adoringly to the ideal of Woman-Beauty; 3) obsession with lechery, with the adulterous triangle, the pepper of incest, and the spice of Christian sin; 4) the professorial passion for the past and the mania for antiquity and collecting" (68). See Blum (1996) for a psychoanalytically inflected discussion of the relation between futurism and the feminine. Many analyses of the futurist poetry of Mina Loy also include discussions of these relations.

[18] As Pankhurst elaborates it, "The militancy of women is doing a work of purification. Nowhere was purification more needed than in the relationship between men and women. . . . A great upheaval, a great revolution, a great blasting away of ugly things—that is militancy. . . . The bad and the old have to be destroyed to make way for the good and the new. When militancy has done its work then will come sweetness and cleanness, respect and trust, perfect equality and justice into the partnership between men and women" (*The Suffragette*, May 2, 1913; quoted in Rosen, 197). Pankhurst's reliance on revolutionary discourse (embedded in the rhetoric of militancy)— complete with images of the new sweeping out the old, utopia upending dystopia, and so on— deepened as government pressure on the WSPU increased, but the Union had represented itself as a military organization from its very inception. See, for example, *Votes for Women*'s inaugural lead article (fn. 4), and Emmeline Pankhurst's 1913 New York City speech "Why We Are Militant." See also Barbara Green's throroughly illuminating account of suffragist Teresa Billington-Greig's critique of WSPU militancy (89–100).

*The Vote*.[19] And in March 1912 Marinetti himself marched with the London Suffragettes during their window-smashing campaign.[20]

## Cultural Alliances

What are we to make of Marinetti's ambivalent and apparently rudderless stance toward women, which embraces suffragism but deplores feminism? Peter Nicholls maintains that, for Marinetti, "woman"—the object of futurist scorn—signified either the remnants of an outmoded gender system, or the symbolic embodiment of a feminine and feminized culture, or both.[21] Yet Nicholls hardly engages the unabashed masculinism of this single-sex male utopia; rather, he seems to imply that since "the feminine" stands for a nineteenth-century aesthetic practice, its material effects as a gender construction are limited. Arguing that "'scorn for women' was . . . rather more complicated than it has often seemed, for it was closely related to the Nietzschean desire for a transcendence of the 'merely' human" (1995, 89), he aims to qualify Marinetti's anti-feminism by linking it to Niet-

[19] The review was written by the suffragist, journalist, and playwright Margaret Wynne Nevinson, mother of the aforementioned futurist painter C. R. W. Nevinson, and married to Henry Nevinson, a leading radical journalist and staunch supporter of suffrage militancy. Her review notes, with bemused sarcasm, that "in his raillery at woman—the war against whose 'pernicious influence' is by no means the least important part of the Futurist programme—in his denunciation of her 'snake-like coils' which have ever 'choked the noblest ideals of manhood,' Signor Marinetti still found time to extol the Suffragette! (Had he an idea that among his Lyceum audience were more than one or two women who would answer proudly to that title?)" (*The Vote*, December 31, 1910, 112).

[20] Marinetti's own recollection of marching with Suffragettes in 1912 ("Suffragettes and the Indian Docks") is a playful study in the vacillation between the scorn for women that he espouses and the *amore* that he vehemently repudiates in nearly all of his manifestoes (and especially in "Against *Amore* and Parliamentarianism" [72–75]). Here he narrativizes his ideological double helix:

> Several of us captain the tide of women along the street where the Ministries are located but the increasing flow and tumult of other legions coming in from the outlying districts compel the mounted police to give the signal for a charge all hell breaks loose as the horses come galloping down on them clubs flying screams pistol shots people knocked down and the crashing of more windows in the stores invaded by the madwomen. . . .
>
> Three hours later in a big room of the large building the suffragettes have taken over as a hotel I was explaining in French with endless semaphoric Latin gesturing out of a miniature painting the aesthetic of the machine plastic dynamism and idolatry of things modern the importance of flying in literature and art to the more attentive of the 1000 women there all of them ugly except one just a meter away who was betraying me by holding Boccioni's hand but promising me an early revenge. (341–42)

[21] In 1989, Nicholls cites Marinetti's somewhat later writings in which "scorn for women" points the way toward what Nicholls sees as a defeminized sexuality; and in 1995 he cites a 1910 preface in which Marinetti "emphasized that his real object of attack was 'the sentimental significance' attributed to women" (89).

zsche's anti-feminism. This is a puzzling move, since Nietzsche's anti-feminism was routed through a ubiquitous misogyny that attributed the corruption of modernity in part to "the feminine"; this Nietzschean thread runs through Weininger, Strindberg, and other heralded theorists of "woman's" fundamental ahistoricity and antipathy to modernity.[22] In any case, Marinetti's ambivalence about women and suffragism was hardly unique among avant-gardists—or within the revolutionary/avant-garde tradition, for that matter. While individual artists and writers such as Nevinson, Hulme, and Gaudier-Brzeska may have eschewed the "feminine" and called for "virility," "hardness," and "masculine precision" in their new abstract art, nearly all of them benefited directly from the patronage of "emancipated" women, and many of them supported women's suffrage.[23] More generally, the issue of women's political rights appeared in both the work and the private activities of the writers and critics who championed the new avant-garde. Frank Rutter, one of the few influential art critics sympathetic to the English avant-garde, was an honorary chairman of a men's pro-suffrage league, for example. The novelist Violet Hunt, Ford Madox Ford's longtime companion, was involved in the suffrage movement and apparently invited Christabel Pankhurst to her famous South Lodge artist gatherings. Rebecca West, literary editor of *The New Freewoman* and author of pungent critiques of patriarchal culture, was a feminist journalist who provided witty (indeed, hilarious) and very sympathetic coverage of the suffrage campaigns in a variety of left-wing London publications.[24]

The fashionable status of suffrage support among members of the art world was enhanced by the British press's reliance on the discourse of hysteria and disease in its accounts of both avant-gardism and suffragism. The

[22] For a thoroughly illuminating discussion of the masculine-feminine schematic worked out by Georg Simmel, Otto Weininger, and other fin-de-siècle gender theorists, see Felski 1995, esp. chaps. 1 and 2.

[23] Nevinson's "Vital English Art" manifesto, quoted earlier, called for "an English Art that is strong, virile, and anti-sentimental" (C. R. W. Nevinson, 80). T. E. Hulme insisted that the primitive and the abstract, both desiderata of modern art, were the equivalents of a masculine ethos, and he apparently elaborated this ethos into a policy of banning women from his Tuesday night gatherings in London (Tytell, 69). Gaudier admired the work of fellow vorticists Helen Saunders and Jessie Dismorr, while consistently praising "strength and manliness" in art (quoted in Wees, 138).

[24] West's coverage of the suffrage movement was always radical to the extent that she supported militancy and understood the difficulties inherent in the frail and disintegrating alliances between suffragists and such male-dominated groups as the Labour Party; she was horrified, however, by Christabel Pankhurst's Moral Purity tracts and only made journalistic sense of their tactical value years later, when universal suffrage had been attained and discourses of sexuality had shifted dramatically. For her early coverage, see "Lynch Law: The Tragedy of Ignorance" (207–14); for her later view see "A Reed of Steel" (243–62).

first Post-Impressionist Exhibition, for example, was described in various newspapers as "the output of a lunatic asylum," "the source of the plague," and "the exact analogue to the Anarchist movements in the political world" (Wees, 22, 23, 26), and even reviews in such counterculture publications as *The New Freewoman* questioned the "sanity" of the new art.[25] At the same time, press accounts of WSPU militancy were narrated in the language of lunacy and morbid egomania. For example, a *Times* lead story reporting the window-smashing raid of March 1, 1912, declares that "were it not for the calculated and determined manner in which this work of devastation was carried out[,] one would suppose it to have been wrought by demented and maniacal creatures: and even . . . a survey of the scene rather suggests that the mischief was done by people of unstable mental equilibrium" (March 2, 1912, 8).[26]

Interestingly, the Suffragettes' "demented and maniacal" behavior was periodically linked to displaced and/or depraved artistic aspirations. One physician wrote to the *Times* diagnosing the militant Suffragette as a near-maniac needing "a daily dose of rousing sensations" which could take the form of "ill-judged incursions, without talents, into literature or art" (March 16, 1912, 9), while another physician referred to the Suffragette as "the artistically uneducated who whimpers for the limelight so brutally withheld" (March 18, 1912, 6). Suffragettes do what they do, in other words, because they cannot be artists.

The press's discursive construction of frustrated women and diseased artists was part of its response to the militant identities actively cultivated by avant-garde artists and Suffragettes: in particular, conservative papers such as *The Times* and the *Daily Mirror* hallucinated the shadows of conti-

---

[25] See, for example, Edgar A. Mowrer's "Discipline and the New Beauty" (*New Freewoman*, November 1, 1913, 196–97), or John Cournos's " Battle of the Cubes" (*New Freewoman*, November 15, 1913, 214–15). In 1911 Roger Fry alluded to the critical habit of equating abstract art with mental instability when he wrote that parts of the "cultivated public" have "expressed the desire that all the pictures now in the [postimpressionist show at the] Grafton Gallery should be burned. . . . Such expressions of opinion appear to me to be somewhat exaggerated, I might even have said hysterical, were it not that that is the word which has been applied to myself with a view to explaining the aberration of a mind hitherto supposed to be fairly well balanced" (99).

[26] A *Times* editorial two days later muses that "the suffrage movement, whether right or wrong in itself, is the most striking example in our time of the manner in which a cause can take complete possession of the minds of its devotees, cutting them off, as it were, from all the complexity of life, and simplifying its issues so that they see nothing before them but a success, which is heaven, and a failure, which is hell. There is a kind of mind, the mind of the born fanatic or enthusiast, which desires this simplification of the issues of life rather than any of the material prizes which life can offer" (March 4, 1912, 9). The strain of this argument, which aligns feminine intellectual activity with absolute simplicity and depthlessness, is in fact the foundational thesis of Weininger's *Sex and Character* and surfaces as well in works by Georg Simmel and Thorstein Veblen.

nental anarchy and domestic labor strikes ever hovering behind the specter of militancy. Thus the press effectively created and foregrounded a bifurcated semiotic of militancy. Avant-garde militancy, in its threat to the standards of cultural production, was frustrating and distressing; but Suffragette militancy, which in addition challenged the sanctity of private property and the political organization of gender, was positively dangerous, truly an infectious disease.

The politics of simplification, for instance, could be a complex matter; in the pages of *The Times*, the artist's talent for abstraction could be praised at the expense of the Suffragette's mania for single-issue activism. One particularly revealing *Times* editorial of March 4, 1912, distinguishes aesthetic (good) simplification from Suffragette (bad) simplification, so that artists may be construed as "lucid" whereas "enthusiasts" are merely reductive:

> [T]he very aim of all plots, and of lucid design in all art, is to present reality freed from that complexity and uncertainty of issue; and the artist succeeds when he does so simplify reality and at the same time convinces us that he has not simplified it away. But what the artist does in his work the enthusiast tries to do in life itself. He persuades himself that, for those who can see it rightly, life is already so simplified that there is only one thing worth doing in it, one issue upon which the future of mankind depends. He is the lover of romance, and the object of his love is . . . a cause perfect and glorious, to die for which is heaven. (9)

In some sense this hierarchizing of forms of militancy opened the doors for the surprisingly rapid cultural assimilation of futurism at the expense of an anathematized suffragism. A typical art review headline of the period reflects the archetype/ectype pattern of this cultural formation: "The Hysteria Wave Spreads to Art."[27]

The semiotic links among militants produced by the press (and aptly figured in this headline's metaphor of contagion) were strengthened in the militant discourse produced by the groups themselves. Kobena Mercer explains that the process by which associations of this kind are formed involves not the "uncovering of repressed subjectivities that were always there," but "the historical, social and political bringing into being of new forms of subjectivity and identity" through the use of militant discourse (1990, 7).[28] The characteristic use of militant discourse by both Suffragettes

---

[27] *Bystander*, March 13, 1913, cited in Tickner, 279 n. 18.
[28] See also Stuart Hall 1988, 48–54, on the politics of identity formation.

and avant-garde spokespersons such as Lewis, Hulme, and Pound served, in part, to map out the radical terms, if not the terrain, of their respective struggles. For of course the terrains of the two groups were quite different: the WSPU's militant speech acts took as their referents the bodies of WSPU members, insofar as they aimed to incite physical rebellion and to amass tangible evidence of widespread and incessant civil disobedience.[29] By contrast, the militant discourse of Lewis and Pound was confined mostly to the page: Pound's description of the artist who "must live by craft and violence," whose "gods are violent gods" ("The New Sculpture"), was aimed not at incipiently violent artists but at the texts of their nemeses: "passive" Georgian artists and the critical apparatus that supported them. Nevertheless, the unyielding *terms* of the radical struggles of avant-garde artists and Suffragettes—full force, no surrender, brotherhood/sisterhood against blind, corrupt powers—found a fit in the inflexible "maximalized language" (Furet, 50) of revolutionary discourse. Militancy, in other words, both produced and conformed to an unambiguous structure of discourse that thoroughly polarized and polemicized the marginal groups' relation to the cultural center. Moreover, the militancy of these two groups was enhanced by their status as largely middle-class movements aiming to differentiate themselves from certain qualities of a reified "bourgeoisie." While avant-garde artists flew the banner of "scorn for women" and avant-garde suffragists adhered to a cultural program of "scorn for (sexual) men," both were united in an attack on bourgeois categories of gender, and that attack amounted to a form of pseudo-speciation, since it involved a middle-class repudiation of middle-class values.

If it is true, as Mercer indicates, that militancy offers a set of signs that lend ideological coherence to intersecting and evolving marginal group identities, then we should expect further points of commonality between Suffragettes and avant-garde artists. One such commonality was forged in a rhetorical strategy used frequently by Pound and Lewis, and increasingly by the Suffragettes, whereby press accounts of militant lunacy and disease were reworked and turned back upon the accusers. Ezra Pound's poem "Salutation the Third," which appeared in *BLAST* 1, interpellates a reader who, like a feminized *Times* critic, is a "slut-bellied obstructionist, / [a] sworn foe to free speech and good letters, / [a] fungus, [a] continuous gan-

[29] For instance, when Emmeline Pankhurst, avoiding reimprisonment, slipped into a huge WSPU meeting under the protection of the Bodyguard, delivered a brief contraband speech, and then shouted, "I incite this meeting to rebellion" (295), rebellion ensued. Rarely do performative speech acts work so well. The huge suffrage pageants were initially mounted as a response to Asquith's dismissal of suffragism as an unpopular movement with negligible support.

grene" (45). Similarly, and perhaps more spectacularly, Christabel Pank-hurst's polemic *The Great Scourge* diagnoses nearly all men as carriers of venereal disease and points to their "ignorance and unclean superstition" (197) as accelerators of Britain's "race suicide" (224).[30] Likewise, both groups rely for self-consolidation on a rhetoric of contempt for hypothe-sized general audiences: for example, what Mrs. Emmeline Pankhurst called the "dull and self-satisfied English public" (quoted in Morrell, 57), Ezra Pound gleefully referred to as the "race with brains like those of rab-bits" ("The New Sculpture"). Indeed, this rhetoric of contempt which con-ceives and reifies as an oppressive cultural center a nonporous, undifferen-tiated "public" may be understood as the flip side of militant alliances forged at other times around the sign of "the people."

The two examples of discursive links that I have offered—the rhetoric of disease returned in volleys and the rhetoric of contempt for unsympa-thetic publics—are also, notably, polemical strategies characteristic of the manifesto, and this constitutes a third important connection between mili-tant suffragism and the avant-garde: both groups produced manifestoes and related polemical tracts designed to programmatize anger, to polarize readership, and to recalibrate their own group's revolutionary position within hegemonic liberalism. Their tracts filled contemporary newspapers, rained down on the heads of gallery-goers, and plastered street corners, representing militancy as a war of words. But beyond this manifestic mili-tant textual alliance, it is difficult to locate additional commonalities be-tween the Suffragettes and the avant-garde artists. We cannot find them in historical accounts, for example, which treat suffragism as a female civic activity unconnected with the largely male vorticist movement.[31] And it is

[30] As both of these examples make clear, the language of disease—here taken up as a reverse discourse (but familiar also as a component of republican polemic, especially in its inflections of corrupt sexuality)—is intimately tied to a gendered ideal of transparency and hygiene. The de-bauched feminine carnality of the "slut-bellied obstructionist" threatens to occlude and rot the health of unfettered speech, while the unenlightened superstitions and profligate practices of the syphilitic man threaten the health of the entire polity. But the disproportionate disadvantages for the Suffragette in this militant reappropriation of the language of hygiene are manifest: in order to occupy the rhetorical position of the diagnostician, the Suffragette must work against a whole set of cultural assumptions that associate sexual disease with the feminine. Pankhurst cannot easily coin or invoke a "gigolo-loined obstructionist"; on the contrary, it takes her six months of serial-ized editorials to build up a polemical case against male sexuality.

[31] Even Miriam Hansen's subtle account of the vorticist/Hulmean social aesthetic misses the is-sue of commonality and instead critiques what she sees as George Dangerfield's dated, impres-sionistic treatment of labor unrest, Ulster unionism, and Suffragette militancy in Georgian En-gland. "What made Suffragettes, Orangemen and the labor movement indeed comparable within a larger pattern was their tendency to shift political action from the chambers of Parliament to streets, factories, courtrooms and secret meeting-places," writes Hansen (357). She then equates this "tendency" with the general fashion, shared by the avant-garde, of repudiating liberalism and

no easier to find them in the "original texts" of the movements themselves, precisely because the commonalities between such apparently different groups tend to be suppressed in the very discourse that tentatively allies them. Apart from the obvious reason why "the feminine" was deployed regularly as an evaluative and pejorative category in nineteenth-century art criticism, as we have seen, commonalities were further obscured by the self-representations of the Suffragettes themselves. Martha Vicinus has argued that suffragist leaders played with the roles afforded by a "separate spheres" ideology, consciously transforming the idealism traditionally ascribed to women into a form of spiritual polemic (252). Susan Kingsley Kent, arguing from a slightly different perspective, shows that in their attempts to overhaul the gender categories that made possible the double standard of separate spheres, the suffragists made use of a reverse discourse that incorporated into their tactics of resistance some of the very categories and taxonomies of the dominant order (15–16). These were, after all, women who dressed in white, wore big hats, and went shopping a lot; as Jane Marcus has observed, when Suffragettes smashed fancy shop windows in Bond Street, they were liberating mannequins that looked just like them.[32]

Any attention to the potential commonalities between Suffragettes and the avant-garde, then, must take into account a long-standing aesthetic and political ambivalence exemplified by Marinetti's 1910 textual relation to women and feminism; more specifically, it must acknowledge the avant-garde's need to distance itself from a radical movement that was, at least on the face of things, middle-class, middle-aged, reformist, and feminine. It is in this light, however, that we may pursue one particularly intriguing suppressed commonality. As Lisa Tickner's massive study of suffrage pageants and productions has shown, a sizable number of Suffragettes *were* artists, many of them exceptionally talented and ambitious artists. They designed posters, banners, postcards, cartoons, and murals for suffrage organizations; they received royalties for their designs; and they ranged from amateur seamstresses to middle-aged painters who had exhibited widely in England and France. Many of them had attended the

humanism. But, as Stuart Hall and Bill Schwarz have shown, the "rejection of Victorian liberalism was often sufficient, in its own right, to promote alliances between groupings which, according to the more familiar, standard political classifications of today, appear to have little in common" (113).

[32] See Marcus 1989: "It . . . doesn't take a Freudian to explain the effect of feminine sexual solidarity in those masses of huge, flower-bedecked Edwardian hats as they marched in the West End, smashing the icons of their oppression while wearing them as emblems of class and gender" (145).

Slade, London's progressive art school, which produced most of the vorticists. Several suffrage artists developed theories of artistic composition and
production, for example, Mary Lowndes's wonderful 1909 pamphlet on
suffrage banner making, which lays out a praxis of color and plane that at
points seems to anticipate Kandinsky's 1911 tract "On the Spiritual in Art"
(parts of which appeared in *BLAST* 1).[33]

But however "avant" the training or experience of the suffrage artists—
and many of them were actually traditional or commercial watercolor
artists—suffrage art decidedly was not the abstract art valorized by Hulme
and Lewis. Rather, it was somewhere between "decorative" art and commercial art, the two most salient critical targets of vorticist polemic, which
dismissed "decorative art" as "banal and obvious" (*BLAST* 2:46) despite its
importance for the work of Matisse and Kandinsky, and ascribed to commercial art "false and filthy standards" (*BLAST* 2:47).[34] Suffrage art was
hardly banal or filthy, but often it was both decorative *and* commercial:
iconographic, illustrative, and explicitly political, it sold in enormous
quantities and circulated in the mail and across British cities as the coin of
struggle. Thousands of marching women held it aloft in spectacular
pageants. It was public, discursive art; by virtue of its extensive production,
it interpellated just the same mass audience celebrated by Marinetti and
reviled by Lewis and Pound.[35] And frequently it was produced collectively
and anonymously—in the manner of the Omega workshop "factory," and
in contradistinction to vorticist art, which, as we have seen, was made by
competitive artists who adopted a name and a code principally to fend off
Marinetti's colonizing gestures. In short, Pound's oxymoronic description

[33] The Lowndes pamphlet, an exemplum of decorative theory, is reprinted in Tickner, app. 5.
[34] Norma Broude has shown how the operative hierarchy of much modernist art criticism
placed decorative art at the bottom of an order dominated by abstract art, and she provides ample
evidence of the hierarchizing of "decorative" art according to a gendered code. In Broude's argument, Kandinsky, though profoundly influenced by the Jugendstil decorative style, differentiated
his work from what he called "mere geometric decoration" by positing significant abstract art as
that which calls forth "vibrations of the spirit." Lewis's trenchant critique of decoration was no
doubt fueled by his rivalry with Fry, and as late as 1915 Lewis was still demonizing Fry as a shill of
decorative art: in *BLAST* 2, in his "Review of Contemporary Art," he writes that "the most abject,
anaemic, and amateurish manifestation of this Matisse 'decorativeness,' or Picasso deadness and
bland arrangement, could no doubt be found (if that were necessary or served any useful purpose) in Mr. Fry's curtain and pincushion factory in Fitzroy Square" (41). For a review of modernist art criticism and its denigration of "the domestic" and the decorative, see Valerie Jaudon
and Joyce Kozloff.
[35] Jane Marcus has argued that suffrage poster art, with "its borderline status between commercial art and painting . . . *translated semiotically the signs of commodity fetishism into a deliberate
feminist fetishism*" (1989, 144). That is, a good deal of the suffrage art produced before the war may
be read against the commercial fashion art that reflected and created women's oppression within
patriarchy.

of vorticism as "a movement of individuals for individuals, for the protection of individuality" (quoted in Levenson, 79) and Lewis's ingenuous redefinition of "popular art" as "the art of the individuals" (*BLAST* 1:7) effectively de-aestheticized all collective, political art.[36]

Incongruous though the praxis and style of the art of the Suffragettes and the vorticists may have been, the fact remains that one suppressed commonality between the two groups—their strategic production of an art that constituted and advertised a radical group aesthetic—brought both of these oppositional and self-differentiating groups into national focus. Each group worked with chiasmatic disadvantages: while the fine artists in the suffrage campaign had unprecedented access to a wide audience, they received none of the critical attention that was devoted to their postimpressionist contemporaries. And while the vorticists were attended by a loyal literati press, they nevertheless were forced to show their art in the limited setting of the small gallery, where they faced a depressingly low level of sales and circulation. Christabel Pankhurst's sister Sylvia reluctantly gave up her fine arts career to design banners for the suffrage campaign, while Wyndham Lewis grudgingly confined his artistic polemic to "the small public interested in these matters" (*BLAST* 2:38).

Interestingly, the suppression (indeed, the unwriting) of the bond of art production between Suffragettes and vorticists is itself made manifest by Lewis and Pound in their announcement of an explicit anti-bourgeois alliance between the two groups.[37] It appears on the last page of the original version of *BLAST,* and was probably composed very late in the militant campaign, during the height of the May-June painting slashings of 1914: "To suffragettes. A word of advice. In destruction, as in other things, stick to what you understand. We make you a present of our votes. Only leave works of art alone. You might some day destroy a good picture by accident.

[36] Lewis frequently equated commercialism with a kind of debased populism: beating the drum of aesthetic autonomy, he insisted, in the next issue of *BLAST,* that "the moment [the artist] becomes USEFUL and active he ceases to be an artist. We most of us nowadays are forced to be much more useful than we ought to be. But our painting at least should be saved the odour of the communistic platform or the medicine chest" (40). Lewis's doctrine of the separateness of art from life was by no means confined to vorticism: Fry and Bell, for all of their investment in the collectivism of the Omega Workshop and of avant-garde ideals, understood art in terms of rarification, not politicization (C. Harrison, 47–50), and Mark Cheetham documents the exclusivity of the rhetoric of purity which propped up the continental abstract aesthetic (119–38).

[37] This tactical suppression may also be understood as a mode of rivalry. As militants competing for claims and positions against a bourgeois cultural center, the two groups marked out an overarching rivalry within which they mounted various efforts to delimit and compartmentalize their own (and each other's) competing grievances and entitlements. Nowhere is this mode of rivalry more evident than in Lewis and Pound's notice of an explicit anti-bourgeois alliance between the two groups, "To Suffragettes."

Then!—mais soyez bonnes filles! Nous vous aimons! We admire your energy. You and artists are the only things (you don't mind being called things?) left in England with a little life in them. If you destroy a great work of art you are destroying a greater soul than if you annihilated a whole district of London. Leave art alone, brave comrades!" (151–52).[38]

The alliance coheres around common *energy*, which marks out artists and Suffragettes from the rest of London. Energy, in fact, constitutes the very vortex that names the vorticists: for, as Pound tells us at the end of *BLAST* 1, "The vortex is the point of maximum energy" (153). Suffragettes, at least as they are interpellated here, stand as eccentric bundles of vortex energy in an inert city, and this fact alone secures the salutary textual alliance among "brave comrades." But of course *BLAST*'s acknowledgment of this commonality is strategic: the Suffragettes are avatars of political energy and therefore are *not* artists. Not being artists, they cannot know a good work of art and might unwittingly destroy one. If they are "good girls" who stick to politics and don't mess with art, the vorticists will cede them their own votes—which, they subtly stress, hold no value for the artist. For the artist-agitator is *not* the political agitator; rather, the artist is the individualist whose cause, Lewis tells us, is "NO-MAN's." In belittling and dismissing the (bourgeois) political aims of the Suffragettes, Lewis's avant-garde manifesto simultaneously enhances his own group's artistic claims to anti-bourgeois autonomy. Indeed, the manifesto embraces only the *formal* properties of Suffragettes as they are discursively reconstrued and compartmentalized in a carefully controlled militant alliance. We recognize this model from Marinetti's manifestic attack on women, feminism, and parliamentarianism which simultaneously celebrates such (Suffragette) characteristics as "courage, audacity, and revolt"; "the punch and the slap"; "aggressive action" (41).

It is important to stress that *BLAST*'s explicit militant notice to "brave comrades"—almost always referred to by historians as a "salute"—does indeed signal the production of new allied identities. The vorticists *create*, on the one hand, a Suffragette who knows nothing of art, only energy, discipline, and destruction, and, on the other hand, an avant-garde artist who energetically guards the new art against any intrusive bourgeois influences or threats. That historians have overlooked the complexity of this polemical relationship stems in part from the fact that the fabrication of these

[38] Wees speculates, with Walter Michel, that the first and last eight-page signatures of the extant *BLAST* were added while the journal was already at press (163). If this is so, then the warning to the Suffragettes would have concluded the original, unaugmented version of the journal, which was probably composed in May, a month in which at least seven paintings were slashed.

new, fictional identities occurs in manifestoes, which, as we have seen, are usually read as transparent documents rather than as inflected discursive formations. We have also seen how the manifesto's characteristic use of the pronoun "we" simultaneously animates a polemical voice of hortatory urgency and claims for its nascent group all good things, including moral infallibility. So exactly what identifies the "we" of this new avant-garde, so eager as it is to jettison past art and artistic identity? For one thing, the new avant-garde positions itself against, even as it cultivates, a public reception of incredulity and suspicion.[39] The very title of Marinetti's 1910 tract "The Pleasure of Being Booed" instantiates the hostile relation of avant-garde production to the critical apparatus of its uncomprehending reception, and anticipates *BLAST*'s predictable dismissal by the (previously sympathetic) art critic P. G. Konody as "wildly extravagant and often ungrammatical nonsense" (Cork, 263). In their public inscrutability, however, the new avant-gardists are not unlike their Suffragette contemporaries, also self-marginalizing in tactics and doctrine, whose "arguments"—both discursive and nondiscursive—become increasingly unreadable except from a subject position within Suffragette militancy. Government figures such as Chancellor Lloyd George and Prime Minister Asquith had long been confounded by the rancor steadily directed at them by the Pankhursts.[40] By 1912 even the WSPU membership itself had begun to splinter around the tactical issue of intelligibility: the Union's seemingly random destruction of property had come to require, at least according to its dissenters, "too much explanation."[41]

Yet the "we" created in *BLAST* and other avant-garde tracts shares more with the "we" of the Suffragettes than just the public's incomprehension. The new English avant-garde forcefully abjures the heterosexual cult of "sentimental" carnality associated with earlier art movements such as sym-

[39] Unlike other Edwardian art groups—such as the New English Art Group, which aimed for middlebrow press reviews by men of letters—the "we" of the new avant-garde plays to the public from a deeply interiorized position; "reaching the public" is construed as a nearly impossible venture, and *BLAST*, with all of its inscrutable epigrams and appellations, smugly identifies itself as "an avenue for all those vivid and violent ideas that could reach the Public in no other way" (1:1).

[40] Andrew Rosen reports the Suffragettes' reactions to the "torpedoing" of the 1911 Conciliation Bill (which would have opened the way to limited suffrage for women): "WSPU members heckled Asquith severely at the City Temple on 28 November. Women shouted, unfurled banners, and blew police whistles. Unable to continue his speech, Asquith departed." The next day Lloyd George, breakfasting with C. P. Scott, asked him, incredulously, "But what can they hope to achieve by attacking him [Asquith]?" (155).

[41] Dr. Louisa Garrett Anderson, upon resigning from the WSPU (quoted in Rosen, 156). Even Pound, writing a mildly sympathetic piece on Suffragettes for *The Egoist* (under the pseudonym "Bastien von Helmholtz"), cannot read Suffragette intentions and complains that they "should destroy *only* national property" (1:3 [July 1914]; rpt. in Bonnie Kime Scott, 369; emphasis added).

bolism and impressionism, and even contemporary movements such as *die Brücke*. In Marinetti's utopian future, "the carnal life will be reduced to the conservation of the species, and that will be so much gain for the growing stature of man. . . . *Amore*—sentimentality and lechery—is the least natural thing in the world" (72–73). *BLAST* expands the injunction against *amore* into an allegory of art: "The Past and Future are the prostitutes Nature has provided. Art is periodic escapes from this Brothel" (1:148).[42] The new avant-garde, then, equates *techné* with the disparagement of traditionally rendered sexuality, encoding into its warrior credo the break with symbolist or fauvist representations of parasitic feminine carnality, and marking the creative beginnings of an abstract art that controls masculine machinelike forms within fields of static tension.[43] Pound was to inflect this injunction against craven sensuality somewhat cryptically in an advertising prospectus for the forthcoming *BLAST*, the caption of which read, "No pornography. End of the Christian Era."[44] He might well have added "Death to Sentimentality," since the asceticism offered by Pound, Hulme, and most continental avant-garde groups *avant la guerre* as the cure for modernity's deterioration contained a strong current of anti-sentimentalism. Indeed, according to Suzanne Clark, anti-sentimentalism

[42] Lewis's polarization of art and female sexuality is of a piece with coeval continental theories of abstract painting in which "the feminine" was construed as a Platonic principle antithetical to the production of abstract ("pure") art. Mark Cheetham provides a fascinating analysis of Piet Mondrian's "drive to purify the feminine in order to clear the way for abstraction" (126) in an argument that dovetails with the thesis that the exclusivity underlying the early modernist rhetoric of purity contributed to Nazi ideologies of race purity. Cheetham quotes from Mondrian's 1912–14 *Sketchbooks:* "Woman is against art, against abstraction . . . in her innermost being" (122) and concludes convincingly that Mondrian's "ruthless purification . . . can be seen as nothing short of an aesthetic eugenics based on the discrimination of gender" (123). My own understanding of this representative early modernist misogyny differs from Cheetham's in that my emphasis rests on the historical contexts in which the rhetoric of purity performed its cultural work. For the importation of such ideas to England by acolytes such as Lewis and Pound (whose literary circle also admired Weininger's *Sex and Character*, a kind of scientistic blueprint for a modern metaphysics of misogyny) was necessarily modified by a cultural context in which the consideration of female suffrage rights had been part of the public sphere discourse for at least half a century, and in which the specter of feminist militancy definitively challenged the validity of such abstractly (and inconsistently) "feminine" properties as passivity and domesticity. Female militancy, in other words, further complicated the already incoherent gendering produced in bourgeois ideology.

[43] Carol Duncan argues that the fauves and *die Brücke*—continental avant-garde contemporaries of the futurists and vorticists—painted "powerless, defaced nude[s]" which were "inversion[s] of the Symbolist *femme fatale*" (302), and that these nudes were distinct from previous nudes in "the compulsion with which women [were] reduced to objects of pure flesh, and the lengths to which the artist [went] in denying their humanity" (298). While determining the degree to which modern artists "denied the humanity" of their nude models seems to me an especially tricky affair, it is certainly possible to see in these nudes the debasement of femininity by anxious partisans of progressivist modernity.

[44] If pornography is, literally, writing about prostitutes, then Pound's injunction is an exact literary cognate of Marinetti's ban on painting *les femmes des ateliers*.

is constitutive of the modern aesthetic; in her reading, "sentimentalism" is for modernists the watchword of bourgeois ideology, loaded with unhealthy (and unartistic) attachments to family, love, pathos, religion, sorrow, *feeling*.[45]

## Militant Hygienics

Another source of the distinct modernist bifurcation between feminine subjective sentimentality and its constructed opposite, masculine objective experimentalism, has been copiously documented and analyzed by Rita Felski: that is, the parsing out of culture into, on the one hand, historically embedded and objectively concrete modern (masculine) productions and, on the other hand, the ahistorical, unchanging (feminine) matrix against which the magnitude of such productions may be judged.[46] From this angle, femininity and modernity are locked in an antithetical—albeit dialectical—relation; yet, as Felski shows, the logic that underpins the relation is thoroughly circular, since it takes for granted that femininity must always remain outside the ambit of modernity. Suffragettes were determined to historicize femininity at every turn—witness, for example the historical pageants with which the suffrage movement began—and to create monuments of their own magnificence. Part of their plan to do so involved bringing "woman" into alignment with militant subjectivity, recreating her in the image of the citizen of a rigorous, hygienic new world. This program, which is the subtext of *The Great Scourge*, duplicates and complicates the agenda of the masculinist avant-garde, as we shall see.[47]

The anti-sentimental asceticism deployed throughout *BLAST*'s manifesto marks vorticism's self-differentiation from the perceived excesses of earlier movements and, more disingenuously, from the "Latin temperament" (for which read sensuality) of its rival, futurism.[48] But if we are ade-

[45] See Clark, esp. Introduction and chap. 1.
[46] See Felski 1995, chap. 2, esp. 48–57.
[47] By no means is this outline applicable to the *non*-masculinist avant-garde of England, that is, the Bloomsbury-Omega axis. Within the aesthetic ethos of that group, masculinism itself was a form of irredeemable bourgeois instrumentality, and located as far from an avant-garde sensibility as one could get. In fact, it is possible to understand the Bloomsbury-vorticist hostility in these terms: vorticist masculinism represented for Bloomsbury acolytes an unregenerate form of the gender retrenchment promoted by revolutionary discourse. It is interesting, in this regard, that in an era saturated by artistic manifestoes, no one associated with Bloomsbury-Omega ever produced a manifesto.
[48] Note that Peter Nicholls (1995) argues that this is precisely futurism's relation to its forebear, symbolism, which, he persuasively shows, exemplified for Marinetti the decadence of thick meaning and cloistered poetic space. See esp. 89–92.

quately to map out the relation between the English avant-garde and the Suffragettes, this futurist-vorticist metaphor of asceticism must be read alongside Christabel Pankhurst's sudden editorial calls, in 1913, for a Suffragette program of militant asceticism. In fact, the exceedingly polemical *The Great Scourge and How to End It,* brought out at the end of 1913, ignores the aesthetic issue of cultural sentimentality (except where it hoodwinks women about the "joys" of marriage), and instead concentrates on a program of sexual continence for the entire British male population. As with its contemporary avant-garde productions, *The Great Scourge* was received either enthusiastically or with dumbfounded incomprehension; interestingly, versions of the latter mode continue to characterize the book's reception, as some libraries still catalogue it with medical texts.[49]

Indeed, although Pankhurst periodically creates connections between sexual restraint and artistic creation (made also by the London avant-garde), her main argument *is* fundamentally medical.[50] Whereas the trendy countercultural publication *The New Freewoman* (for which Pound wrote) discussed human sexuality in 1913 in logical-philosophical terms, and the futurist-vorticist axis that emerged in 1913 revised aesthetic discourse to accommodate a critique of culturally constructed sexuality, Pankhurst's 1913 tract takes up the topic of sexuality in a carefully crafted discourse of anti-sentimentality and pure objectivity. As I shall show, by using such a discourse Pankhurst simultaneously positions herself against the bourgeois medical writers who had heatedly come out against women's suffrage (for "medical" reasons), and within a discursive formation that sought with scientific precision to contest bourgeois constructions of heterosexual marriage and sexuality. Thus she devises a suffragist oppositional discourse that both acknowledges and differentiates itself from other (avant-garde) contestations of Edwardian "common sense."

[49] Perhaps the most absurd example of critical incomprehension comes from Pankhurst's own biographer, David Mitchell, who accounts for *The Great Scourge*'s initial popularity by hypothesizing its appeal to "ferocious spinsters . . . and to long-suffering wives who relished a vicarious revenge" (226).

[50] As Pankhurst puts it in one editorial, "Art is creative. Sexual excess is a waste of man's creative energy" (231). Jonathan Rose points out that "waste" and its antonym "efficiency" were Edwardian keywords which "pervaded discussions of imperial policy, industrial organization, social legislation, personal hygiene, and religion" (117). He shows that "efficiency" had, by 1903, become a banner for radically different groups, from Fabian socialists to conservative imperialists. The Edwardian cult of efficiency visibly underpins *The Great Scourge*'s sweeping appeals to abstinence and self-control. To wit: "Prostitution involves a futile and wasteful expenditure of men's energy—energy which they greatly need to enable them to hold their own in science, art, athletics, industry, and commerce" (192). Note that by this particular enumeration of qualities, Pankhurst ironically situates abstinence within the Victorian cult of manliness.

Pankhurst's editorials maintain that an epidemic of venereal disease is disabling sexually active women and crippling the English birthrate, that 75 to 80 percent of British men are infected, and that their infection is disseminated through and perpetuated by their "partnerships" in prostitution. At every turn of her argument, Pankhurst carefully situates her (undoubtedly inflated) epidemiological account of venereal disease within a framework of individual agency.[51] Prostitution, she declares, is the manifestation of the "unnatural" economic and sexual enslavement of women; individual men will not eschew the brothel until they are "re-educated" (197) and can see women as equal partners rather than as sexual slaves; and this reeducation cannot begin to be useful as an intervention in the economic, cultural, and physical "enslavement" of women until their political enfranchisement has been achieved.[52]

Today's feminist readers of *The Great Scourge* understandably have been troubled by its normative moralism and eugenic assumptions. I have no desire to rehabilitate the ideological foundations of Pankhurst's arguments; nevertheless, I do want to detail further the relation between *The Great Scourge* and some of its contemporary medical, economic, and literary discursive formations in order map out what I take to be Pankhurst's attempt to enter into the universalizing discourses that had been formative in the historical exclusion of women from universal subjecthood. Specifically, *The Great Scourge* may be framed as a tactical entry into several Edwardian public discourses that intersect with the avant-garde and medical fields of discourse already mentioned: first, the anti-liberal assault mounted by a loose phalanx of social groups that included vorticists, Ulster Unionists, and collectivists; and second, the discursive "sex war" that had been mapped out for several decades in medical tracts, New Woman novels, reform movements, and anti-suffrage polemics. Since both of these discourses helped to structure ongoing debates about modernity and its relation to women, they provide us with an outline for understanding the British suffrage movement's relation to the opposing forces of modernity *avant la guerre*—empiricism and radical individualism.

[51] The epilogue to *The Great Scourge* is an exposé of a scandal known as "Picadilly Flats": a London brothel was raided in the summer of 1913, but individual clients—many of them highly placed in government and industry—were protected. Susan Kent notes that the case "confirmed for many feminists their belief that the private behavior of many M.P.'s rendered them incapable of legislating or administering law disinterestedly" (155).

[52] Note the form that Pankhurst's libertarian analysis takes. Her political approach to women's disadvantages in patriarchy operates as a sort of wolf in sheep's clothing, whereby what seems to be systemic critique is in fact neither class based nor economically based nor even gender based, but rather turns on state-enforced volunteerism.

As Stuart Hall and Bill Schwarz have shown, anti-liberalism in the decade before the war was constituted by heterogeneous political forces, each driving a separate wedge into the cracks of the rapidly deteriorating Liberal Party. Suffragists challenged the liberal rationale that offered limited suffrage as a means for *virtual* representation of "the masses" (including women, laborers, and the poor), and radicals like Pankhurst aimed to expose the ideological inflection of those economic policies by which the liberal state obstructed the political empowerment of women. The liberal laissez-faire mandate, for instance, ultimately made possible what Pankhurst regarded as the free market in prostitution—for Pankhurst the most dramatic and palpable locus of women's economic dependence. So *The Great Scourge* recasts the whole idiom of selective liberal protectionism—which images government as a passive "nightwatchman"—to reflect its link with patriarchal dominance. "It is said by hypocritical opponents of Votes for Women," she writes, "that women must not vote because men protect them already. Women will not listen to that excuse any longer, now that they know what men's protection means" (189). Men's protection means, among other things, men covering their own backs by defending prostitution as a legitimate market response to their own "natural" sexual needs. When Pankhurst vigorously and repeatedly challenges the "compulsory" nature of male sexuality, she is in part attempting to dissever the politics of prostitution from the yoke of the "natural market" ideology of free trade economics. When, at the same time, she follows a rhetorical tradition of connecting prostitution to "slavery," she essays to expose the joints between economic coercion and sexual subjection.[53] It is in this context that the form of sexuality implicitly proffered by her text need not necessarily be read as coercion or subjection but rather may represent the exercise of choice: in *The Great Scourge,* celibacy registers the repudiation of the concept of sexuality as a free market "protected" by men. Celibacy is therefore, paradoxically, meant to represent the most "liberated" form of sexuality imaginable.

Pankhurst's anti-liberalism also contains a goodly measure of radical conservative imperialism—a measure present as well in *BLAST*'s nation-

[53] The suffrage movement's widespread use of slavery as a metaphor for female sexual oppression is troubling and ubiquitous. References to "lynching" and "masters and slaves" appear frequently in Emmeline Pankhurst's speeches. There is perhaps some influential overlap between the British adaptation of this discourse (e.g., the title of Rebecca West's early assessment of the Pankhursts, mentioned earlier, "Lynch Law: The Tragedy of Ignorance") and the powerful speeches and writings of the civil rights leader Ida B. Wells, who delivered her famous oration "Southern Horrors: Lynch Law in All Its Phases" on over forty occasions in England and Scotland in 1893.

alistic construal of competing Anglo-Saxon and Latin "races." Pankhurst charges that "men are constantly infecting and re-infecting the race with vile disease, and so bringing about the downfall of the nation" (189). The integrity of "the race" corresponds to the health of the English nation, whose self-assigned management of other races helped to create and sustain its own economic vitality. But by 1914 England's "health" was threatened on just this front, as imperial dissolution seemed increasingly possible both at home (in Ireland) and abroad (in India and China). Here the semiotic force of imperial England may figure in Pankhurst's fears about "race suicide" (188). After all, Pankhurst's purchase on the vote was, however synecdochally, a purchase on empire; any diminishment of that empire literally and symbolically devalued the vote. In this sense Pankhurst's emphasis on racial disease may be read alongside the fanatical militancy of the Ulster Unionists, who were at that moment drilling for civil war. Both Pankhurst and the Orangeman Sir Edward Carson cast their militant violence as panaceas for the deteriorating empire—at a time when, as Hall and Schwarz put it, "the issue of Ireland condensed the anxieties about Britain's imperial position as no other could, for if the empire were to be dislocated at its very centre its prospects looked bleak" (101). In other words, whereas Votes for Women could be (and was) figured by anti-suffragists as the fatal symptom of a crumbling empire, Pankhurst proposes that voting women will nurse Britannia back to health.

There are even more explicit reasons to consider the Unionists with the Suffragettes. Carson—who, like several Suffragettes, was celebrated in *BLAST*'s list of forces to "BLESS"—had stymied the Liberal government with a brand of unrestricted militancy: if human blood had to be spilled for the Union, he repeatedly declared, the Orangemen were ready to spill it. And yet, as Suffragettes never tired of pointing out, the Unionists were neither banned from meeting in public nor tried and imprisoned for their violence. Indeed, Pankhurst argued, the English government had a history of capitulating to—and even venerating—militant causes such as the Orangemen's: Lloyd George himself had "declared that 'the kingdom of politics is like the Kingdom of Heaven, it suffereth violence, and the violent take it by force.'"[54]

---

[54] Christabel Pankhurst, "Militant Methods," in *The Great Scourge* (119). The Suffragettes' strained insistence on the boundaries of "justifiable" and "unjustifiable" (or "humane" and "reckless") violence seems of a piece with the rivalrous parceling of grievances and tactics among militant groups which is evident in the pages of *BLAST*. When Suffragettes began to slash paintings in 1914, for example, *The Suffragette* made a point of comparing "the damage to a picture of man with the potential killing of thousands of 'real' men by Edward Carson's Ulster militants" (May 8, 1914; quoted in Fowler, 115).

While the imperialism of *The Great Scourge* resonates with other forms of white racist anti-liberal discourse, Pankhurst's deployment of a normative idiom of female sexuality (according to which "normal women" believe that "sexual intercourse where there exists no bond of love and spiritual sympathy is beneath human dignity" [197]) requires a different context. For *The Great Scourge*'s institutionally scientistic body of work is of a piece with an antecedent body of writings about the female body. One kind is the "social purity" writing exemplified by Josephine Butler's late nineteenth-century assaults on the Contagious Diseases Acts: Butler and others argued that the acts' "regulation" of prostitution through the enforced speculum examinations of prostitutes in garrison towns helped to figure the female body as a repository of disease; her melodramatic narratives villainize above all the powerful medical doctors acting as dangerous agents of a misogynistic state.[55] Another kind of writing, the medical and sexological discourse against which Butler's generation of feminists chafed, particularized the female body in detail, "saturating" it with sexuality. By the late 1910s medical discourse dominated the logic of much of the anti-suffrage sentiment that appeared in the editorials and letters published in newspapers such as *The Times*. One notable example is the infamous letter of March 1912 by the bacteriologist and surgeon Sir Almroth Wright, in which he argues that a woman's physiology interferes with her capacity for rationality, and is therefore ultimately responsible for her unthinkable public violence. This violence, to complete the curve of his circular thinking, is symptomatic of a pathology that blinds the Suffragette to the unwritten social codes of the civilized world.[56]

Pankhurst's book incorporates and reworks these two kinds of writing. First, she drops Butler's melodramatic narratives and turns the discourse of demonized doctors into a tool *against* the misogynistic state. Quoting

[55] See Kent, 119–29, for an account of the animosity and contempt felt for the medical profession by feminist social reformers. Butler's generation of feminists developed a rhetoric of "social purity," which, on the one hand, figured prostitution as both a model and a metaphor of patriarchal vice and, on the other hand, figured purity as the spiritual apotheosis of human nature. Ironically (but not surprisingly), their understanding of purity is directly at odds with that of the contemporary continental theorists of abstract painting (described at length by Cheetham in his first chapter) who inflect purity with "masculine" rather than "feminine" values.

[56] Wright expanded this "militant hysteria" letter (*The Times*, March 28, 1912) into a book titled *The Unexpurgated Case against Woman Suffrage*, which came out in early 1913, a few months before Pankhurst began her *Great Scourge* editorials. It was repudiated even by Mrs. Humphrey Ward, a leading anti-suffragist; it was also widely reviewed (often sympathetically, if not exactly favorably) and acknowledged to be one of the most radical anti-suffrage publications of 1912 and 1913. In Rebecca West's amusing account of the feminist book reviewer's distress at being asked constantly to review such works, she describes her pain on being "enveloped in the fog-like featureless gloom of Sir Almroth Wright" (*Clarion*, November 21, 1913; rpt. in West, 223).

carefully and extensively from contemporary American and English physicians, she ironically conscripts those physicians as willing allies in women's battles against conspiracy and vice: "Doctors [are at last] breaking through the secrecies and traditions of long years," she proclaims, "and sounding the note of alarm" (196). Second, through the continuous deployment of the slogan "Votes for women, chastity for men!" she inverts a standard cultural representation of gender by interpellating (and making available for interpellation) politically active women and sexually passive men. Vicinus has observed that Pankhurst's "speeches were filled with exhortations to independence, freedom, and action; she never spoke of woman's woes and helplessness, but talked of her equality and power" (256). Unlike other reformists, Pankhurst never forces woman into the complementary role within a political model of a universal rights-bearing male. Woman's power is not limited to republican maternity, and equality is never construed asymmetrically: "The power of maternity is something which women have in addition to their other powers. The power of maternity corresponds with the power of paternity, and not to some other power or quality in men" (226). But the slogan "Votes for women, chastity for men!" assumes that the choice for chastity *has* already been made by women— who have had due cause to reflect long on such matters.

In the New Woman novels of the 1880s and 1890s, chastity was an ideological sign that figured prominently in characters' struggles for independence and self-control. As Ann Ardis has persuasively shown, celibacy represented a way for a New Woman protagonist to "possess her 'self' in a culture that conceives of a sexual relationship as a man's 'possession' of a woman. . . . [C]elibacy seems to be a necessary means of self-protection when confronted with the aggressive demands of the New Man, the man who wooes her with Darwinian law" (110). Extending to the New Man this possibility of self-control through chastity, Pankhurst ironically creates a subject position not unlike that created by Marinetti and Lewis: no longer a slave to his Darwinian body, this New Man can turn his back on "unwholesome flesh" (Marinetti), clean up the public's "filthy standards" (Lewis), and escape from "this Brothel" into Art. Whatever else its effects, then, *The Great Scourge* renders meaningless such gendered evaluative terms as "virility" and "manliness."

Finally, Pankhurst rewrites previous medical-sexological discourse by ignoring the female body and avoiding almost completely any rhetoric of contaminated female sexuality; instead, she particularizes and spectacularizes the male body, saturating *it* with pathological sexuality. Her discussions are bold and unflinching: on the subject of nocturnal emissions, for example, she blithely quotes an expert's opinion that the semen of continent men may "be easily gotten rid of by an involuntary emission during sleep once or twice a month, a state of things which is perfectly natural" (208).[57] And her wry tone as she urges the medical profession to "cure" male sexuality (with bromides, if necessary) matches the patronizing antisuffrage sermonettes presented by the likes of Almroth Wright.

Out of Pankhurst's program of self-control for men and political control for women emerges a future she casts as utopian (albeit eugenic) in its freedom from disease and sex-based injustice. *The Great Scourge*'s regulation of male sexuality includes a repudiation of the brothel as a place where control is lost, identity blurs, social formations collapse. Control of the body—the code of this new order—everywhere patterns the discursive fabric of militancy. Sexual self-control defines New Women and New Men of England; oral control steels the hunger-striking Suffragettes bound to silence by prison rules; military control galvanizes the Bodyguard as they receive the truncheon blows meant for Emmeline Pankhurst.

*The Great Scourge,* then, may be read as a reactive polemic that creates radical subject positions, first and foremost, for women who had been pathologized as hysterical or syphilitic bodies. And, just as important, it may also be understood as an *intertextual* construction by a woman who had, at the time of its writing, a predominantly textual relation to militant suffragism: *The Great Scourge* was written during Christabel Pankhurst's long exile in Paris, where she read every daily paper from London even as she moved in avant-garde circles that included Valentine de Saint-Point, author of the "Futurist Manifesto of Lust." Pankhurst was reviewed in *La Revue de Paris* by Jean Finot, who described her tract as "an exceedingly passionate and unusual book, despite a surfeit of feminist propaganda" and urged that it be translated into French (D. Mitchell, 227–28).[58] *The Great Scourge* was, then, like much avant-garde polemic, calculated to shock and polarize a reading public already reeling from the unprecedented physical violence of Suffragette militancy. As a participant in the militant discourses circulating in prewar London—discourses that constructed identities and alliances across a strikingly broad spectrum of political interests—*The Great Scourge* insisted on gender and sexuality as

[57] This passage alone provoked gasps of astonishment from radicals and conservatives alike. See, for instance, the bewildered letter to *The New Freewoman* (October 15, 1914) from the radical theorist R. B. Kerr. See my discussion, in Chapter 5, of the tactic in feminist polemics of particularizing the male body, and the consequent de-universalizing of the masculine subject attendant upon this spectacularization. See Deem, esp. 511–14, for a further discussion of this tactic.

[58] See David Mitchell, 205–9, for a partial account of Pankhurst's activities in Paris, and especially for a description of her avant-garde social circle.

sites of insurgency, as had the vorticists, the futurists, and even the "Life" sensualists associated with *The New Freewoman*. To put it another way, we may say that *The Great Scourge* offered one blueprint of the reconfiguration of gender and sexuality within the prewar avant-garde.

I want to return to what is by now, I hope, an obvious point: the actions of the militant Suffragettes were making literal (and in fact mapping out) to an astonishing degree the metaphors and metalepses of iconoclasm used by the English avant-garde, including Marinetti's attack on sensual luxuries and his equation of war with hygiene, *BLAST*'s hit list of oppressive cultural figures, and Pound's exhortations to "craft and violence" ("The New Sculpture"). In the final year of militancy, Suffragette artists were among the most active iconoclasts of the movement, and police raids yielded caches of bombs, paraffin, wire cutters, and hatchets in the studios of artist-arsonists (Rosen, 191–93).

The most historically accessible case in point is the slashing of Velázquez's Rokeby Venus by the Suffragette artist and arsonist Mary Richardson, whose undercover alias was "Polly Dick." (Truly.) The painting has been discussed by Edgar Snow as a work that disrupts, and perhaps even disproves, the concept of the male gaze.[59] But Richardson said she disliked the painting, and gave it four blows of an ax to protest the government's unremitting re-arrests of the hunger-striking Mrs. Pankhurst. Richardson explained that she had "tried to destroy the picture of the most beautiful woman in mythological history as a protest against the government for destroying Mrs. Pankhurst who is the most beautiful character in modern history" (quoted in MacKenzie, 261). Hers, then, was an attack on representation—in particular on the inadequacy of women's representation in and by patriarchy. Snow's analysis notwithstanding, Richardson associated the Rokeby Venus with a government of oppression. And Wyndham Lewis's warning to "LEAVE ART ALONE" notwithstanding, Richardson's political *and* aesthetic sensibilities were perfectly intact: she knew what she was doing when she slashed Velázquez's goddess of love. The painting had been purchased through a public subscription appeal in 1906 after it had been thoroughly popularized and admired by the New English Art Club (Fowler, 112), a group of faded moderates scorned by the emerging avant-garde of Lewis and Pound. Richardson's vandalism, in other words, had taken as its object a "national asset," one that represented a solidly bour-

---

[59] Although Snow's thesis is provocative, at no point does it acknowledge—or even indicate any awareness of—the painting's fate at the hatchet of "Polly Dick."

geois notion of what *The Times* called "the perfection of Womanhood" (quoted in Fowler, 112). Implied in her act is an aesthetic and decidedly avant-garde judgment, which, not coincidentally, forced the closing of the very museums that were the targets of Marinetti's early exhortations, as this passage from the first Futurist Manifesto illustrates: "So let them come, the gay incendiaries with charred fingers! Here they are! Here they are! . . . Come on! set fire to the library shelves! Turn aside the canals to flood the museums! . . . Oh, the joy of seeing the glorious old canvases bobbing adrift on those waters, discolored and shredded! . . . Take up your pick-axes, your axes and hammers, and wreck, wreck the venerable cities, piti-lessly!" (43).

While the hortatory urgings of this passage match Suffragette activity almost prophetically, the emotional charge of Marinetti's exhortations re-calls us to the English insistence on control. It is apposite here to take some note of the official WSPU slogan, "Deeds, not words!" one of whose inter-texts is undoubtedly the Italian epigram *fatti maschii, parole femine*— "male deeds, female words." Among the Suffragettes' many tropings of gender can be seen, in their "Deeds, not words" slogan, the material enact-ment of the avant-garde rhetoric of violence, which both literalizes the Italian epigram's catachresis and reverses its terms: Suffragettes commit deeds; vorticists and futurists are all talk.[60]

In reopening the archive on modernism, my suffragist counternarrative is offered not as the "good" modernist unconscious, "truer" because mar-ginalized in subsequent histories. All the figures of these narratives are in some way compromised, and none can be unproblematically recuper-ated—as if such a thing were possible, or even desirable. As Fredric Jame-son has written, there can be no unproblematic recuperation of "nonhege-monic cultural voices," for "only an ultimate rewriting of these utterances

---

[60] Nicholls's 1989 discussion of Charles Maurras's "passéism" unwittingly points up the irony of this epigrammatic transposition. Arguing that futurists followed a cultural attitude about gender that had been schematized a few years earlier by Maurras, Nicholls describes that scheme as a con-trast "between a 'womanly' preoccupation with the material (especially phonic) properties of lan-guage on the one hand, and a virile literature of action on the other" (1989, 207). "Deeds, not words" also bears an obvious and important relation to the late nineteenth-century anarchist method of "propaganda by deed." There is no doubt that the militancy of avant-garde rhetoric *avant la guerre* is directly indebted to the lines laid down by Bakunin and Kropotkin, the latter of whom declared in an 1877 manifesto: "Experience has spoken! Far be it from us to go for the way which is pacific and legal. We are for the violent way which has proved itself! Let us leave the radi-cals to the pacific twaddle" (quoted in Cahm, 83). See Peter Starr's illuminating discussions of the force of contagion disseminated by the anarchist movement, and his argument that "the deed" of violence was widely perceived as the epicenter of the spread of social hysteria (176–80). Pankhurst's articulation of her project to the anarchist agenda was undoubtedly calculated to pro-duce an unprecedented semiotic form of (female) militancy.

in terms of their essentially polemic and subversive strategies restores them to their proper place in the dialogical system of the social classes" (1981, 86). And yet we may take Jameson's imperative one step further. On the one hand, the categories of the "hegemonic" and the "marginal" can be shown to be profoundly relational; but on the other hand, we need to stress that no amount of revision, reinterpretation, or re-dialogizing can undo the power dynamic in the parasitic relation between the English avant-garde and the English Suffragette movement. The "energy" and iconoclasm of suffragism, adopted and redeployed by a gender-conscious avant-garde, dovetailed with an anti-bourgeois agenda expressed in revolutionary discourse. Both groups were invested in unmasking what they took to be the "false" universalism of the bourgeoisie; both groups, it may be deduced, anticipated a "true" and transcendent universal. A few subsequent historical facts about these groups, then, should give us pause: first, the fact that both the militant Suffragettes and the militant avant-garde took up arms for God and country at the moment World War I was declared; and second, the fact that, after the twenties, Pound, Lewis, and Marinetti all made careers of twinning art and fascism, while Christabel Pankhurst became an evangelical millenarian Christian. This shift in the direction of critique suggests, at the very least, a confluence of revolutionary discourse with absolutist forms of universalism. And yet I must hasten to add that modernist groups using revolutionary discourse were not always fated to wind up in reactionary camps. Therefore, with this proviso in mind, and in order to widen the vista of modernist critiques of modernity, I now turn to other forms of engagement with revolutionary discourse—and its absolutism—exemplified by some contemporaries of the Suffragettes, vorticists, and futurists. These competing instances of cultural interventions are to be found in the works of Dora Marsden, the imagist publicity machine, and, above all, Mina Loy.

# 4 Modernists and Gatekeeping Manifestoes

## Pound, Loy, and Modern Sanctions

The case of the Suffragettes and the vorticists helps to focus an important question that concerns the relation of the avant-garde to the bourgeois universalism it sought to overhaul. For there can be no doubt that the universalism of the bourgeois subject was under attack and revision by the likes of Marinetti, who, broadly speaking, posited an alternative revolutionary universal subject, or by Tristan Tzara, who envisioned a universalism that went no further than collective idiosyncrasy, or by Pound and Yeats, who held to a premodern ideal of artistic aristocracy. In all of these cases, modernity presented a constant double pressure toward, on the one hand, collective efficiency and, on the other hand, individualist expression. When this double pressure became especially intense in the years surrounding the First World War, the avant-garde program of integrating the realms of the political and the aesthetic was increasingly threatened by the Scylla of bourgeois instrumentalism and the Charybdis of solipsistic aestheticism. And the problems for *women* of entering into the avant-garde project of critiquing the bourgeois regime entailed a further barrier, which, though diffuse, is in evidence everywhere in the radical literary and political organs of modernism: that is, the difficult task of negotiating the frequently competing aims of feminism and avant-gardism. In modernist journals and little magazines, the tension between social activist forms of feminism and avant-gardism is thick; in order to investigate this tension and its political ramifications, I will examine some of the effects of political debates, polemical tactics, and newly theorized representations of sexual identities as they were articulated in proto-modernist "counterculture" journals such as *The New Freewoman*, with the aim of following the path of gender's construction in the print culture where modernism was produced. From such a vantage point, the relations among modernism, "implicit" feminism, and explicit suffragism may turn out to be more binding and overdetermined than histories of modernism or feminism would lead us to suspect.

We have seen, in the previous chapter, the discursive relation between militant suffragism and the English avant-garde as it was created and deployed in the Edwardian popular press and in some of the more outspoken publications of each oppositional group. Dora Marsden's sequential run of journals, *The Freewoman*, *The New Freewoman*, and *The Egoist*, provided a set of forums for further links between the avant-garde and feminism. The first two of her journals, both short-lived (November 1911–September 1912, and June 1913–December 1913, respectively), moved increasingly in editorial focus from individualist feminism to de-gendered individualism, a focus taken up more or less permanently when *The New Freewoman* became *The Egoist* in January 1914.[1] With this editorial shift came a gradual prominence of contemporary (and in some cases avant-garde) works of art and literature, as well as literary and art criticism, and the concomitant diminution of polemical political commentary.[2]

*The New Freewoman* offers us an especially interesting example of how the mode of self-presentation of one branch of feminism might be read alongside an increasingly dominant mode of self-presentation used by the avant-garde. For both the feminism and the avant-gardism represented in the pages of *The New Freewoman* seek deliberately to create a constricted and highly self-conscious audience, a deliberately sectional (i.e., nonuniversal) audience: despite the journal's respectable circulation numbers, no general "reading public" is interpellated and no note of popular solicitation struck. Marsden sets the tone for this putatively exclusionary audience in 1911, when in her inaugural editorial for *The Freewoman* she declares that there are probably no more than ten "freewomen" in Britain. The remainder of the female population are "Bondswomen," that is, "the women

[1] The subtitle of *The Freewoman*, first "A Weekly Feminist Review," was changed to "A Weekly Humanist Review." When the journal became *The New Freewoman*, Marsden used the subtitle "An Individualist Review," which remained the subtitle for *The Egoist*.

[2] Frequently it is the fate of avant-garde collectives to fall to one side or the other of the political-aesthetic divide. Compare, for an example of the opposite trend, Peter Wollen's description of the Situationist International after 1962: "The earlier artistic goals and projects either fell away or were transposed into an overtly political (and revolutionary) register within a unitary theoretical system" (122–23).

who are not separate spiritual entities—who are not individuals." According to Marsden, it is only when a woman becomes an individual that "she *is* free, and will act like those who are free."[3]

Marsden's consistent appeals to a constricted and self-selecting audience stem in part from her commitment to radical philosophic egoism, which she presents in a variety of formats that include the mode of individualism advanced by Max Stirner and another formulated by advocates of political anarchism such as Benjamin Tucker, a regular writer for her journals.[4] Radical egoism contracts and subordinates social issues to a theory of individual will; and to this end Marsden repeatedly militates against the "falsehood" of socially or rhetorically constructed groups. "There *is* no corporate life. There are only individuals, geographically situated near to, or at a distance from, each other" (*New Freewoman*, August 1913, 65).[5]

But Marsden's resistance to a collective "we," particularly in relation to feminism and suffragism, issues also from her own earlier experiences as a member and organizer of the WSPU, and from her personal disagreements with Mrs. Pankhurst's broadening political and semiotic claims for "the Vote." According to Jane Lidderdale and Mary Nicholson, Marsden chafed under the directives of the WSPU's highly centralized militant organization, with its demand for unquestioning allegiance and obedience (54–55).[6] Her carefully crafted *New Freewoman* editorials, aimed at "a very limited number of individual women" who "can not be lumped together in a class, a sex, or a movement" (June 15, 1913, 5), are of a piece with her incessant denunciations of militant suffragism and the ubiquitous "we" with which the WSPU interpellated its feminist audience. Marsden's "we," by contrast, is thoroughly unmanifestic, very nearly a royal "we," barely hanging together as a pronominal entity. As *The New Freewoman*'s purview

[3] *Freewoman*, November 23, 1911, 1–2. Hereafter the three journals will be cited parenthetically in the text.

[4] In Michael Levenson's account of Stirner's philosophic egoism, "man," for Stirner, "was no more substantial than 'divinity.' Both were abstractions; both represented the displacement of more fundamental egoistic drives. . . . Stirner's aim was to free the ego from any slavish attachment to a 'higher' calling" (64–65).

[5] Bruce Clarke's thorough study of Marsden's political philosophy characterizes her individualism as "an early modernist form of philosophical idealism. It is overwritten by an evolutionary vitalism that organicizes and reinscribes the ego-ideal as the 'living,' or preideational, self. Vitalism and anarchism both postulate a unitary, metaphysical life force . . . which drives individuals into differentiated selfhood and then unifies those atoms relative to a common telos, for instance, Whitman's visionary 'democracy'" (72).

[6] In this Marsden was not unlike another ex-WSPU member, Teresa Billington-Greig, who, as Barbara Green has shown, broke away from the Pankhursts because of the yoke of emotional control they imposed on their followers; Green argues that Billington-Greig resisted the manipulation of spectatorship by which the Pankhursts achieved so much popular success (see chaps. 1–3).

grew in scope and notoriety, taking on a broader pool of contributors and introducing a literary section at the urging of Rebecca West, its "we" came to stand for fewer and fewer readers, as Mark Morrisson's study of the magazine's marketing techniques shows. This "we" may be militant, but it is hardly revolutionary. "We *are* 'common,'" declares Marsden to her detractors, but "this does not mean, either on our lips, or on others', that we are like everybody else. *Tout au contraire!* It means that we are egoistic, individual, selfish. To be 'common' with the 'fine' [i.e., from the perspective of 'refined' people] means to be in the bonds of self-ish motives and to see others in the same; not to be under sway of the fine concepts; the 'noble' emotions; to be running *amok* of the whole cultural structure. And so we are" (July 1, 1913, 25).

Although Marsden's sophistic reinvention of "the popular" and "the common" strains the limits of rhetoric (and syntax), the contradictions in her "we"—"we are individuals"—are hardly disabling for Marsden. They allow her to recast "the common" as an anti-bourgeois identity and to separate it from the homogeneity of the masses. The semantics here adumbrate a rhetorical tactic that will be found a year later in the pages of *BLAST.* There revolutionary discourse is simultaneously invoked and revised so that "the people" are reclaimed in limited numbers as discrete subjects with aesthetic or philosophical faculties. Wyndham Lewis claims that *BLAST* is "popular, essentially," but "popular art does not mean the art of the poor people, as it is usually supposed to. It means the art of individuals" (1:7). Lewis's manipulation of the revolutionary rhetoric of "the people" is consistent with his profound distrust of movements, collectives, and *fraternité* generally.

In their reworkings of revolutionary discourse, both *BLAST* and the *Freewoman* series deliberately constrict their supposed appeals to political and social change. This calculated effect is perhaps more dizzying in the case of *The New Freewoman,* since it is difficult to imagine feminism as a program—even Marsden's individualist brand—apart from a foundational construal of women as a social group, however provisionally or strategically or tenuously that group holds together.[7] The feminist organ that seeks rhetorically to constrict feminism's interpellated audience in effect takes on an avant-garde aura of rarity and cultish originality and rejects the means of social reproduction by which political change—in

[7] Cf. recent feminist debates about identity and difference, wherein advocates of the former concept insist that "woman" is valuable as a provisional site of strategic political alliance (e.g., Felski 1997), against the wide array of positions that argue against identity (e.g., Nicholson 1995; Cornell). See Anderson 1998 for an overview.

this case the recognition or formulation of women's (universal) rights—
might be advanced. This is a conundrum that resurfaces in second-wave
feminism of the 1960s, for example, in such avant-garde works as *SCUM*
(the Society for Cutting Up Men), the singly authored manifesto by Valerie Solanas, as we shall see in Chapter 5. But *SCUM* might just easily be
the progeny of *BLAST,* wherein Lewis, claiming that "great artists in England" (a grouping in which Lewis presumably includes himself) "are always revolutionary" (*BLAST,* 1:7), uses "revolutionary" to mean ruptures
with the past acted out *by individuals.* Solanas, Marsden, and Lewis all
share a profound distrust of movements, collectives, "politics," and *fraternité* generally, even in spite of their struggles to make a place for their own
movements.

But when Lewis and Marsden rework revolutionary discourse for their
own ends, something more than self-contradiction occurs: they create
simulacra, rather than repetitions, of anti-hegemonic insurgency. In their
usage, revolutionary discourse becomes referentless, less a reanimation of
earlier struggles against seats of power than a staging of self-representation
through a familiar (even popular) syntax of hortatory utterances. We may
recall from Chapter 3 Lewis's manifestic declaration in *BLAST* that "our
*cause* is NO-MAN's"; Marsden had made much the same claim a year earlier
when she decreed that "*The New Freewoman* has *no* Cause. The nearest approach to a Cause it desires to attain, is to destroy Causes" (July 1, 1913, 25).
Both of these aphoristic quips suggest an appropriation of "the revolutionary" which undercuts any identification with social change; the result is
that the whole notion of "revolutionary change" comes to be little more
than a sign of the iterability of revolutionary discourse. With their repudi-
ations of political "causes," the anti-modern modernists Marsden and
Lewis are thrown back on the other horn of the modern dilemma: extreme
unintelligibility produced by extreme individualism. For Marsden and
Lewis, the stand against modern assimilation ensures its opposite: political
atomization.

As we have seen, *BLAST*'s taking up of revolutionary discourse was as
much a response to the threat of futurism's colonization of the English
avant-garde as it was to the opportunities offered by the ambiguities of
revolutionary avant-garde discourse. By laying out a series of interrelated
manifestoes, *BLAST* created a subject position whose "we" could at once
signify a select and self-limiting group *and* the uncountable artists of an
immanent future of literary and cultural change. In this respect, *BLAST*
represented something of a public relations improvisation on its only successful English predecessor, the anti-manifesto "*Imagisme*/A Few Don'ts by

an Imagiste" of 1913.[8] In fact, imagism's self-presentation affords us a look at a first-run model of modernist revolutionary polemics not only for *BLAST* and vorticism, but also for the self-presentation of Marsden's quasi-feminism. With the aim of returning to Marsden's use of modernist tactics, and ultimately in order to ground a reading of Pound's simultaneous attraction to and suppression of the various feminisms of Marsden and Mina Loy, I will first elaborate at some length Pound's use of the manifesto form and the consequences of that use for the renovations of "masculinity" that we have come to associate with Pound, early modernism, and revolutionary discourse generally.

## Recuperating the Manifesto Form

That Pound's founding double tract of the imagist movement should be referred to universally as a "manifesto" is one of English modernism's most telling ironies. Of course, it has come by this appellation for some obvious reasons. "*Imagisme*/A Few Don'ts by an Imagiste" deliberately gives an impression of being the first text to bear the imprimatur of a nascent movement of avant-garde poets called imagists. Like many other aesthetic manifestoes, the tract positions this movement within a field of contemporary movements, but claims for imagists a central place in a closet-utopian program of literary change. Pound's imagist tract also functions in certain prominent respects like the Italian futurist manifestoes, wherein, as Marjorie Perloff has written, "theory . . . *is* the practice. . . . To talk about art becomes equivalent to making it, and indeed most historians of Italian Futurism agree that the series of fifty-odd manifestos published between 1909 and Italy's entrance in to the war in 1915 were the movement's literary form par excellence" (90). The difference is that "*Imagisme*/A Few Don'ts by an Imagist" precedes anything resembling an imagist movement or school. As several historians of modernism have argued—Martin Kayman perhaps most explicitly—imagism was more a historical fiction than "a relatively real 'school'" like vorticism (53); imagism's "creation" occurred in a brief and cryptic series of texts designed to advertise Pound's own explicit proposals for the improvement of contemporary (and, particularly, American) poetry.[9]

However tempting it may be, then, to think of these inaugural essays as manifestoes, it might be more productive to read them not as manifestoes

[8] All citations of F. S. Flint's interview "*Imagisme*" and Ezra Pound's "A Few Don'ts by an Imagiste" are from *Poetry* 1.6 (March 1913), 198–200 and 200–206, respectively.
[9] See Kayman, 63–65ff., for his account of imagism *as* a literary history.

but as reactive responses to the manifesto's implicit popular appeal and sensational London reception, a reception shaped in part by Marinetti's futurist assaults and in part by the coverage in the national press of syndicalist manifestoes and radical labor tracts.[10] In this reading the relations between English modernism and its audience can then be linked with English feminism's relation to modernism's audience.

The story of the composition of "*Imagisme*" and "A Few Don'ts by an Imagiste" is well-known.[11] F. S. Flint wrote the first of the two imagist tracts in early 1913 at Pound's request and under his direction; Pound then cut and rewrote it for publication in Harriet Monroe's new Chicago-based journal *Poetry*. "*Imagisme*" appeared in the March 1913 issue; it was signed by Flint and followed by the somewhat lengthier "A Few Don'ts by an Imagiste," signed by Pound himself. In choosing Flint for a coauthor, Pound had chosen someone who, in a substantial review essay, "Contemporary French Poetry" (*Poetry Review* [August 1912]), had recently established himself as an authority on French literary movements and "isms." Flint's "coverage" of *imagisme* amounts to an exclusive literary scoop. As he informs his readers, he has been "unable to find anything definite about it in print," presumably because it is a movement that is utterly *un*-public, accessible by none of the usual discourses of the literary public sphere, intelligible only by means of the method of reporting Flint has chosen—that is, personal, almost secretive contact with the cloistered individuals of imagism.

Flint begins by describing the literary outlines of this English group with the French name: its members "admit" that they are "contemporaries of the Post Impressionists and the Futurists" but point out that "they had nothing in common with these schools. They had not published a manifesto. They were not a revolutionary school; their only endeavor was to write in accordance with the best tradition." If this founding document of imagism presents its group in contradistinction to other competing avant-garde groups, the distinctions are key: this is *not* a revolutionary group; it

[10] David Kadlec outlines Pound's confused relation to the polemics of contemporary anarchist and syndicalist groups in London: "The conflict and strife in Pound's work during the time around *BLAST* is also a conflict of discourses, a false bridging of terms and sympathies." Kadlec charts Pound's efforts in the early months of 1914 to link his own radical program for poetry with the "revolutionary *elan* of the striking workers" who had been part of the general labor unrest in England (1028).

[11] Most commentators agree that Pound solicited Flint as his "interviewer," wrote much of the interview himself, and then further edited Flint's revisions of the interview. See Longenbach, 31–33; Kayman, 55–64; and Ruthven, 67–72, for variations within this standard account.

does *not* take up the revolutionary discourse of the manifesto; and it aligns itself with, rather than opposing itself to, some notion of a traditional literary past. In fact, the grievances and goals for disruptive change conventionally codified in the numbered lists contained in aesthetic manifestoes have been ironically recast by the imagists as "a few rules" of literary composition, which, Flint informs us, were "drawn up for their own satisfaction only, and they had not published them." Had not published them, that is, until Flint "offered" to take up the task of handling these public matters. Flint enumerates the three heretofore undisclosed rules—two of them fairly straightforward guides for composition, and the third a tenet of vers libre—before revealing the existence of yet another mysterious doctrine of imagism that has been withheld deliberately from the literary public sphere.[12] This is, in Flint's words, "a certain 'Doctrine of the Image,' which they had not committed to writing; they said that it did not concern the public, and would provoke useless discussion." Unwritten, unpublic, unavailable for discussion, this "doctrine" is like unto an artifact of premodern gnosis which, through its hermeticism, absents itself from the bourgeois sphere of consensus and debate. For Pound and Flint, to imagine a "useless discussion" is to inhabit a perspective outside the precepts of modernity: such a move involves either sheer cynicism or absolute faith, neither of which can circulate as modern currency.

Thus, in the space of just three paragraphs, Flint repeats to the point of insistence a portrait of the imagist group opposing itself to (in part by erasing itself from) "the modern public" and its circulating printed media. As an anti-manifesto, "*Imagisme*" adopts a strategy that is already clearly marked: Pound invokes the new Continental avant-garde method of creating an audience through revolutionary discursive forms, and in the same moment repudiates that practice.

In Chapter 2 I drew on Lauren Shumway's concept of "stylistic terrorism" to describe that either/or discursive configuration of the avant-garde manifesto which makes it possible to mandate certain forms of cultural production and unequivocally dismiss all others.[13] But Pound's "mandate" for imagism is rather more tangled. We might read Pound's subtle journal-

---

[12] John Tytell argues that Pound's earliest intimations of imagism's first and second "rules"—"Direct treatment of the 'thing,' whether subjective or objective," and "To use absolutely no word that did not contribute to the presentation"—were connected to his growing association with the anti-democratic, anti-Romantic T. E. Hulme in 1911, who opined to Pound that "all a man ever thought would fit onto half a sheet of notepaper. The rest is application and elaboration" (73).

[13] See also Shumway, 57–58.

istic manipulation of this kind of discursive field alongside Michael Levenson's persuasive appraisal of Pound's ambivalence toward the new avant-garde methods of self-promotion: "On the one hand, his inclination is to publicize and to legitimize new aesthetic doctrine"; but on the other hand, fearing that "widespread diffusion will undermine the essentially elite nature of the modern renaissance," Pound aims ultimately "to avoid the democratization of art." He therefore "exploits the particular character of mass culture—its susceptibility to publicity, celebrity and fashion—but at the same time he defines himself against the logic of mass appeal, the dissemination of high cultural values" (148).

This apparent ambivalence toward publicity may also be understood from a slightly different perspective as one facet of Pound's canny understanding of the causal links between literary publicity and the perception (and even the production) of literary merit. K. K. Ruthven argues just this point in a broader thesis that explores Pound's propagandizing role as a literary critic. Ruthven maintains that, for Pound, getting hold of the means of production of literary criticism "was a more urgent task . . . than writing any number of poems whose merits would never be noticed until a revolution in critical discourse had been achieved. For only in that way would it be possible for Pound to create the taste for his own poetry and other writing he approved of" (42). Pound's "conviction that literary texts make their way in the world not by some supposedly intrinsic merit as literature but by claims made on their behalf by criticism" (61) led him to jury-rig reviews of his own volumes of poetry, according to Ruthven; more important, for our purposes, it produced early on a drive to control the creation of the organs and language of critical discourse in which "new" poetry might be received and contextualized. The first and most salient example of this career drive was the creation of a referentless "imagist" critical apparatus—referentless because "les Imagistes" at that moment meant only seven poems by two people united more in romance than by poetic style. In imagism Pound created for himself a concrete structural foundation for subsequent critical elaborations, one that began to posit an anti-modern ethos based in a pre-republican contraction of the universal field.

The "formal doctrine" made possible by Pound's strategic introduction of imagism to an American poetry magazine's readership contains critiques of the methods and products of the two competing contemporary movements that Flint names at the beginning of the "*Imagisme*" article: postimpressionism and Italian futurism. Between them these two quasi-groups form an intertextual field (characterized principally by notoriety) within which the terms of imagism may be seen in sharp relief.[14] From this specific contemporary perspective, imagism's reported resistance to public discourse seems at once aristocratic and ingenuously naive. Indeed, the sole and single-minded determination of the "group"—"to write in accordance with the best tradition, as they found it in the best writers of all time"—bespeaks a kind of monastic and anachronistic dedication to scholarship and letters; Flint confesses to a sense of amazement at their "earnestness" and tolerates their *snobisme* because it is of a "dynamic form, with a great deal of sound sense and energy behind it; and they are stricter with themselves than with any outsider." It is, in other words, the *snobisme* of a disciplined, cloistered coterie, bound by aristocratic codes and largely unconcerned with the affairs of the contemporary world.

This is, in any case, the intended effect of the rhetoric of "*Imagisme*"— an effect made stronger by Pound's negotiation (and ultimate erasure) of the manifestic pronoun "we." In Kayman's account of the composition history of "*Imagisme*," Pound wrote an "interview" between himself and Flint; Flint would not sign it, however, and instead drafted it into an article which he returned to Pound. This Pound went over closely, making careful cuts and several changes. One important change involved the excision of all direct speech: any information about *imagisme* was to be shunted through Flint, the chosen interlocutor. Linked to this change is the transformation of all personal pronouns to an unspecified "they": neither Pound nor H. D. nor Richard Aldington (the only three extant *imagistes*) are named, nor are they numbered. With this move, the "interview" collapses into special reportage of the transmission of rare formal doctrine. In Ruthven's reading of the "*Imagisme*" stratagem, Pound hoped to evince a rising sense of intrigue in Harriet Monroe, editor of *Poetry:* "The elusive *imagistes,* she would read, 'had not published a manifesto,' but now here was Flint actually supplying her with their hitherto unpublished poetic. How could *Poetry* turn down the opportunity to be the first journal in the world to print the *Imagiste* manifesto, especially when it had the opportunity also to publish concurrently an essay by Ezra Pound called 'A Few Don'ts by an Imagiste,' whose recommendations were remarkably consistent with those *Imagiste* principles reported by Flint?" (71). How indeed, given the premium placed on rarity and opacity in the essays? But the question of the disappearance of the manifestic "we" does not stop here with the evaporation of any direct access to *imagisme;* it requires some fur-

[14] The summer of 1912 in Paris had seen, for example, the showing of Duchamp's *Nude Descending a Staircase,* a performance by the heavily postimpressionist Ballet Russes, and the publication of Apollinaire's study *Les peintres cubistes.*

ther probing if we are to understand Pound's deliberate manipulation of contemporary avant-garde rhetoric and the manifesto form.

For Pound's eschewal of "we" in *imagisme* suggests a self-marginalizing group to which *no one* is offered access or the chance of self-alignment.[15] We have seen how the "we" of the manifesto polarizes fields of discourse into "us" (with whom an audience is invited to identify and to whom are attributed all good things) and "the rest of you" or "them" (against whom an audience is urged to oppose itself). Pound upends this manifestic convention, exposing its fiction but also transmogrifying it into another polemical configuration: on one side the cloistered and sparsely numbered "school" known only as "they" (whom the audience is invited to admire but not to identify with or to join) and on the other side "you"—the privileged but ultimately excluded reader. Pound hammers home these restraints on "you" when, in "A Few Don'ts by an Imagiste," he lays out reference after reference designed to discourage too much familiarity between unschooled reader and erudite *imagiste*. In fact it is difficult to imagine many beyond Pound who might follow his advice to "consider the discrepancies between the actual writing of the Greek poets and dramatists, and the theories of the Graeco-Roman grammarians, concocted to explain their metres," or to "let the candidate fill his mind with the finest cadences he can discover, preferably in a foreign language . . . e.g. Saxon charms, Hebridean Folk Songs. . . . If you want the gist of the matter go to Sappho, Catullus, Villon, Heine when he is in the vein, Gautier when he is not too frigid."

Pound's reversal of the manifestic "we" issues in control of heterogeneity. He produces a new kind of literary "manifesto" in which the univocality of the speaking position is explicit rather than hidden (as it had been in the pseudo-populist "we" of Marinetti's futurists). The uncountable numbers characteristically represented by "we" here close down into a stringently restricted "school." And "a school," Pound had informed his *Poetry* readers two months earlier, "exists when two or three young men agree, more or less, to call certain things good."[16] Or even when, as in this case, a young woman agrees to append a schoolish-sounding moniker to her initials: "H. D., Imagiste." From a movement to a school, from a manifesto to

15 Pound's policing of membership extended to the management level of imagism. To take the most famous example, Amy Lowell's self-insertion into the editorial side of things infuriated Pound, who wanted her financial backing but not her aesthetic or strategic guidance. See Hanscombe and Smyers, 181–84, and Ruthven, 106.

16 Michael Long has characterized Pound's intolerance of heterogeneity as a preference for Dante over Shakespeare, finding in Dante "an articulated moral and intellectual coherence more seamless and austere (so he thought) than Shakespeare's heretically tolerant mess" (105).

a credo, Pound effects a shrinkage of avant-garde goals while sustaining an illusion of avant-garde kinship and familiarity.

In fact, in August 1912—the month when Pound signed Hilda Doolittle's poem with his inspired new name for her—Pound had been leading a life divided between spectatorship in the expansive world of the Paris and London artistic avant-garde and intimacy in a sequestered world characterized by the ascetic literary traditionalism of his new friend and mentor in anti-bourgeois polemic, William Butler Yeats. James Longenbach has chronicled Pound's ambitions "to be part of Yeats's inner circle ... to establish just Yeats and himself as London's most exclusive, most mysterious society of all" (12); and, according to Longenbach, Pound and Yeats's cohabitation in the London countryside for three winters from 1913 to 1916 helped to create for Pound a coveted "sense of poetic aristocracy, meeting in private, ignoring the demands of a vastly inferior public" (26).

The blueprints for this project of setting elite art and poetry against a hostile or uncomprehending public—or, more specifically, against a bourgeois public—are evident in the early "*Imagisme.*" Pound sharpens the antagonism a year later in a group of anti-bourgeois essays[17] that include the pseudonymously penned "The Bourgeois" (signed "Bastien von Helmholtz"), wherein he declares that "the bourgeoisie is a state of mind. It is as a term of opprobrium, used by the bohemian, or the artist in contempt of the citizen" (53). Pound's defining metaphor then moves from mind to body: the bourgeois is "the stomach and gross intestines of the body politic and social, as distinct from the artist, who is the nostrils and the invisible antennae." Pound's language bespeaks an obsessively itemized "body politic" in which the artist is markedly *alien,* and one would not be surprised to hear of the artist's special scanner vision; but Pound instead resumes the abstract language of social condemnation: "bourgeois" is "a term which is the censure of a whole code of morals and of ethics" (53).

Raymond Williams, addressing precisely this kind of modernist codification of artistic class antagonism, insists that "no question is more important to our understanding of ... modern movements than the ambiguity of bourgeois" (1988, 5). Among the various permutations of modernism's critique of the bourgeoisie, he singles out for description a strain of a nineteenth-century critique mounted from a quasi-aristocratic position

> which was to survive, pathetically, into the twentieth century, to be taken up by even the most unlikely people: the claim, indeed the asser-

[17] See, for example, "The Serious Artist" and "The New Sculpture."

tion, that the artist was the authentic aristocrat; had indeed to be, in the spiritual sense, an aristocrat if he was to be an artist. An alternative vocabulary gathered behind this assertion, from Arnold's culturally superior "remnant" to Mannheim's vitally uncommitted intelligentsia, and more individually in the proposition—eventually the cult—of "the genius" and "the superman." Naturally the bourgeoisie and its world were objects of hostility and contempt from such positions, but the assertion did not have to be made very often to extend to a wholesale condemnation of the "mass" that was beyond all authentic artists: now not only the bourgeoisie but that ignorant populace which was beyond the reach of art or hostile to it in vulgar ways. (6–7)

This is the "ignorant populace"—"the vulgo," the "matinee girls," the "race with brains like those of rabbits," the "mentalities of a loathsomely lower order"[18]—who increasingly populated Pound's fictional reading public, and against whom he was to direct his literary polemics of the next decade.[19]

But despite having elaborated this rigidly polemical field within which a select group of artists occupied an embattled moral and aesthetic high ground, Pound still had need, in the years 1912–14, to negotiate a broader kind of revolutionary discourse as well. As Wyndham Lewis was to put it later, "If you were a 'movement' [in 1914] you were expected to shout. One was surrounded—one was hemmed-in—by mob-orators" (Michel and Fox, 58). How then to formulate an aristocratic "shout" and still be heard among the mob-orators? How to preserve one's doctrinal purchase on a

---

[18] See Pound ["Bastien von Helmholtz"], "John Synge and the Habits of Criticism": "There is no truce between art and the vulgo. . . . The consumer, the digestive man, fears the dynamic man. He is perfectly right to do so. The dynamic man exists. Nothing can inhibit his existence" [54]; "The New Sculpture," 67, 68; *Ezra Pound and Dorothy Shakespear: Their Letters, 1909–1914*, Ed. Omar Pound and A. Walton Litz (New York: New Directions, 1984), 316.

[19] Pound displayed more antipathy toward his American audience than his English audience. Kayman has argued that Pound sought to make *Poetry* "into a force for the sort of 'Awakening' that he firmly believed in" (56), an awakening that would shake the American literati out of what he perceived to be their parochial stupor. His habitual casting of America as a cultural outpost seems to have served several purposes, not the least of which was to establish a critical foil against which he could foreground his American "discoveries" (such as Robert Frost and H. D.) who had escaped the country's dangerously outmoded cultural values. For example, according to J. J. Wilhelm, in 1918 Pound actually paid an American reviewer to attack American provincialism and to praise T. S. Eliot as a nonprovincial writer (207). Earlier, Pound had pseudonymously responded to a critical exchange in the pages of *The New Freewoman* concerning the strengths and weaknesses of American literature; he parodically assumed the persona of a Pennsylvania Dutch champion of provincial dialects who has "long feared the influence of older culture," and who closes his "letter" with a proposal for further American cultural insulation: "The first step is the establishment of the Murhkn langwidg with its own patentud fonetick, protectud by the gulorious staars and stripes.—Deidtrisch Pheffenschneider" (October 15, 1913, 178).

fiction of past exclusivity while competing for the kind of critical attention paid to more explicitly plebeian movements, such as the approving observation, made by Harold Munro, that the Italian futurists possessed "precisely the spirit which actuated men in the early days of the French Revolution" and represented "the reaction of a suppressed vitality against a tyrannous and antiquated power"?[20]

One way was to project an aura of revolutionary impatience and restlessness with (and a commitment to the inevitable overthrow of) the regime of the *modern* oppressor, the "bourgeoisie." To this end, Pound distinguished between the bourgeois ("the consumer, the digestive man") and "the oppressed": "There is a constant and irrefutable alliance between art and the oppressed. . . . The oppressed have never set a hand against their artists, but the half taught have always done so" ("John Synge," 54). In this rhetorical sleight of hand, "the oppressed" corresponds simultaneously to two very distinct classes. On one reading, "the oppressed" signifies a proletariat class whose integrity and (aesthetic) subsistence is threatened by an unspecified class that is lexically recognizable as a depraved and counterrevolutionary petite bourgeoisie. From this perspective we see Pound availing himself of the "people's will" of revolutionary discourse. On another more subtle reading, however, the solidarity of "the oppressed" with "their artists" suggests a kind of prerevolutionary feudal loyalty between peasants and patronizing aristocracy. Pound, in other words, has it both ways: he inscribes revolutionary values within a prerevolutionary social gestalt.

Another way for Pound to preserve this careful rhetorical configuration was to adopt the gender codes of revolutionary discourse while at the same time creating and sustaining the patronage links between his own handpicked artistic charges and the powerful women of London's cultural circles.[21] Pound's coding of creative works of art rests on a fundamental association of "the feminine" with anti-art forces. His explicit 1918 declaration that he had still "to be convinced that any woman ever invented anything in the arts"[22] (apparently forgetting H. D.'s role as inventor of imagism)

[20] *Poetry and Drama* (December 1913), quoted in Perloff, 35–36.

[21] Ruthven argues that in "Hugh Selwyn Mauberly"—a revisionist "literary-history-poem" of London before the war—Pound creates a portrait of "the titled female culture vultures at whose salons British class distinctions are momentarily suspended and sexual opportunities appear to abound" (40). Ruthven's phrasing is interesting: it associates aristocratic women with sexual debauchery, and yet it acknowledges the democratizing process of the bourgeois public sphere within which "class distinctions are momentarily suspended." Pound was the beneficiary of both aspects of this paradoxical portrait.

[22] *Ezra Pound and the Visual Arts*, quoted in Ruthven, 102.

was already subtly present in his earlier prescriptions for art and literature. This specifically modernist doctrine of the anti-feminine was formulated in part by one of Pound's mentors, T. E. Hulme, whose poetics, argues Naomi Segal, were characterized by "a marked preference for the 'clean.'" Hulme "advocated 'a poem which is all dry and hard, a properly classical poem'" (Segal, 242), and this sentiment is echoed in Pound's praise of the poems of (the ungendered) H. D. to Harriet Monroe: "Objective—no slither; direct—no excessive use of adjectives, no metaphors that won't permit examination. It's straight talk, straight as the Greek!" (quoted in Hanscombe and Smyers, 153). That Pound is apparently un-ironic in his characterization of H. D. *and* Greek culture as "straight" suggests that he means no more than that H. D.'s poetry avoids the "slither" of what Pound and Hulme characterized as "feminine" writing, feminine culture; by the very same token, H. D.'s lack of "slither" paradoxically helps to rehabilitate an association between poetry and hygienic masculinity. And in this bifold characterization we may correctly recognize once again the revolutionary opposition between rhetorical transparency, unfettered truthfulness, visibility—coded masculine, of course—and the "slither," interestedness, and intrigue of depraved feminine culture, what Pound commemorated in his description of Victorian and Edwardian culture as an "old bitch gone in the teeth." [23]

Notwithstanding Pound's deployment of this aesthetic avant-garde discourse, here and in numerous other writings, he nevertheless had to work under the directives of the powerful women who published his work in journals.[24] These included not only Harriet Monroe at *Poetry* and Dora Marsden and Rebecca West at *The New Freewoman*, but also, a few years later, Jane Heap and Margaret Anderson at the *Little Review* and Harriet Shaw Weaver at *The Egoist*. Frequently Pound shouldered his way into these journals by asking for increasing amounts of space and autonomy from their editors. That is, Pound never allowed himself to be merely a contributor to the woman-run journals where his work appeared; he always sought, and was usually granted, a sub-editorship or some other official position whence he could establish his own uncontested seat of literary influence within the journal. For example, in 1917 he inaugurated his position as foreign correspondent for the *Little Review* with a letter informing Margaret Anderson that "*The Little Review* is perhaps temperamentally closer to what I want done??? . . . I want an 'official organ' (vile

[23] See "Hugh Selwyn Mauberly," in *Selected Poems of Ezra Pound*, 64.
[24] For a useful overview of Pound's editorial relations to modernist publishers, see Marek, chap 6.

phrase). I mean I want a place where I and T. S. Eliot can appear once a month. . . . I must have a steady place for my best stuff" (quoted in Hanscombe and Smyers, 180–81).

His directives to Harriet Monroe were no less proprietary: he argued with her over *Poetry*'s motto, "To have great poets there must be great audiences too," which he thought too "democratic" for his own aristocratic literary aims, and he nagged her about the quality of the poetry that he expected to see published in *Poetry*. In Kayman's analysis, Pound sought "to make this new and influential magazine into a force for the sort of [American] 'Awakening' that he firmly believed in"; and to this end he worked to establish "his personal critical standards" as "the [editorial] policy of *Poetry*" (56). At virtually the same time, Pound was working on Dora Marsden to give him a number of pages in *The New Freewoman* for a literary section which would be funded by an unnamed patron (John Gould Fletcher): "I don't want to 'boss,'" Pound wrote to Marsden, "but if I am to make the page efficient, I must follow my own scheme" (quoted in Lidderdale and Nicholson, 68). In the face of Marsden's suspicious reluctance to yield territory to Pound, he tried to persuade the wealthy Amy Lowell to buy *The New Freewoman* for him (Kayman, 56), and even referred to the journal as "our left wing" in a letter to Harriet Monroe. And when Richard Aldington became its literary editor in December 1913, Pound wrote confidently to his friend William Carlos Williams that "Richard is now running the *NF*" (quoted in Ruthven, 79).

Ruthven has argued that Pound's method of promoting literary talent always involved "the workings of a literary politics which uses the space at its disposal to keep potentially useful people on side" (88); and of course this method would necessarily require a continuous expansion of the "space at his disposal" by whatever means possible. But most accounts suggest that Pound exercised a markedly diluted version of this kind of empire-building henchmanship on the male editors for whom he also wrote in these same years.[25] By contrast, in Jayne Marek's words, "his attitudes indicate a belief that women seldom had solid critical or editorial capabilities, yet might prove useful as sources of publication or money for Pound and his chosen companions. Given such opinons, it is not surprising that Pound made numerous attempts to control the editorial direction of women's literary magazines" (179). Although Marek's position is only one among many staked out on the issue of Pound's colonizing masculinism

[25] These include A. R. Orage's *The New Age*, Wyndham Lewis's *BLAST*, and W. L. Courtney's *Fortnightly Review*.

(as we shall see shortly), it is nevertheless a valuable starting point for an examination of Pound's dealings with *The New Freewoman*.

## *The New Freewoman:* "So Post-everything"

*The New Freewoman* started out as London's alternative feminist journal for a surprisingly large and rapidly assimilated readership, Marsden's exclusionary claims to the contrary notwithstanding.[26] Ronald Bush, taking issue with critical accounts of Pound's predatory relation to *The New Freewoman* (and Ruthven's in particular), calling them "terribly reductive" (B. Scott, 354),[27] points out that Rebecca West first solicited Pound's work for *The New Freewoman,* and that Dora Marsden was in any case anxious to dissociate herself from parliamentarian feminism and to provide a forum that would instead link "the struggle of feminism to the goal of liberating the life principle in every human being" (355). Furthermore, Bush maintains, Pound's critical support of the work of a handful of women poets suggests that his androcentric aesthetics were theoretical rather than pragmatic.

In spite of Bush's forthright acknowledgment of those aesthetics, his defense of Pound nevertheless rings hollow. It is true that Bush conscientiously reminds us that a prominent theme in Pound's later works—"that 'the female is a chaos'" (353)—began to take shape in these early London years, and then dutifully directs us to Pound's postscript to his 1922 translation of Rémy de Gourmont's *Natural Philosophy of Love* (1902), without mentioning anything in particular about the postscript; Bush then admits apologetically that "there is no question that [Pound's] work flaunted machismo, and that he frequently characterized both modernist style and culture itself as masculine achievements" (354). But ultimately Bush ignores the practical implications of Pound's literary expansionism. For

[26] Several early issues of *The New Freewoman* featured a full-page promotion titled "Some Opinions on *The Freewoman*," which sampled endorsements (and a few advantageous condemnations) from a variety of individuals and journals, including Havelock Ellis, H. G. Wells, the *Chicago Evening Post,* Mrs. George Bernard Shaw, and Charles Lapworth, editor of the *Daily Herald* (who writes that he and Mrs. Lapworth were "leading the life of tramps in Italy" when they "were first introduced to *The Freewoman*" and "fell in love with its fine, upstanding, vigorous attitude towards 'Life Problems'") (July 1, 1913, 40). See Mark Morrisson's exhaustive and ingenious study of the journal's subscribers, which leads him to conclude that most subscribers to *The New Freewoman* lived "in the terrace houses, maisonettes, and less spacious or modernized houses of the lower-middle classes. Almost none of them owned the house in which they lived" (465 n. 35).

[27] Bush critiques a short article by Ruthven titled "Ezra's Appropriations," which appeared in *The Times Literary Supplement,* November 20–26, 1987, 1278, 1300–1301; this article forms the abstract for Ruthven's 1990 book, *Ezra Pound as Literary Critic.*

when Pound took on the job of literary editor of *The New Freewoman* from the ailing Rebecca West in August 1913, he intended from the start to sever "his" territory from the rest of the journal. As he put it to Dora Marsden, "I don't suppose a literary page will queer the editorial columns" (quoted in Lidderdale and Nicholson, 68). If we understand the verb "queer" here to mean "taint" (as the "straight" Pound undoubtedly meant it), then the proposed cordon sanitaire between "editorial columns" and literature—which rapidly became Pound's effective policy—created a kind of schizophrenic split in the pages of the journal. While Dora Marsden and her contributors debated questions about suffragism and prostitution, democracy and environmentalism, Pound and his contributors took up art and literature from the pedantic perspective of his own poetics. There were divisions especially among art reviewers: those few who had been writing for Marsden before Pound signed on tended to continue to call for a production of art and literature that was anti-intellectual and entirely spiritual, while Pound's own poems (which appeared frequently in *The New Freewoman* after his arrival) were explicitly intellectual and often polemical.[28]

The letters from *The New Freewoman*'s readership reflect the schism: despite the burgeoning number of pages devoted to art and literature, readers remained solidly engaged by Marsden's increasingly disaffected individualism. Nevertheless, as a result of Pound's intercessions and self-promotion, the journal steadily came to be perceived as a literary organ;[29] and when, in November, some "disappointed American friends" wrote to say that "they imagined that *The New Freewoman* was 'to stand for something,'" Marsden replied that "it stands for nothing. . . . All that we require of it is that it remain flexible and appear with a different air each issue." Another reader wrote plaintively that she could no longer grasp "the im-

[28] Marsden herself participated in this spiritualist poetics: "It is this thing, a soul, which it is the province of art as distinct from science, to make chart of. . . . Art is the scientific spirit applied to soul, observing, collating, noting. . . . A poet concerning himself with ideas is a sad spectacle; so ill-employed, busily propagating illusions" (October 15, 1913, 166). A few months later she censures the "charlatan artist" who pretends "to follow the motions of the soul, but who follows merely the idea"; in particular she attacks F. T. Marinetti for ruining a "genuine emotional impulse" by "plunging it into ideas" (November 1, 1913, 181–82).

[29] Pound took every opportunity to refer to *The Egoist* as a journal notable primarily for its literary pathbreaking. In 1917 he wrote, "I do not think it can be too often pointed out that during the last four years *The Egoist* has published serially in the face of no inconsiderable difficulties, the only translation [of Gourmont, Gabalis, Joyce, and Lewis]" (quoted in Longenbach, 92). Although Gourmont's and Gabalis's serializations had been done when the paper was still *The New Freewoman*, Pound never acknowledged this fact. His retrospective myth cast *The Egoist* as "a quiet literary review" (*Egoist* 1.4 [February 16, 1914], 76), rather than an evolving sequence of feminist-individualist journals.

port of a paper so post-everything as *The New Freewoman*," to which Marsden rather cryptically "restate[d]" the journal's "position" that "the use of ideas should be strongly discouraged (except perhaps for mental gymnastics)" (November 15, 1913, 203).

At this point it is worth pausing over Bush's fleeting reference to Pound's postscript to Gourmont's *Natural Philosophy of Love*. For it is there that Pound advances a startling biological theory of artistic creation involving sperm and masculine fertility, and presaging Yeats's rumored monkey gland transplant a few years later. In a postscript characterized by nothing so much as "slither," Pound holds that "the power of the spermatozoid is precisely the power of exteriorizing a form." That is, sperm—the male "essence"—may signify and make visible the hardness, the contour of creative expressivity. While woman can be understood biologically as "the accumulation of hereditary aptitudes, better than man in the 'useful gestures,'" it is man alone who accounts for "the 'inventions,' the new gestures, the extravagance, the wild shots, the impractical, merely because in him occurs the new upjut, the new bathing of the cerebral tissues in the residuum, in *la mousse* [i.e., sperm] of the life sap" (vii–viii).[30]

Given Pound's penchant for body metaphors—for example, in his characterization of the bourgeois man as "the digestive man"—I don't even want to try to untangle the psychosexual paideuma of this latest masculinist twist to his habitual biologism. I merely wish to point out the implications for *The New Freewoman* in this nascent theory. In view of Pound's theory of sexual "essence," the woman-identified *New Freewoman*'s most "useful gesture," so to speak, can only be one of facilitation and provision. The Marsden-West axis has given him a welcome—and perhaps more effective—access to a countercultural reading public; it has acted as the matrix out of which "exteriorizing a form" has become possible. In contrast to this "useful gesture," however, it is clear enough that the journal's principal value for Pound lies in the resultant creative acts by men that can be marshaled in the service of avant-garde masculinity, that is, the form of masculinity that Pound has begun to revamp as an explicitly artistic property (and one that, in his theorization, helps to retain a hold on the aristocratic artist's universal aesthetic privilege). These are the cre-

[30] Pound, a promoter of Rémy de Gourmont's fictional and nonfictional prose, had serialized a translation of *The Horses of Diomedes* in *The New Freewoman* almost as soon as he had been made its literary editor. J. J. Wilhelm notes that Pound "admired the following aphorism from Gourmont's *Litanies de la Rose*: '*Femmes, conservatrices des traditions milésiennes*' (Women, preservers of Milesian traditions) . . . and he also liked the insight: That women preserve the basic chthonic feeling . . . but defined [the adjective] negatively: 'people who have no sense of "civilization" or public order'" (206).

ative acts—the "inventions," "new gestures," "new upjut"—of his coterie of contributors.

An awareness of this gendered symbiosis between male form and female conduit becomes evident in a letter, signed by five male contributors to *The New Freewoman*, which urges Marsden to de-feminize the journal's name. Marsden reprints the letter for her readers, defending its signatories as "a group of contributors, to whose generous support the paper has owed much from its start"—apparently forgetting that three of them, Pound, Richard Aldington, and Allen Upward (all friends and all connected by Pound's imagist "school") had only begun to publish in her journal four months earlier, while the remaining two, Huntley Carter and Reginald W. Kauffmann, wrote almost exclusively about spirituality in art and about anarchy, respectively. The men's letter offers a show of gratitude to Marsden for "establishing an organ in which men and women of intelligence can express themselves without regard to the public," but then goes on to complain that "the present title of the paper causes it to be confounded with organs devoted solely to the advocacy of an unimportant reform in an obsolete political institution" (December 15, 1913, 244)—that is, organs concerned with women's suffrage.

It is difficult to imagine that any potential readership in London in December 1913 could have confused *The New Freewoman* with *The Suffragette, Votes for Women,* or any other suffrage journal. In nearly every one of her previous twelve *New Freewoman* lead articles and editorials, Marsden had devoted large amounts of space to attacks on suffragism, the Pankhursts, militancy, "The Cause," parliamentarianism, chastity, and organized feminism. Richard Aldington, soon to become the journal's new literary editor, had contributed to *The New Freewoman*'s pages such misogynist pieces as the satirical "Un Dialogue Dirisoire" ("The English write from the desire of imaginary women, their own being too repellent") (October 1, 1913, 155) and "Un Monologue Dirisoire" ("The most unpleasant, discourteous and ignorant animal in the world is a middle-aged, middle, middle-class Englishwoman. Even the exact phrase 'middle, middle-class' does not cover all the types; there are innumerable and offensive gradations") (October 15, 1913, 168).

What *does* seem to be at issue in the male contributors' protest over the journal's name is in fact a twofold concern. If, for Pound, "the female is a chaos," then the journal title's explicit reference to a feminist ideology could effect a sort of contamination by association. And the semiotics of a title such as *The New Freewoman* are complex: on the one hand, it echoes that earlier literary and cultural moniker of feminine sexual independence, the New Woman, who had disrupted, among other things, the aesthetic categories of masculine and feminine. On the other hand, Marsden's title suggests a new and indeterminate kind of woman no longer bound by cultural or political law. Again, if the female is a chaos, then the new freewoman may well be a citizen of that centerless state.[31] Pound's repudiation of the aesthetics of chaos had come in his three-part *New Freewoman* article "The Serious Artist," where he declared aphoristically that "good writing is perfect control" (November 1, 1913, 194), a sentiment seconded just a few pages later in Edgar Mowrer's pronouncement that "the need of the present age is *discipline*" ("Discipline and the New Beauty," 196). The uncontrolled freewoman, in this reading, may well be antithetical to "good" art.[32]

The other issue that underlies the male contributors' anxiety about their journal's title concerns its overt reference to gender, and in this they seem to be joined by Marsden herself. Marsden's central aim in her editorials for both *The Freewoman* and *The New Freewoman* is to expose the constructedness of all social and philosophical categories of thought. Her critiques range across the categories of "women," "types," social classes, races, and, finally, language and ideas, always with the goal of showing how these illusory constructions fetter the autonomy and "life substance" of the individual. In short, she champions differences between rather than sameness among the constituencies of social and epistemological categories, and so understands liberation to "mean" differently for every individual.

The category of gender presents Marsden with a thorny problem, however, since most of her theorization of gender evolves in polemical opposition to what she perceives to be the "womanliness" of suffragism. While her trenchant contestations of suffragism also involve an understanding of Mrs. Pankhurst's "Cause" as a muddle-headed conflation of the political

[31] Pound's repeated insistence on the importance of cultural centers and capitals may be of some interest in this connection: in a letter to Harriet Monroe, he stresses that "America is a colony until she can make a capital" (quoted in Zinnes, 290). And in an editorial that explicitly links American provincialism with centerlessness and artistic chaos, Pound opines that "the value of a capital or metropolis is that if a man in a capital cribs, quotes or imitates, someone else immediately lets the cat out of the bag and says what he is cribbing, quoting, or imitating" (*Poetry* 5.5 [February 1915], 227). Metropoles allow for the policing of literary production. And if centerlessness makes for chaos as well as provincialism, then the semiotic contrast between a new freewoman and an egoist is indeed worth noting.

[32] Bruce Clarke argues that Pound's "mature" essay "The Serious Artist" was the result of Marsden's pressure on him to articulate a clear poetics of artistic intellectual commitment (108–17). Clarke's massively documented thesis is poised against two other readings of the relationship: the view that Pound was an androcentrist who bent Marsden to his will by steering the paper away from feminist issues, and the view that Pound and Marsden were equal partners in a joint attempt to merge his brand of new literature with her platform of radical individualism.

with the spiritual, she takes the Suffragettes' various strategic reconstructions of gender (using the "angelic woman" as the political avatar of righteousness, for instance) to be unself-conscious reifications of a sexual "type." What this amounts to is Marsden's confusion of gender's outward manifestations with its social functions. In nearly all of her editorials attacking "The Cause," Marsden construes the gendered roles of women as the end results of individual adoptions of social codes—as a mode, in other words, of what we might call false consciousness. But in doing so she negates the possibility that a patriarchal social system may overdetermine—or at least determine—the social configurations of gender. Always the libertarian, Marsden believes in absolute individual agency to the exclusion of the influence of social systems.

An example taken from outside the category of gender may be helpful here. In a November editorial about the Welsh coal mining strikes which had been in effect for several months, issuing in violence and instigating considerable debate in the press, Marsden chides the *miners:* "One is supposed to be grateful to them for the dangers they undergo to provide us with coal. We are not grateful. Why on earth a body of people should conceive it their 'work' to toil and moil underground to produce the rest of the people's coal is beyond our comprehension. . . . When one realizes that [the threat of death] befals [sic] a heavy proportion of all the 'workers' concerned in it, one is driven to the conclusion that there is something radically wrong with miners and all self-elected victims" (November 1, 1913, 184). In Marsden's cosmology of individualism, all individuals and groups seeking redress from a governmental body are merely the blind products of what she calls elsewhere the "tyranny of democracy." Not only are such groups of individuals guilty, first and foremost, of willing the necessity of labor upon themselves, and then trading their souls for the false security of identity offered by group-based alliances (note her scare quotes around "workers"), but also all those who suffer as a result of their collective dissidence—in fact, all those who suffer *in any way*—are self-elected victims.

It should be pointed out that this complete rejection of all alliances, however strategic or rhetorical they might be, stands in stark contrast to the militant alliances we have seen criss-crossing the English suffrage movement. But Marsden's refusal to countenance identity across diversity exerts an interesting and problematic pressure on the construction of gender offered *within* the pages of *The New Freewoman*. In the first place, we find in those pages an array of articles and editorials that display an extraordinary grasp of the limits and contingencies of sexual categories. For example, in one editorial Marsden elaborates an argument that *all* women are on sale, and therefore the only salient difference between wives and prostitutes is that the prostitute "wants the purchase money on the spot [while] the prospective wife can afford to wait." This is an argument made by a variety of avant-garde women writers, including Emma Goldman, Isadora Duncan, and Olive Schreiner. But from there Marsden moves to a conclusion that "women do not need more protection; they need less. They should be taking upon themselves the responsibility for their own protection and maintenance: which can only be achieved by the augmentation of their own individual power" (August 1, 1913, 64). There is an obvious ideological (and perhaps insurmountable) tension between Marsden's recognition of what Goldman called the systemic "traffic in women" and this later, somewhat halting skepticism about the need for social intervention in the sex-gender system. For, according to Marsden, whereas the disease is social, the cure must be entirely individual.

Marsden's contributors do not necessarily share her unyielding insistence on individual agency: in a fascinating article titled "Intermediate Sex Types," one E. B. Lloyd reports on a visit to the "intermediate human sexual types" exhibit at the International Medical Congress held in London. The exhibit not only displays a spectrum of sexuality that includes (but is not limited to) "male" and "female," but also occasions Lloyd's critique of "the injustice and brutality of our social and legal persecution of people of this [intermediate] type at the present day." Lloyd grasps the exhibit's important implications for the social construction of gender. He concludes that, "generally speaking, Nature abhors a hard and fast line just as it does a vacuum; and as we are now aware the chain of sexual continuity shows no break of any note, either on the physical or on the mental side, in its subtle gradations from the most womanly woman to the most manly man. Indeed we have learned that, for most thoughtful people at any rate, such antiquated abstractions as 'Man' and 'Woman' *per se* will at no very distant date have to be relegated to realms of the philosopher's Absolute" (October 1, 1913, 155–56). Lloyd's argument ultimately issues in a plea for tolerance of homosexuality ("Uranianism"), but his observations also contribute to the journal's repeated attempts to broaden out categories of gender and to challenge their stability.

That Lloyd's article is conspicuously devoid of any victim-blaming makes it uncharacteristic of the journal as a whole, however. For while Marsden may endeavor to dilate "gender" in the interest of establishing absolute difference among individuals, she nevertheless tends to recognize only the feminine as a gender, and to attribute gender only to women. That is, in Marsden's treatment of social sexual divisions, masculinity is an invisible universal norm: women are gendered, and men are not. So, for example, Marsden defends a generic "Poor John," who must work to support his wife while competing with women in the marketplace; from Marsden's point of view it is not "poor" John who is implicated but his wife, who ought not to have gotten John into this bind in the first place through her participation in what Marinetti was to call "the legal prostitution of marriage" (*New Freewoman*, August 1, 1913, 64).[33] Marsden's ascription to man of universal subjecthood and to woman of indexical sociosexual marking—differentiating woman from the abstracted individualism of the universal male subject—is of a piece with the modernist–avant-garde lexical category of "woman," as we have seen in Marinetti's "scorn for women" and Pound's allegorical-biological dichotomies, as well as in the coding of revolutionary discourse. Within this framework, women who are "liberated" are women who have distinguished themselves from other women. This is not to say that in Marsden's catechism women should strive to be "like" men. But it *is* to suggest some connections between Marsden's individualist brand of feminism and the Anglo-Italian avant-garde's "endorsement" of feminism: for both understand feminism in terms of an activism that aims to break up and dissolve the pejorative category of "the feminine." Given this implicit program, it is easy to see why the trajectory of the title of Marsden's journal would move increasingly away from the image of the free woman and toward her apotheosis as an ungendered (that is, de feminized) individual. It is also easy to see why such avant-garde acolytes as Pound and Aldington would wish to distance themselves from a title that called attention to its own deviation from an ungendered (i.e., masculinized) avant-garde poetics.

I noted earlier that segments of Marsden's readership were confused by her increasingly trenchant rebuttals of organized feminism. Marsden's insistence on difference among women (and their difference from "woman"),[34] her campaigns to destabilize taxonomic categories of women, her exfoliation of individualism against a starkly undifferentiated social terrain of class, gender, and politics, and her tautological measurements of individual

---

[33] See also for comparison Olive Schreiner's *Women and Labor:* "The wife or mistress, [who] lives by the exercise of her sex function alone," is a short step away from "the prostitute, who affects no form of productive labor" (104).

[34] Marsden's insistence on individualism and difference may be thought of as a kind of inversion of strategic essentialism. Generally speaking, whereas strategic essentialism posits sameness within a self-conscious theoretical frame that tacitly acknowledges but effectively ignores difference for the sake of systemic argumentation, Marsden's strategy is to acknowledge tacitly but effectively ignore sameness and the political grounds for essentialism.

agency against a Nietzschean yardstick of psycho-spiritual strength all combined to *preclude,* in effect, anything like a workable feminist ideology. The reader who described *The New Freewoman* as "so post-everything" might well have specified "post-feminist," to which Marsden no doubt would have agreed readily. In addition, I have been suggesting that the constricted scope of Marsden's apolitical feminism helped to construct an audience from which the English avant-garde soon benefited. For by the time Pound engineered imagism as a literary movement propped upon a rhetorical repudiation of "the vulgo," Marsden had already alienated various segments of "the vulgo." Supporters of the Pankhursts had withdrawn their subscriptions as Marsden stepped up her attacks on Mrs. Pankhurst's "death wish" (calling the Cat and Mouse Act[35] "extremely good government" [July 15, 1913, 44]); and Marsden herself had cultivated horrified reactions from another segment, the bourgeois literati, who, through the voice of Mrs. Humphrey Ward, characterized *The Freewoman* as the "dark and dangerous side of the 'Woman Movement'" (July 1, 1913, 40).

Conversely, however, Marsden also benefited from her association with Pound's avant-garde: she extracted a small, centralized readership that associated new forms of artistic expression with new forms of individual freedom. The implicit linkage between the "free love" aspects of Marsden's libertarianism and the "free verse" of non-Georgian poetry was to become more pronounced in the next few years, especially, as Carolyn Burke has argued, with respect to "liberated" women poets such as Mina Loy.[36]

## Producing the Avant-garde Woman

If Pound's carefully calibrated avant-garde audience found a measure of compatibility with an individualist feminism that avoided broad or unqualified public appeal, then it makes sense to inquire into the fate of the relations between other contemporary formulations of feminism and the wider avant-garde audiences with which they were linked. The widest

[35] The Cat and Mouse Act was the colloquial name for a parliamentary act designed to staunch the effects of Suffragette hunger strikes: when a fasting prisoner was deemed sufficiently ill to be released from prison, she was given a "license" which granted her a short period of convalescence at home. Upon the expiration of the license, the prisoner was re-arrested and returned to prison. This process continued (theoretically) until her prison term was served in its entirety.

[36] In "The New Poetry and the New Woman: Mina Loy," Burke makes savvy connections between the "free feet" of Isadora Duncan's dancing and Mina Loy's writing, which, in turn, Burke speculates, "confirmed the popular view that free verse probably led to free love" (43). This argument is elaborated in the "Interlude I" chapter of Burke's *Becoming Modern.*

avant-garde audience was of course the one cultivated by Italian futurism, "the first artistic movement of mass society,"[37] through Marinetti's whistle-stop tours of Europe, mass-distributed manifestoes, and allied newspapers such as *La Voce* and *Lacerba*.[38] As we have seen, futurism's relation to feminism was double-edged and strategic at best. For example, while Marinetti eventually came to support the campaign for women's suffrage, he did so for the cynical reason that he believed women's voting would deal a final, mortal blow to what he viewed as the hopelessly corrupt and antiquated system of parliamentarianism (Tisdall and Bozzolla, 162–63). This self-serving attitude toward women's rights had been noted by English Suffragettes as early as 1910, when Margaret Wynne Nevinson caustically observed that "it was not the Suffragette's desire for liberty that aroused the Signor [Marinetti]'s admiration, but merely her method of enforcing her demands." Toward the end of her critique of Marinetti, however, Nevinson marked out the contours of a debate that would come to problematize the self-representation of the few avant-garde women who took on futurist identities: "The Suffragettes and Signor Marinetti are at one in deploring the existence of the serpent-of-old-Nile type of woman. But while the Futurists hold women responsible for what they consider a degenerate type of man, the Suffragette maintains that the erotic woman is a product of man's absolutism—a product that is declining rapidly along with man's unlimited control of the things that matter" (112). Whereas Nevinson sees the "amorous woman" as a product of patriarchy, Marinetti, in good revolutionary fashion, sees her as an atavistic throwback to earlier decades of aristocratic corruption; Suffragette and futurist alike agree only that this "type" of woman exists, and that she must be eliminated.

During the next five years the terms of this disputation took on new inflections in the work of two futurist-associated women writers in particular, Valentine de Saint-Point and Mina Loy. Their differing treatments of the amorous woman help to illuminate various relations between feminism and the avant-garde. Saint-Point, a Parisian painter, writer, and dancer (whose choreography and technique were often compared to that of Isadora Duncan), made her debut as a futurist revolutionary when she lectured on futurism in Paris and Brussels in 1912. She produced two manifestoes, "Manifesto of the Futurist Woman" (1912) and "Manifesto of Lust" (1913), both of which won for her a high profile of notoriety within conti-

---

[37] Germano Celant, quoted in Perloff, 37.
[38] *Lacerba* broke with futurism in 1915; for an overview of its publishing history, see Tisdall and Bozzolla, chap. 9.

nental avant-garde circles.[39] The "Manifesto of Lust," in which she declared that "art and war are the great manifestations of sensuality; lust is their flower" (71), especially drew commentary from futurists and avant-gardists. As late as 1917, Pound was pseudonymously summarizing her platform in a belated but approving *Egoist* review:

> She is . . . averse to feminism of the suffragette type; it is too virtuous to please her and too much bent on social reform.
>
> But what she attacks most vigorously is *clair de lune* sentimentality. Love, she holds should be of *women's* life (also) a thing apart: (not "'tis women's whole existence"). . . . Valentine de Saint-Point carries her re-volt against weeping sentiment startlingly far, for it drives her to glorify *la luxure* [lust]. (4.5 [May 1917], 62)

Pound's provincial shock at Saint-Point's glorification of lust presum-ably stems from his expectations for her gender, but in fact the few women avant-gardists who joined the futurists' ranks in Saint-Point's wake gener-ally did tend to limit themselves (or be limited) to polemics involving fem-inine sexuality—its corruption, rehabilitation, expression, bourgeois re-pression, and liberation. According to Cinzia Sartini Blum, Saint-Point, as "the first Futurist woman," is responsible both for this trend and for the limits it imposed on the substance of futurist women's writing: "While re-acting against Marinetti's association of woman with the constraints of family, pacifism and sentimental love (obstacles to the heroic destiny of man), [Saint-Point] nevertheless circumscribed women's ambitions within the complementary and mutually exclusive roles of selfless mother and in-spiring lover. These two roles were well within the scope of action tradi-tionally reserved for women. . . . [T]his first provocative attack on restric-tive mores also charts the boundaries of the subversive territory explored by futurist women" (1996, 105–6). Saint-Point, in other words, stuck to the sexual agenda preordained by Marinetti. Her unquestioning adaptation of a "Futurist Woman" is of course strongly reminiscent of the women of an earlier republican public sphere who were more or less hamstrung by the gender coding of revolutionary discourse: Saint-Point's Futurist Woman will help to channel rather than restrict the "hygienic" sexual energy of the revolutionary futurist man, will support the revolutionary platform from within her own appropriate separate sphere, and will eschew divisive po-litical "interest" in its various forms of feminism and separatism. Approxi-

[39] Valentine de Saint-Point was also the aunt of the baronne de Brimont, Christabel Pankhurst's chief social connection and chaperone at several exclusive Parisian literary salons during Pankhurst's exile there. See D. Mitchell, 208–9.

mating the rhetorical moves we have seen in Wollstonecraft, de Gouges, and others, Saint-Point seeks to bring other women into line, to recalibrate the role of woman within a utopian program predicated on new masculine virtue, and to repudiate aspects of "the feminine" deemed counterrevolutionary or corrupt.

Blum's argument does not specifically take up revolutionary discourse or avant-garde configurations of gender, but it does offer a reading of the Italian futurist Enif Robert's novel *Un ventre di donna: romanzo chirurgico* (1919), which illustrates the effects of masculinist avant-garde prescriptions on the work of women futurists. Robert's experimental novel, stamped literally with Marinetti's imprimatur,[40] is about a woman's unyielding futurist fight to cure her own fatally diseased womb. While the novel rehearses a number of masculinist futurist conventions, including an insistence on the protagonist's militarism and fearless impatience, Blum nevertheless concludes that *Un ventre di donna* ultimately lays bare the predicament presented by futurism to women in the movement. In Blum's reading, Robert's protagonist demonstrates her incontrovertible difference from futurist protagonists in the very fact that she is alienated through her "exceptional status (hysterical behavior, diseased body, confused gender identity)." Robert's heroine is neither a "Futurist superman" nor a "model of emancipation to other women in the way that the Futurist hero is." Rather, she lives a "story of inner conflicts and malaise which we cannot find in the male Futurists' texts," since those male texts (exemplified by Marinetti's 1910 novel *Marfarka il futurista*) present a hero's unambiguous lust for heroic death. Such a death is simply not available to a woman suffering from an incurable womb—literally, from terminal hysteria. In addition to marking its heroine indelibly with un-futuristic ambiguity and chronic malaise, Robert's novel "allegorizes the limits of the strategy generally adopted by the Futurist women: to follow an avant-garde prescribed by a male-centered movement which does not seriously threaten the social organization of gender" (1986–87, 25–26).

The bind for the futurist woman is clear: to write as a *woman* means to write from a subject position under fire, especially if one writes in the idiom of revolution. One must either take as one's topic the ideological rehabilitation (or even defense) of that subject position in order to ensure intelligibility to one's audience, or risk being delegitimated by a program geared to forging new links between revolutionary art and masculinity. Further, to write as a *feminist* is to challenge "the social organization of

---

[40] Marinetti appended one of his own manifestoes to the beginning of Robert's novel.

gender" on which futurism is based; it is to call attention to sexual difference even while seeking to repudiate it.

Given that any feminist subject position within futurism must constantly work a double shift—speaking even as it clears a legitimate space
for itself—I cannot agree with Blum that Valentine de Saint-Point is "responsible" for the self-circumscription evident in much of the writing by
futurist women. For as I have shown, it is crucial for cultural historians to
understand the definitive role of overdetermined discourses and audiences
in structuring the difficulties women have had creating polemical speaking
positions for themselves. I therefore want to reengage Saint-Point's efforts
to align herself with futurist men (and against women) from the perspective of the discursive options available to women of the historical avant-
garde. After all, we have seen (for example) how Dora Marsden's individualism conceives of liberation as the successful effort of the individual to
distance himself or herself from a "group" or "type," and how this creates
for feminism an intractable game of optics: one is feminist insofar as one
differentiates oneself from a mass of unreconstructed women. A political
conundrum of this kind seems to me to be dependent less on originary
practices by individual writers than on implicit contracts struck between
writers and audiences engaged in convention-laden polemical discourses
and the ideology that underpins them.

The always polemical writings of Mina Loy may be juxtaposed to those
of Saint-Point as a way of developing this point. Loy, who lived in Italy
during the years of futurist ascendancy, produced poetry, plays, and manifestoes that challenged the "social organization of gender" and its encoding
in avant-garde discourse. Her writings deploy a dialectical method that
ironizes and undercuts futurism's authoritative disdain for all things feminine, including maternity and conception. And while her challenges sometimes partake of the eugenic individualism of the futurist mode in which
she wrote, she nevertheless contests both directly and by example most of
the stark constructions of gender on which futurist rhetoric depended.

We may begin by comparing Loy's and Saint-Point's disparate treatments of the futurist tenet equating woman with irrational chaos, instinct,
sentimentality, and prudery. Saint-Point engages this tenet to celebrate
woman's "essential" biological powers. The fulfillment of woman's heroic
biological destiny lies, according to Saint-Point, in the rearing of new generations of male- and machine-identified futurists;[41] it is futurist woman's

[41] That is, in her role of republican motherhood. In the "Manifesto of the Futurist Woman,"
Saint-Point casts the role of woman as mother and nurturer in much the same way that this role

unique task to inspire and galvanize heroic new men (a version of which we have seen elaborated during the French revolutionary days of Thermidor). Futurism's recasting of "woman" girds Saint-Point's repudiation of the "political, 'cerebral' mistake of feminism" (Blum 1986–87, 14), a repudiation we have seen practiced dogmatically by Marsden and endorsed by Marinetti. And in this position Saint-Point differentiates herself from other women (women "who only think what I have dared to say") by championing a brand of lust linked to virility, pugilism, and conquest, and categorically dissociated from "the ill-omened debris of [feminine] romanticism" ("Manifesto of Lust," 71–72). In short, Saint-Point gives back to futurism its own reverse image essentially unaltered.

Mina Loy's response to this tenet of female irrational chaos is far more diffuse than Saint-Point's, because it is intersubjective, personalized, and frequently satirical. It stretches through several of the works that she produced while in Florence, where she lived with and was then estranged from her English husband, where she bore three children and lost one in infancy, where she cultivated a friendship with the Americans Mabel Dodge, Gertrude Stein, and Carl van Vechten, and where she exhibited paintings at the First Free Exhibition of International Futurist Art. These were the years when she experienced what she called "the throes of conversion to Futurism."[42] She allied herself with the iconoclastic energy of futurist aesthetics and—just as important for her critique of futurism—had affairs with Marinetti and Giovanni Papini, the political editor of *Lacerba*.

Loy's initial enthusiastic embrace of futurism as an artistic and cultural program may be seen in her "Aphorisms on Futurism" (1914), which Caroline Burke has described as "a manifesto set like a long poem" (1987, 37), but which, significantly, is devoid of any self-identifying pronouns. No declaration of "we" is involved in Loy's paean to expansive futurist energy; as a painter and a poet she appreciates but does not explicitly represent futurism's revolutionary revision of traditional aesthetics. Her manifestic discourse is limited to futurist-inspired exhortations, such as "DIE in the Past / Live in the Future" and "ACCEPT the tremendous truth of Futurism / Leaving all those—Knick-knacks—" (1996, 149, 152).

By the end of 1914, after she had been through her sexually and emotionally disappointing affairs with Marinetti and Papini, her enthusiastic echoes of futurism gave way to probing analyses of futurism's platforms

---

was created during the French Revolution: woman supports the Republic by producing strong, healthy, well-schooled citizens of the new world.
   [42] Letter to Mabel Dodge (1982, lxvii).

concerning women and heterosexuality. From 1914 to 1916 she produced a number of remarkable critiques of futurism's relation to Woman and futurists' relations with women, including the unpublished "Feminist Manifesto" (1914), the poem sequence *Songs to Joannes* (published 1915), the unpublished play *The Sacred Prostitute* (ca. November 1914), and the play *The Pamperers* (1916; published 1920). These pieces probed the Manichaean rift between the sexes wrought by futurists and their continental progenitors. In them, as in a host of other works, Loy plays with futurism's taxonomical constructions of "woman" and extemporizes her own alternative taxonomies of "man"; she also highlights deferred spaces of meaning between "woman" and "man" and so unhinges futurist certitude about the ontologically gendered foundations of avant-garde poetics.[43] Finally, throughout her work Loy simply refuses to give up any of her own claims to avant-garde authenticity.

This is not to say that Loy's tracts are "feminist" in any conventional sense. In fact, although the unpublished but distinctly futurist "Feminist Manifesto" was, according to Loy, the product of her own burgeoning sense of "feminine politics," the manifesto is more of an attack on contemporary brands of feminism than on Marinetti's reductive dichotomizing of women into mothers and mistresses. Suffragists like Christabel Pankhurst had long asserted the superiority of women's character over men's; suprafeminists like Marsden insisted on the transcendence of individual egos over the "types" generated by a gender system. Loy's manifesto occupies another polemical space entirely. Sounding the avant-garde note of anti-parliamentarianism, the "Feminist Manifesto" opens with an address to women advising them to "cease to place [their] confidence in economic legislation, vice-crusades and uniform education," and then shifts to the central issue: women must "be *Brave* & deny at the outset—that pathetic clap-trap war cry, *Woman is the equal of man*—for She is *not!*" (153). No amount of Nietzschean self-differentiation from social types will reveal a basic transsexual core of Stirnerian ego; no amount of individual will, of the kind exhorted by Marsden, can wish away the political, social, and biological components

[43] Here I depart from the majority view that sees in Loy's work an acknowledgment of unbreachable ontological differences between the sexes. I suggest instead that Loy is committed to showing the instability of the divide that separates "man" from "woman." While it is true that in the "Feminist Manifesto" she declares man and woman to be "enemies" whose interests intersect only in the "sexual embrace" (1996, 154), it is also the case that she is always at pains to show how "enmity" between the sexes derives from positions of relative power within patriarchy. And in her cosmos it is the job of avant-garde artists of all sexes to expose the ideological shell game that offers biological and cultural differences as transcendental Difference. "The Feminist Manifesto" is reprinted in *The Lost Lunar Baedeker*, hereafter cited by page.

that accrue to gendered subjectivity. As we saw at the close of Chapter 1, in Loy's view "man" simply does not offer an adequate model for women who are beginning to grapple with the constructedness of gender, and women should therefore "leave off looking to men to find out what you are *not*—seek within yourselves to find out what you *are*" (154).

But what women *are*, in this manifesto, is hamstrung by cultural roles. Loy urges women to break free of the traps of "Parasitism & Prostitution—or Negation"; she chafes against the separate-spheres gender complementarity advocated by futurists (and their revolutionary precursors); but finally she casts women squarely within reproductive ideology. Even as the manifesto critiques marriage and the worship of virginity, it nevertheless asserts a futurist-hygienic ideal involving unsentimental sex and woman's "right to maternity" (155).[44] And this maternity "right" is tied to the most corrupt component of the contemporary birth control movement: the eugenic argument that certain "undesirable" populations must be offset by the offspring of "superior" women.[45]

But if woman's only real claim to equality with revolutionary men must be routed through a logics of biology, there is a subtext of equality involving a sex war, in which Loy suggests that both sexes can lay equal claim to victimization by that disease of modern ennui, parasitism: "Men and women are enemies, with the enmity of the exploited for the parasite, the parasite for the exploited. . . . The only point at which the interests of the sexes merge—is the sexual embrace" (154). The indeterminate syntax makes it difficult to tell just who is the "exploited" and who is the "parasite." If woman is parasitic, then man is abject and exploited; by the same token, man may just as easily feed off woman's sexuality (or inspiration, or wealth). Loy seems uninterested in making heroes or villains out of men or women, since her phrasing everywhere turns all parties into both the parasitic and the exploited, hinged together by "the sexual embrace."

[44] By contrast, Loy backs away from stark anti-sentimentality in *Songs to Joannes*, where she demonstrates that sex is easily as affect-laden as "love." See Clark chap. 1, for an analysis of modernism's anti-sentimental compulsion.

[45] The manifesto declares, "Every woman of superior intelligence should realize her race-responsibility by producing children in adequate proportion to the unfit or degenerate members of her sex" (155). It is difficult to ignore an exhortation like this, which is at once supremacist and, as DuPlessis avers, vague (for who, after all, counts as "intelligent" in Loy's world?). The manifesto form is of course the genre of broad strokes and exaggerations, but in many of Loy's poems and polemics there persists an attitude toward "Negroes," Italians, and the uneducated poor that is characteristic of the most pernicious eugenics in modernist theories of the masses. DuPlessis asserts pivotally that "for Loy, autonomous sexuality and her 'freewoman' brand of autonomous feminism involved a radical claim to maternity" (274). My version of this argument develops in the direction of the cultural contradictions that surrounded the figure of the woman artist. For a fuller treatment, see Lyon 1998.

More important to Loy, I think, is the project of critiquing avant-garde discourse—exploring, in particular, the aporias and insupportable contradictions arising from the gendering of aesthetics and the gendering of "morality" as well. Loy's formulation of women's systemic disadvantages is rooted in an understanding of and participation in the apparatus of avant-garde production, which is to say that she wrote as a self-identified woman artist, and a feminist at that. Unwilling to hand over the term "woman" to Marinetti's museum case of corrupt history, Loy wielded it as a conceptual weapon to deconstruct avant-garde masculinism.

The urgent subject of the sexual embrace would become the centerpiece of analysis, reconfiguration, and satire in her next three polemics. But here in the "Feminist Manifesto" it plays an almost standard futurist role as the bedrock of "real" physical experience underlying the social illusions generated by marriage, physical purity, and virtue: dismantle the illusions and you liberate the sexual woman. Loy's proposal for the violent elimination of these illusions is also standard futurist fare, shot through with hyperbole and histrionics and directed *against* the female body: "the first self-enforced law for the female sex, as a protection against the man made bogey of virtue—which is the principal instrument of her subjection, would be the *unconditional* surgical *destruction of virginity* through-out the female population at puberty" (154–55). Loy had earlier warned women that only "Absolute Demolition" would "bring about reform" (153); but this type of demolition, however figurative, writes women back into the futurist prescription that locates aberrancies within women's sexualized bodies, insofar as Loy advocates the surgical alteration (and "correction") of women's bodies. And from this point on, the manifesto takes its pace from revolutionary discourse: women must see to the genetic upkeep of the race; offspring should be the result of vigorous, hygienic sex (rather than "outworn" coupling [155]); women must detach their sexuality from "honor, grief, sentimentality, pride and consequently jealousy" (156); and so forth. Not until the manifesto's final article does Loy return to her opening challenge of futurist precepts: setting herself "in defiance of superstition," she proclaims, that "there is *nothing impure in sex*—except in the mental attitude to it" (156). Deviating markedly from Saint-Point's championing of *lust* (which "drives the great men of business who direct the banks" [1913, 71]), Loy reintroduces and re-semanticizes the "sex" of "the sexual embrace." Whereas for Saint-Point "lust is the expression of a being projected beyond itself" (71), for Loy, "sex" constitutes a rare overlap of subjectivities. The intersubjectivity of sex (rather than the unilateral drive of lust) holds for the future "an incalculable & wider social regeneration than it is possible for our generation to imagine" (156). Sex, unlike lust, is therefore not simply a one-sided manifestation of the life force—the role assigned it in Marinetti's declaration that "there is nothing natural and important but coitus, whose purpose is the futurism of the species" (72); it is an even more dynamic composition of both bodies and psyches.

In fact, the dynamism of this perspectival vision informs the long poem *Songs to Joannes,* and is the shaping force behind Loy's iconoclastic conceptual and visual sensibilities. In that poem Loy examines the gaps in phenomenological meaning that are produced by futurism's gendered and polarized discursive field. Many of *Songs'* themes, if not its networks of images, are developed through heterogeneous vantage points, and it is significant that the putative addressee of the poem, "Joannes" (modeled on Giovanni Papini), appears not to have access to the poem's multiple vantage points; his blinkered conceptual apparatus limits his field to just a narrow strip of the poem's physical and emotional territory.[46] Irony in this sense is structural to the poem: Joannes sees little of what the reader sees, and what the reader sees is subject to parallax shifting. In a series of short irregular poems, we are shown the fragments of a discontinuous sexual and intellectual relationship; but we are also shown alternative fragments, equally discontinuous, of a relationship that *might* have been. In short, we are made to see, almost immediately, that "what is" is only one of several sets of charged fragments, the presence of which undermines any definitive claims to comprehensive representation. Furthermore, the "meaning" of all those fragments is shaped by a kind of negativity and constructed through invocations of emptiness or void, or by suggested absences, frequently indicated in the poem by blank or white space or by verbal images of whiteness or blankness.

Poem 18 provides a good example of how negativity works in *Songs.* This short imagist poem foregrounds the meaning of "night" as something that is positively rendered only by its relation to the negative space of a landscape:

Out of the severing
Of hill from hill
The interim
Of star from star
The nascent
Static
Of night.

[46] It is significant that Papini, political editor of *Lacerba,* was the theoretical point man for futurism's political agenda.

Structural and constitutive meaning inheres *between* stars, *between* hills, and in the contradiction of "nascent / Static." The poem is generated by a powerful indeterminacy which equates "severing" with an act of creation: night (a matrix unto itself) is birthed out of a sluice of its own making, and in that act of self-creation, night produces the contours of its own context.

Although this kind of meaning holds little significance within any field of positivist discourse (such as futurism's), here and throughout *Songs,* it is the *matrix* that bears the weight of meaning. The matrix produces the poem's various concrete configurations; equally important, the foregrounding of the matrix in the poem relativizes the value of those various configurations. Put still another way, the dialectical movement of negativity is the focal point of the poem's parallax vision. The negative dialectics of avant-garde practice are powerfully at work throughout *Songs:* the poems push toward a subversion of the Real (the obvious or apparent) in an effort to conceptualize what the Real obscures: that is, the freedom of the Possible, the unobvious, the undecipherable. Herbert Marcuse famously understood avant-garde literature as an effort "to break the power of facts over the word, and to speak a language which is not the language of those who establish, enforce and benefit from the facts" (447–48). This formulation of negativity has been a ready tool in the tradition of Marxist analyses of futurist and historical avant-garde practice. What is crucial to my argument about Loy's negativity, however, is that her project is launched precisely against futurism's participation in hegemonic constructions of (hetero)sexuality: whereas futurism advertises its avant-garde assaults as *tout court* anti-bourgeois, Loy refigures futurism's sexual politics as blindly bourgeois and slavishly "amorist."

In fact, the critique of *amore* animates more than a few of Loy's pieces from this time, and especially the enormously amusing (but still unpublished) satire of futurism, *The Sacred Prostitute.* The play's cartoon-like futurist character (called "Futurism") makes solemn aesthetic pronouncements about art and culture which are shown to stem directly from his uncontrollable compulsion to seduce women and to be unconditionally adored by them. Loy's play—originally titled "Futurist Dialogue"—reverses the structure of many of the plays written for the Futurist Synthetic Theatre. In those plays (produced mostly by Boccioni), women are, as Caroline Tisdall and Angelo Bozzolla put it, "either silly creatures adorning art galleries and drawing rooms, boring wives with inept lovers, or electric dolls" (157). By contrast, *The Sacred Prostitute* offers a rogue's gallery of *male* types. There is "The Idealist," the man who sees women as annoying obstacles to the vital experiences available in life. There is the "Tea Table

Man," who hopes to attain sexual intimacy with women by befriending them, consoling them, shopping with them for lingerie while holding to the strictest standards of sexual protocol. There is "Another Man," who opines that "the ethereal type [of woman] always gets beaten—every pore of her skin cries out for it—no healthy man could resist" (2).[47] There is the amorous Don Juan, who explains his philosophy of seduction by insisting, Hamlet-like, that a man must be cruel to be kind to women; he has "enticed those sleeping beauties from their nests of illusion—and showed them themselves. It is no fault of mine if they gave those selves to me and if, with my passing, very little was left" (2). And last, there is "Futurism," who introduces himself to the other characters by handing around a "tome" titled *Women I Have Had* (9).

The relation of "Futurism" to a "hermaphroditic" character called "Love" is the focus of the play. As soon as he has assembled an audience of male characters, Futurism begins to stake out the territory of his intended conquest. He declares that the mysterious Love is feminine: in spite of its hermaphrodism (which Futurism ignores), "Love is a feminine conception spelt 'Greed' with a capital 'G.'" Futurism delivers a futurist tirade against love, and then drags Love across the floor by the hair. But when the other male characters, not wishing to be witness to another man's sexual triumphs, leave the stage abruptly, Futurism is transformed. He carefully releases Love, cooing. "Excuse me, I hope I didn't hurt you. I have to do that for the sake of my reputation. *Never* believe anything a man says about women, when there is another man present!" (11).

Having thus revealed Futurism's veneer of machismo, the play becomes an exposé of futurist self-contradiction, double standards, and personal motives. After repeated unsuccessful efforts to seduce the exasperating non-character Love (who seems oblivious not only to the sexual appeal of futurism, but also to Futurism's imaginary script), Futurism resorts to pleading with Love in the name of sentimentality and soul—those "passéist" qualities that Marinetti condemned in Woman as the great impediment to Futurist Man's development. "I have an infinite need of tenderness," Futurism tells Love (11). "You're the most feminine thing I've ever found—that's why I love you so" (16). (This to a "Hermaphrodite.") But when his tactics continue to fail, Futurism sputters, "Women are so illogical." "So are you," Love patiently retorts. Incredulous at her ignorance, he informs her that "Futurism is diametrically opposed to logic" (17).

---

[47] *The Sacred Prostitute* is an incomplete manuscript (Beinecke Rare Book and Manuscript Library, Yale University).

Loy satirically invents and reveals the personal motives behind futurist bombast; even Marinetti's doctrine of words-in-freedom, which advocates the breaking of syntax and the elimination of auxiliary words,[48] becomes a target of her exposé: Futurism [tells Love]: "You take too long saying things. If you left out all the adverbs and adjectives and used the verb in the infinitive, I might have a chance to get what I want—before my train leaves. Why can't you love-me-love-me-love-me?" (16). Adjectives and adverbs may gum up the language, but what is more important, they slow down the seduction game—especially as it is played by men like Futurism, who see no conflict between speed and passion: "My love is eternal and my train leaves in fifteen minutes," Futurism bellows at the unflappable Love (15).

Thus *The Sacred Prostitute* exposes Italian futurism's elisions between "impersonal" aesthetic values and personal sexual politics. Moreover, it shows just how old-fashioned those personal politics are: the character Futurism is an amorist, and in this he represents nothing more than an updated version of the "passéist" Don Juan. Midway through the play, these two characters compare notes on their respective seduction techniques and find that, despite generational differences, they are dealing from the same deck. They discuss, for example, the tactic of pitting women against one another, and Don Juan sums up the desired results: "Insult the sex, to catch the demonstrated exception" (19). That is, mount a masculinist attack on woman as a category ("annihilate woman completely," as Futurism puts it), with the aim of drawing individualist women—women who, like Saint-Point, distance themselves from Woman—into the camp (and the beds) of futurists.

In short, the play illuminates the paradoxes entailed in gender ideology. Italian futurism's hysterical pronouncements against women can be made convincingly against futurism itself: it is illogical, instinctive, amorous; it is, in fact, nothing more than a gendered "I" disguised as a universal "we."

To claim, however, that *The Sacred Prostitute* effectively contests futurism's masculinism is to overlook the important fact of its immediate reception: the play was never published, nor did it circulate beyond the small local futurist audience (and the possession of Carl Van Vechten, Loy's agent in America). Carolyn Burke's account of the play in her biography of

---

[48] In "Technical Manifesto of Futurist Literature" (May 11, 1912), Marinetti insists that:

1. One must destroy syntax and scatter one's nouns at random, just as they are born.
2. One should use infinitives, because they adapt themselves elastically to nouns and don't subordinate them to the writer's *I* that observes or imagines. . . .
3. One must abolish the adjective, to allow the naked noun to preserve its essential color.
4. One must abolish the adverb, old belt buckle that holds two words together. (84)

Loy casts it in purely personal terms: Papini had broken off from Loy because of her affair with his public rival, Marinetti, and the play, says Burke, was an attempt to "show Papini how to turn the tables on his antagonist" (1996, 180). By mocking Marinetti's masculine posturing, Loy hoped to give Papini "an opportunity to forgive [her]."[49] This reading is unsatisfying to the degree that it confines a literary critique of ideology to the role of a personal "solution"; it seems likely to me that the unstageable play represents something more than a solution to Loy's broken heart, since in its unwieldiness it ranges across contemporary feminist issues such as prostitution and hygiene, birth control, and the role of "Nature." Loy may have kept the play private in order to avoid alienating herself from the Italian futurist community in 1914 or 1915, for whom feminism was largely unintelligible except as a form of bourgeois recuperation. Prizing as she did the "twenty years added to [her] life from mere contact with [Marinetti's] exuberant vitality" (quoted in Burke 1996, 180), Loy may have written herself into a tight spot from which it was impossible to escape cleanly into the arms of futurist avant-gardism or the solaces of feminism. Her own public career as a poet had only officially begun in 1914 with the appearance of some of her poems in the New York journals *Camera Work* and *Trend;* she still had but little sense of the politics of her transatlantic audience, and no doubt relied on her futurist contacts as a major source of critical conversation. To challenge futurism on the paradoxes of its gender coding would have been to write against or across futurism, and this was a risk that Loy may have intentionally avoided while still living in Florence. Whatever its immediate, local reception, *The Sacred Prostitute* remained largely a private response to the inconsistencies of futurism and its management of feminist individualism.

It was not until 1920—three years after Loy's temporary move to New York—that her second dramatic critique of futurism was published; and although *The Pamperers* was written in 1916, by the time it appeared in *The Dial* (New York), futurism had been conflated with and superseded by other European and New York avant-gardes. *The Pamperers* is a burlesque of the avant-garde's assimilation by monied society, one that suggests that some women are equipped to be better futurists than men. The play's action takes place at an endless art soirée where avant-garde reputations are made and broken; the plot involves the Pygmalion-like transformation of a dim-witted, cigar butt–collecting street bum named Loony into a futurist-talking avant-garde "genius" named Houston Loon, the Vitalist. The trans-

[49] Loy, unattributed quote in Burke, 1996, 180.

forming artist is a woman named Diana, a steely hostess who grooms, educates, plays the muse to, and introduces the new Houston Loon—all in an evening's work. "There are only two kinds of people in society," Diana declares sardonically, "geniuses and women" (69). In Loy's play the woman is the artist, while (male) "geniuses" are merely the found objects (the cigar butts, as it were) with which artists like Diana work. In 1903 Otto Weininger may have declared with confidence that "there is no female genius, and there has never been one ... *and there can never be one*" (189). But in 1916 Diana the *über*-artist violates the cordons sanitaires of originality, genius, and male authorship by declaring mockingly, "I have never met a genius I couldn't manage" (75). Working with the machinelike efficiency of a true futurist, Diana mass-produces geniuses. In fact, it is the play's thesis that women promote geniuses, and geniuses both use and depend upon women. Diana has memorized a monologue which she delivers to Loony as proof of her avant-garde credentials:

I am the elusion [sic] that cooed to your adolescent isolation, crystalized in the experience of your manhood ... (Oh do stop blinking at me, or I can't go on) ... I am that reciprocal quality you searched for among the moonlit mysteries of Battersea Bridge.
    I come to you with gifts those other women had not to give
    I am measured by the silence of inspiration, tuned to a laudatory discrimination ... made of the instigatory caress ... I know the moment to press the grape to thy lip ... put ice on your head; for I am the woman who understands ... so *do* tell me what you are going to make with those cigar-ends? (70)

Diana is the second-generation Futurist Woman, a parody of earlier novitiates who took up as doctrine futurism's prescriptions for gender. She plays the elemental muse with icy precision and reverses the muse role by *managing* geniuses; this new configuration suggests that geniuses and women do not constitute distinct, essential identities for Loy. They are social creations, mutually imbricated in a discursive field of cultural value. Loy is interested to show the contingent functions of "woman" and "genius" *as aesthetic terms;* and in doing so, here and throughout these Florence writings, she produces a substantial ideological critique of gender in modernity. More specifically, her work playfully effaces the avant-garde's enabling hierarchies of artist/woman-muse-hostess, creation/reproduction, genius/sentiment.

Futurism's gender codes come back to haunt it in *The Pamperers:* the genius-woman dyad proves to be more malleable than perhaps Marinetti would have wished, for in the play's closing dialogue, Diana schools Loony on the *true* nature of genius:

> Throw out your chest and don't walk heels first . . . remember
> It takes a genius five minutes to acquire what it takes five centuries to breed into us. (77)

Genius means adaptability, and Loy broadly satirizes the ease with which the hegemonic forces of social fashion can assimilate an artistic avant-garde. But this sardonic portrayal of artistic aspirants and social managers (who, as one character says, "now have the genius served directly to the consumer" [69]) should not obscure Loy's more subtle treatment of gender—a treatment that Virginia Kouidis seems to miss in her understated observation that "the play mocks the insincere disciples of art" (16).

In fact, Loy retrieves Woman from her futurist role as a site of chaotic energy (where "women are only animals, they have no souls," as *The Sacred Prostitute*'s "Futurism" puts it [12]), and reinstates her with a vengeance as patron and agent. Genius is reduced to social serviceability, and woman is put forth as a metonym of society. We have come full circle from Marinetti's early characterization of "passéism" (wherein social woman is the ruination of artistic man), through futurism's valorization of the instinctive woman who supports the revolutionary program of heroic man's avant-garde development, and finally to futurist man's dependence on social woman—a dependence not unlike that of the symbiosis between parasite and exploited in the "Feminist Manifesto." Far from being a machinelike force of revolution, Loony displays an instinctive knack for seductive social behavior.[50] And far from being a centerless source of sexual debauchery or chaotic energy, Diana works with machinelike efficiency, insight, and singlemindedness.

Loy's dramaturgical and polemical explorations of gender and social roles, of avant-garde discourse and feminist debate, of personal experience and aesthetic distance all serve as instructive foils to the libertarianism of Dora Marsden and the masculinist revolutionary program of Valentine de Saint-Point. In this light, Loy's enthusiastic reception by early modernists such as Eliot, Williams, and Pound suggests a heightened level of misreading on their part. Pound, for example, coined one of his three famous descriptive terms of imagism specifically in response to Loy's poetic method. "Logopoeia," which Pound glossed as "the dance of intelligence among

[50] Early in *The Pamperers*, a character in Diana's social circle declares, "I don't want to know anything about Marinetti but I respect him . . . he has a clean collar I am willing to accept the creed of any man who wears a clean collar" (68).

words and ideas," signified for him the ambiguity and self-referentiality of language. According to Ruthven, Pound produced the term "when trying to think of what to say about the poetry of Mina Loy, in whose work he could 'detect no emotion whatever'" (121). Pound was no doubt referring to the poems that had been appearing in New York—poems such as "Parturition" and *Songs to Joannes*. Yet it is difficult to imagine *any* reading of these poems that does not take into account the profound emotional tension of such lines as those in number 11 of *Love Songs*:

> Dear one at your mercy
> Our Universe
> Is only
> A colorless onion
> You derobe
> Sheath by sheath
>     Remaining
> A disheartening odor
> About your nervy hands (1996, 56–57)

Loy's literal dis-heartening—an onion peeled down to nothing by the "nervy" hands of a futurist conjure artist—could hardly be drawn more tautly. Similarly, the emotional continuum stretched between experience and allegory in these lines from the extraordinary poem "Parturition" depicts an emotional state which imagism, for all of its syntactic precision, is incapable of rendering.[51] In this moment the ego actually inhabits the matrix, enters into essence and *narrates* it for an avant-garde audience:

> Stir of incipient life
> Precipitating into me
> The contents of the universe
> Mother I am
> Identical
> With infinite Maternity
>     Indivisible
>     Acutely
>     I am absorbed
>     Into

---

[51] Carolyn Burke favorably compares Loy's "highly visual and kinaesthetic version of Futurist poetics" with the "relatively static Imagist epistemology that Pound tried to repackage in Vorticism" (1987, 38). "Because of its limited focus," Burke argues, "Imagism could not take cognizance of the need for a more conceptual language to convey the poet's reflection upon the emotional states conveyed through the images" (39).

The was–is–ever–shall–be
Of cosmic reproductivity (1996, 6–7)

Loy charts her identification with "infinite Maternity" in a register of modern double consciousness: she watches herself speak as a Mother even as her acute absorption into "cosmic reproductivity" signals a Bergsonian moment of *durée*—the "death of time and space," as Marinetti would call it—in which she preserves her individual ego-I-eye. She scrutinizes and narrates as an avant-garde artist; maternity has given her something that every avant-garde artist needs but few have: to wit, the capacity for parallax vision, which will move her dialectically out of common sense and into knowledge. The passage suggests that it is the humanity of physical experience—touch, motion, warmth—which precedes and creates aesthetic, marmoreal infinitude; and in this suggestion "Parturition" plays with the same tension between the personal and the aesthetic that we have seen in Loy's more explicitly polemical works.

Pound's undiscerning suppression of "emotion" in Loy's poetry may perhaps be read back into the complex relation between feminist writers and the avant-garde audience. As we have seen, Pound wished to set certain literary boundaries so as to reify avant-garde discourse while limiting access to the production and dissemination of avant-garde works. His legendary battles with Amy Lowell over the anthologizing of imagist poetry—battles in which she challenged his control of the movement by insisting that a wide range of practicing poets be democratically represented in the 1914 imagist anthology—demonstrate, among other things, the resentment he felt about what Eliot referred to as "the monopolization of literature by women" (quoted in Ruthven, 75). Of course, at the time, if there was any monopoly at all on the critical discourse produced in conjunction with modernist literature, Pound was the chief stockholder, as Ruthven has argued. Nevertheless, to Pound, Lowell represented not only the untoward influence of literary women on literary production, but also the threat posed to his own self-styled literary aristocracy by the indiscriminate chaos of democracy—a chaos easily conflated with a "female" principle opposed to the "male" principle of "cosmos" and artistic form.[52]

Pound's placement of Loy in a critical space free of emotional chaos—a space ruled by the "dance of intelligence"—tells us something about the terms under which women's literary work gained acceptance in the mod-

[52] See Ruthven, 118, for a discussion of Pound's "heterocosms" of literary production.

ernist movement formed in prewar England. For his response is characteristic of a whole host of High Modernists—at least as they have been canonized—for whom artistic individualism was strongly linked to effacement of temporal politicality. Such a reception may also bear on Loy's decision to keep her "Feminist Manifesto" private: for to write in the revolutionary discourse of the avant-garde manifesto is to invite the scrutiny of those for whom such discourse signals constraints on gender roles. And that scrutiny simply would not understand a feminist manifesto as "feminist."

On one side, Valentine de Saint-Point's manifestoes entered into a futurist public sphere and won approval from a futurist audience while endorsing, rather than challenging, futurism's masculinism. At the same time, the Suffragette manifestoes and revolutionary polemical tracts of Christabel Pankhurst, which not only challenged social constructions of gender but also reversed the gendered assumptions of masculinist sociomedical discourse, were taken by Dora Marsden, Ezra Pound, and others to be the writings of someone with "about as much intellect as a guineapig," who foolishly demanded "a shadow, a useless thing," as Pound put it in "Suffragettes" (367).[53] In other words, the contemporary feminist manifestoes which constituted part of the horizon of expectations for Loy's polemic either reified the masculinism she wished to critique or signified the parliamentarianism associated by avant-gardists with bourgeois politics. The question of how to make feminist demands in the language and mode associated with masculinist polemics obviously troubled Loy, who in 1915 wrote to Carl Van Vechten that "what I feel now are feminine politics—but in a cosmic way that may not fit in anywhere" (quoted in Burke 1996, 187). Certainly they would not fit in with the volumes of manifestoes produced by Marinetti and the futurists, nor would they be suited to the aims of militant and goal-oriented Suffragettes.

Rather, Loy's feminist polemics probe the seam between the political and the aesthetic, between personal experience and avant-garde discursive configurations. Loy's formulation of women's disadvantages in a patriarchal world is rooted in an understanding of and participation in the apparatus of avant-garde production; from such a perspective, the futurist demand for equality between the sexes ultimately means the abolition of the feminine except as a pejorative aesthetic category and the dismantling of "woman" as a social category. This move toward universal masculinity is

[53] For her part, Marsden described Christabel Pankhurst as having only two thoughts: how to torment Prime Minister Asquith, and an obsessive preoccupation with "white slavery." See *The Egoist* 1.12 (June 15, 1914), 223–24.

countered in Loy with a parallel universalism: for Loy, women are the con-stituents of a discrete social group whose experiences may yield a nonessentializing feminist aesthetic. It remains an open question whether the manifesto form could serve such a nontraditional recasting of gender valuation while preserving alliances with an avant-garde readership; but Loy seems to have sensed that her manifesto "[might] not fit in anywhere" because its political position was in tension with the very discourse it sought to use. As we shall see in the next chapter, this is certainly the case as well for second-wave feminist polemicists such as Monique Wittig, a writer in the French avant-garde of the sixties, for whom the scaffolding of Marxist discourse provided both a hortatory speaking platform and a gen-dered prison-house of revolutionary language.

# 5  A Second-Wave Problematic

## How to Be a Radical

Recent histories of modern feminism have tended to focus on the ideological and methodological tensions inhering in second-wave feminism of the 1960s and 1970s. In particular, two sets of questions usually frame this historiography. The first set probes the conflicts issuing from a conceptual dichotomy in Western feminist theory. Called a "paradox," a "divide," a "double gesture," one prevalent incarnation in recent years has taken the form of a perceived binarism opposing feminist essentialism to social constructionism, the result of which is the projection of an unresolvable philosophical conflict between "woman" as a transcendental category and "woman" as a contingent construct. More recently this tension has turned on its axis, emphasizing the continuing impasse between feminisms universal and particular; certainly the figures in Chapters 3 and 4 of this book could serve to illustrate such a narrative: Christabel Pankhurst's insistence on political subjecthood for women who "lived up to" the universal ideal projected in colonial bourgeois ideology stands in chiasmatic relation to Dora Marsden's philosophical repudiation of all universalisms in the name of individualist feminism. Valentine de Saint-Point's embrace of the principle of complementarity between male and female spheres of a "new" (i.e., republican avant-garde) universal subject is opposed by Mina Loy's insistence that the marks of gender make for a permanently uneven playing field, which in turn gives the lie to universalism.

The history of second-wave feminism is a sort of improvisation on all of these oppositions as well as an extended meditation on the gap between Enlightenment ideals and sex equality that we saw in Chapter 2. Naomi

Schor frames it this way: "Second wave feminism is a body of theory born of disillusionment with the promise of the French Revolution to extend access to universal rights to all, a deep loss of faith in the emancipatory promise of the Enlightenment ideal as such" (20). I have been trying to show how feminist disappointment dogs the heels of many subsequent incarnations of the "emancipatory promise" of the French Revolution, and how feminists frequently have had to choose between identifying with or differentiating themselves from a constantly mutating "universal subject."[1] Harking back to the case of Olympe de Gouges, Joan Wallach Scott elaborates on this paradox as it was received by early feminists via the abiding universalist foundations on which rights were being theorized. De Gouges, says Scott, while attempting to negotiate the imperatives of the universal, "at once stressed her identity with the universal human individual and her difference" (1992, 108). Eventually the "existence of [feminists'] particularized critiques of universality" became, in the dualist logic of modernity, "a way of confirming rather than questioning the very notion of the universal" (114–15). As Ann Snitow, Alice Echols, Joan Wallach Scott (1988), and others were at pains to demonstrate in the late 1980s, the dance of the universal reappears in the tensions between radical feminism and cultural feminism, between "equality" and "difference," even between liberalism and radicalism.[2] Snitow reifies the split as one that embodies for feminists the double pressure of "needing to act as women" (i.e., as particularly marked by gender) and "needing an identity not overdetermined by . . . gender" (i.e., a neutral universalist position) (9). In its multiple manifestations, this divide has shaped the course of Western feminism, and the attendant question of universalism has repeatedly come around to an examination of the claims of "particular" groups whose exclusion from access to universal rights "appears to involve a negation of human universality as such" (Balibar, 72). It is especially palpable in the recent chronicles of the

---

[1] Or, alternately, to follow the ideas of Denise Riley, how "women" have helped to form "a kind of continuum of sociality against which the political was set" (30).

[2] For a sampling of the numerous accounts of feminism's shifting divides, see Linda Alcoff, who sees an unresolvable conflict between feminism and poststructuralism; Ann Snitow, who describes a dichotomy between "minimizers" (feminists who seek to minimize and ultimately undermine the category "woman") and "maximizers" (feminists who valorize "woman"); Iris Marion Young, who in "The Ideal of Community and the Politics of Difference," casts the divide in terms of individualism and collectivism; Amanda Anderson (1991), who detects a "cryptonormativism" in the poststructuralist double gesture which attempts to reconcile the divide by conceptualizing it as a "strategic essentialism"; and Teresa Ebert, who articulates a bifurcation between "ludic" postmodern feminists (who are involved in an "anti-totality" project) and "resistant" postmodern feminists (who aim to analyze capitalism in its totality).

various militant, radical, and liberal brands of feminism that formed in the United States in the mid-sixties and the early seventies.[3]

A second, related set of questions framing the new feminist historiography explores the impasses encountered by second-wave feminists as they attempted to articulate social or psychoanalytic theories of gender to Marxist theory and practice. Many feminists who had been political activists under the various banners of Marxism, socialism, and New Left politics came to believe that the analytic tools they had been using to understand class struggle were inadequate for their new task of theorizing feminism. In "The Unhappy Marriage of Marxism and Feminism," Heidi Hartmann wrote that "marxist analysis provides essential insight into the laws of historical development, and those of capital in particular, [but] the categories of marxism are sex-blind" (2); and Sally Alexander wondered how women could "speak and think creatively within Marxism when they can neither enter the narrative flow as fully as they wish, nor imagine that there might be other subjectivities present in history than those of class (for to imagine that is to transgress the laws of historical materialism)" (29). Taken together, these comments revealed a problematic structured by competing taxonomies. Must "women" understand themselves as a social group assimilable to or homologous to "class"?[4] If so, how are they to conceptualize the sexuality that may underpin their social identities? If not, where may feminists create their own subject positions within received Marxist discourse? That is, how might they mark their particularity within the universalizing strategies of left dissent without drawing fire for splitting the movement? As the feminist authors of the "SDS National Resolution on Women" sarcastically put it in 1968: "The much-loved and by now endearingly familiar terminology [of the radical American left] . . . obscures the fact that a so-called secondary contradiction [i.e., between women and the bourgeoisie, secondary to the contradiction between the working class and the ruling class] may in fact be the sharpest contradiction at a given time because people experience it most acutely in their lives. We emphasize that the sharpest contradiction can form the basis for the most immediate struggle against oppression which in turn leads to greater, more effective participation in the total struggle" (257).

These two sets of problems facing radical feminists of the sixties and seventies—that is, how to negotiate the cultural implications of a narrow

[3] For example, Alice Echols's account of this development traces the effects of the gender debate on sixties radical feminist groups as they continually fractured and regrouped under its influence.

[4] Monique Wittig has argued with astounding consistency throughout her career that "women" are a socioeconomic class.

socio-biological grouping called "woman," and how to integrate those negotiations into the extant, barely feminist analytic discourse of the New Left—will frame my investigation in this chapter of the manifesto's role in the production of new feminisms in its second wave. I examine how the conventional and historical determinants of the manifesto form affected some of the feminist polemics produced by women embroiled in debates about their relations to men, to Marxism, to patriarchy, and to other women. I particularly want to ask whether the manifesto form resisted or troubled feminist speaking positions as they were created in the late 1960s and early 1970s in the United States and France.[5] To this end I offer here first a discussion of some second-wave American manifestoes, and then a case study of one little-known French feminist tract, "Combat pour la libération de la femme," which appeared in May 1970 in a small Maoist journal in Paris. The manifesto, coauthored by Monique Wittig, Gille Wittig, Marcia Rothenburg, and Margaret Stephenson, was one of the few early second-wave feminist manifestoes to attempt to engage Marxist discourse in a thoroughgoing way, and its difficulties on this count are instructive. At the same time, its vacillations among the competing strains of feminism it theorizes provides us with a vivid, historicized dramatization of the ideological bifurcations among Western feminisms. Furthermore, the Parisian manifesto's status as an early coauthored work by Monique Wittig—whose adaptations of other forms (dictionary, essay, utopian novel) differ markedly in their postmodern experimentalism from this distinctly non-ludic manifesto—may help to elaborate something like a comparativist perspective on contemporary feminist polemics.[6]

I close the chapter by moving from the Wittig manifesto to manifestoes produced in the 1980s by the poststructuralist feminist Donna Haraway and the media artist Jenny Holzer. These later, more ironic manifestoes cautiously negotiate the form's characteristic use of revolutionary discourse: for example, they deliberately foreground the manifestic pronoun "we" as an index of multiplicity rather than as a signifier of univocality, and, I propose, they need to be understood, like their cousins of the sixties, in the historical contexts in which they were produced. For as we have

[5] Rita Felski has argued that formally based theories of the text cannot productively be used by feminism (1989); yet she tends to connect such efforts with the valorization, by some French *néo-féminine* theorists, of avant-garde forms as particularly "feminine." Felski's line of thinking leads back to Peter Bürger's argument that avant-garde shock tactics rapidly become conventional. Bürger's reading, I contend, misses the important historical distinction between discourse and style. See Felski, 1989 chaps. 1 and 5.

[6] For complex responses to Wittig's more recent critical writings, in particular those addressing the lesbian subject, see Butler, chap. 3; Fuss, chap. 3; and Zerilli, passim.

seen, the revolutionary discourse of the plebeian public sphere—the sphere that marks the production, at least putatively, of the manifesto—often assumes both a speaker empowered to speak for one and all, and an audience organized around acts of dissent against exclusion.[7] Manifestoes may therefore fail to speak *for* unempowered groups within an audience or *to* audiences disempowered precisely by the race and gender exclusions of a falsely universalized radical public sphere. And this possibility raises a further question: How much of a manifesto's effectiveness depends on its ability to dramatize woman's particularity, and how fatal are those dramatizations for her claims on the universal?

## SCUM and Its Counterparts

The Parisian feminist manifesto "Combat pour la libération de la femme" appeared at a time when the manifesto had reemerged as the polemical form of choice for groups such as the Black Panthers, French students, the SDS, and other U.S. student organizations affiliated with the New Left, French laborers, and various strands of the U.S women's liberation movement. Among the women's liberation tracts, Valerie Solanas's notorious SCUM (Society for Cutting Up Men) Manifesto was not only one of the earliest (1967), but also one of the most outrageously militant. It is hardly a "feminist" manifesto in the collectivist sense: like Dora Marsden's "Freewomen," SCUM's "freewheeling, groovy females" constitute a small elite of "individuals" who are defined in part by their contrast to the "Daddy's Girl, passive, adaptable, respectful of and in awe of the male" (15) who make up most of the female population. The "we" of SCUM is Valerie Solanas and People Like Her; but she is the sole signatory of the tract. Laura Winkiel reports that Solanas was disgusted by the faddish popularity of her manifesto among branches of the women's movement (by 1969 the manifesto had attained the status of a kind of bible for many separatist East Coast feminists).[8] For this is a graphically irritable manifesto, brilliant and shocking, and it takes an act of interpretive recuperation to read it as a "heroic" text. SCUM calls upon "thrill-seeking females" to kill "all men

---

[7] Stanley Aronowitz puts the matter of extreme dissent more dramatically: it is "directed against the cynicism of the democratic state which, however much it promises the freedom to participate in governance, merely delivers an *ersatz* public sphere, an imitation of public life" (1987–88, 105).

[8] The SCUM Manifesto was especially esteemed by two groups in particular: Cell 16, a Boston group of militant separatist feminists, and The Feminists, Ti-Grace Atkinson's organization of radical proto-cultural feminists. See Echols, chap. 4. See also Winkiel for a perceptive account and analysis of the manifesto's production.

who are not . . . working diligently to eliminate themselves" (26) and to "take over the country . . . by systematically fucking up the system, selectively destroying property" (25). As a manifesto it advertises at every moment its subversive negotiations of a rhetorical form of revolutionary authority by parodying, in outrageous caricature, the formal aspects of the political manifesto. Its opening sentences demonstrate as much:

> Life in this society being, at best, an utter bore and no aspect of society being at all relevant to women, there remains to civic-minded, responsible, thrill-seeking females only to overthrow the government, eliminate the money system, institute complete automation, and destroy the male sex. . . . Retaining the male has not even the dubious purpose of reproduction. The male is a biological accident: the y (male) gene is an incomplete x (female) gene, that is, has an incomplete set of chromosomes. In other words, the male is an incomplete female, a walking abortion, aborted at the gene state. To be a male is to be deficient, emotionally limited: maleness is a deficiency disease and males are emotional cripples. (3)

From the interpellation of an audience of "thrill-seeking females" arranged around a (literally) iconoclastic program of political, economic, social, and gender anarchy, to the utopian rendering of scientistic biological determinism, offered specifically as a program of eugenics in extremis, Solanas stretches the manifesto form to its limits. The results are uncanny—*unheimlich*—from a generic perspective. SCUM splices the conventional incantatory hortatory prose of the manifesto with highly particularized renderings of inevitability, violence, and recalibrated centrality, thereby undoing the paradoxes of violent threat/static word and rationality/rage that characterize most political manifestoes. What SCUM offers instead is a recipe for more literal violence and less orderly rage, served up by "females" who claim it as their political right. Thus, for instance, SCUM scorns reformists: public marches and student strikes are for "nice, genteel ladies," whereas when SCUM marches, "it will be over the President's stupid, sickening face"; and when SCUM organizes a strike, "it will be in the dark with a six-inch blade" (28).

This manifesto also goes after the male body, particularizing it as the site of a diseased and self-absorbed predatory sexuality, and thereby reversing a whole misogynist rhetorical tradition that stretches back to the male participants in the *querelle des femmes* (and includes notables such as Otto Weininger and Almroth Wright). Melissa Deem has argued convincingly that this reversal of the spectacular body in effect constitutes an attack on the "abstraction of maleness" that is a necessary precondition for the equation of the bourgeois white male with the universal subject; by specularizing the male body, SCUM "contributed to the erosion and questioning of previously established boundaries of the public, the category of the political agent, and the modes of decorum" (512). We have seen that Christabel Pankhurst used a similar strategy, albeit with a tad more discretion, in her 1913 discussions of male erections and nocturnal emissions in *The Great Scourge and How to End It:* by marking male sexuality as concrete, particularized, and out of control, Pankhurst effected a de-universalization of the abstracted, "neutral" male subject for whom the English government speaks.

But Solanas's manifesto takes a more explicitly political tack, since it participates in an anarcho-libertarian tradition according to which individual liberation is linked to the overthrow of capitalism. In a particularly engaging section of the manifesto, Solanas predicts, in the future tense so characteristic of manifestoes, that "SCUM will become members of the unwork force, the fuck-up force; they will get jobs of various kinds and unwork. For example, SCUM salesgirls will not charge for merchandise; SCUM telephone operators will not charge for calls; SCUM office and factory workers, in addition to fucking up their work, will secretly destroy equipment. SCUM will unwork at a job until fired, then get a new job to unwork at. SCUM will forcibly relieve bus drivers, cab drivers and subway token sellers of their jobs and run buses and cabs and dispense free tokens to the public" (25–26).

Like the anarchism promoted in the post-situationist strain of sixties radicalism—itself a mixture of direct action and theatrical improvisation—Solanas's salutary lawlessness bespeaks more a faith in anti-institutional spontaneous intervention than a belief in any kind of careful engagement with systematic critiques of capitalism.[9] And yet by virtue of this very fact—and by her insistent association of patriarchal corruption

[9] At one point, however, the manifesto does explicitly declare that "what will liberate women . . . from male control is the total elimination of the money-work system, not the attainment of economic equality with men within it" (7). For accounts of the divide wrought in the French New Left by the tension between anarchism and Marxism, see Peter Brooks's narrative of the "mai '68" events, in which he maintains that most students of the era exhibited "a lucid mistrust of the totalitarian state socialism, where the state's technological apparatus would infringe individual liberty as much as does capitalism, and proposed instead the direct communism of anarchy, based on the anti-hierarchical, anti-technological form of authority and human solidarity represented by the [student] soviets" (32–33). See also Peter Starr, who develops a very insightful analysis of the Maoist form of activism riven by "the insistence on an absolute and disciplined subservience to the will of the people on the one hand and an anti-authoritarian, even neoanarchist, faith in spontaneous action on the other" (90).

with capitalism—Solanas's manifesto manages, in effect, to span the divide in sixties radicalism that opened between "outrageous" avant-garde performance and the pedagogy of theory.[10] On balance, it is the excess, not the engagement, that resounds in the manifesto; SCUM is the vengeful, victorious daughter of the avant-garde manifestoes of Apollinaire, Tzara, Marinetti, Debord.

Its resemblance to—indeed, its unparalleled trumping of—these forebears has specific implications for SCUM's political efficacy. Though arresting in its irreverence and wit, the manifesto nevertheless illustrates the limits of exclusionary rhetoric (and the gender roles demarcated thereby). "We"—that is, Valerie Solanas—readily takes up that shock tactic, characteristic of several other contemporary left-allied manifestoes, of pitting "liberated" against "brainwashed" women, anticipating what Meaghan Morris calls the sheep-from-the-goats tactics of Mary Daly's cultural feminist rhetoric.[11] In point of fact, though Solanas never intended for it to become a blueprint for separatism, the SCUM Manifesto is separatist on enough fronts to make it a kind of hyper-manifesto: it seeks to polarize rather than negotiate its audiences; it fractures and diminishes its audience beyond coherence; it reviles all men as "half-dead, unresponsive lump[s]" "walking dildo[s]," "completely egocentric" (4); it is viciously homophobic in its cracked depictions of male homosexuality as the last-ditch attempt by men to be women; it demeans virtually all forms of sexuality as "a gross waste of time" (18); and it imagines only a handful of "real women."

Solanas's "we" is strategically singular: anything more inclusive would preclude the possibility for random action in the name of feminist anarchism; anything more inclusive would fix identity, thwart performativity, register a sexed normativity. Anything more inclusive would, in short, reify a category called "women" whose political history would most certainly outstrip its utopian possibilities. In her negotiations of the manifesto's daunting pronoun, Solanas ultimately sacrifices collective politics, except in the most fantastic sense of the phrase, and this entails a dichotomizing of the terms of election and address ("we"/"you") that takes place *within* the category of "women": "The conflict, therefore, is not between females and males, but between SCUM—dominant, secure, self-confident, nasty,

---

[10] For a bracing and useful discussion of "outrageous" feminism, see Ebert, 255–70.

[11] Morris offers a withering critique of Mary Daly's *Gyn/Ecology*, which, she argues, constructs a category of women "othered" by their patriarchal contamination. Daly's banishment of these "Painted Birds" from her elect circle underpins the rhetorical essentialism she uses to create and define her audience: women who are "like us" are not "like them"; truth is "here," aberrancy is "there." See Morris, passim. For a historical discussion of radical feminism's "drift" into cultural feminism, see Echols, chap. 6.

violent, selfish, independent, proud, thrill-seeking, free-wheeling, arrogant females, who consider themselves fit to rule the universe . . . —and nice, passive, accepting, 'cultivated,' polite, dignified, subdued, dependent, scared, mindless, insecure, approval-seeking Daddy's Girls" (25).

While Solanas's "we" charges most women with ideological complicity (like Marsden, she calls into question the whole possibility of provisional politics), the "we" of SCUM at least avoids the fate of the imploded "we" evident in other American feminist movements. The pro-woman Redstockings group from New York, for example, sought to create a separatist position with the broadest possible appeal to all women. To that end, their 1970 "Redstockings Manifesto" eschews involvement with or indebtedness to any other (masculinist) political programs. Its first six sections are composed of short, sober declarative sentences such as, "We identify the agents of our oppression as men" (273) and "We identify with all women" (274). The manifesto's seventh section—its call to arms—is predicated on just this rhetorical sobriety: "In fighting for our liberation we will always take the side of women against their oppressors. We will not ask what is 'revolutionary' or 'reformist,' only what is good for women. The time for individual skirmishes has passed. This time we are going all the way" (274).

Uncomplicated in its relation to its audience (all women), "Redstockings" neatly totalizes a unified audience of "women." In doing so, however, it places itself on the side of revisionary Marxist feminists of the period, for whom the category of woman is a "class" analogous to a victimized proletariat: "Women are an oppressed class"; "All power structures throughout history have been male-dominated and male-oriented"; "*All men* have oppressed women" (272–73). Although its pro-woman focus here remains intact by virtue of its claim to the lowest rung of a reconceived class system, the Redstockings group was doomed to splinter under the strain of such an undifferentiated speaking voice. For in spite of identifying its "best interest as that of the poorest, most brutally exploited woman" (274), "Redstockings" paradoxically bases its agenda on experiential "consciousness-raising," holding this to be the "only method by which we can ensure that our program for liberation is based on the concrete realities of our lives" (274). "We" here becomes an impossible pronoun, signifying both an imagined group of "brutally exploited" victims *and* a group of women testifying to their mutual differences.[12]

The stark distance between "all the women" of the Redstockings Manifesto and the "few good females" of the SCUM Manifesto does not entirely

---

[12] For an account of the Redstockings' breakup, see Echols, chap. 4.

depend on the rhetorical exigencies of the manifesto form. I have re-marked on the ideological gulf, which split the U.S. women's movement from its beginning, between those who held that women's exploitation de-rived principally from capitalism, and so perceived women's liberation as a struggle to be mounted from within the left, and alternately those who blamed capitalism *and* male supremacy *and* men generally for women's oppression, and so saw liberation as a struggle of women against men and men's institutions. Given the terms of this division, however, and given es-pecially the endless possibilities for ideological permutations between these two polar positions, we may easily see how the manifesto form would participate in, rather than attenuate, the misconceptions among individual groups that sprang up as the women's movement proliferated. The mani-festo's conventional use of hortatory rhetoric tacitly enforced a kind of monolithic indifference to difference. Yet the intense competition for a valid "we" within a cacophony of univocal "we's" made clear the very dif-ferences among women that many speakers did not wish to recognize.[13]

## Left Feminism's Dilemma

Although the Wittig manifesto "Combat pour la libération de la femme" shares with its U.S. counterparts many of the same difficulties concerning alliances, left sectarianism, univocality, and scope of address, the horizon of expectations for the French manifesto is somewhat different, and perhaps more indeterminate, than that within which U.S. women's liberation mani-festoes were at first received. "Combat" was one of the earliest second-wave feminist manifestoes in France. According to *Ms.* magazine's foreign corre-spondent, its signatories were virtually the first of the French feminist ac-tivists—only a very small "handful of discontented militants"—in what was perceived to be largely an American struggle (Servan-Schreiber, 30).[14] "Combat" was something like a map that preceded its territory, to borrow Baudrillard's phrase; and its publication in a Maoist journal in 1970 con-nected it to an audience defined principally by its relation to the events of

[13] "A Black Feminist Statement" by the Combahee River Collective—only one of numerous contemporary responses by black women to this totalizing "we" of white feminism—icily ob-serves that no "ostensibly progressive movement [including the women's movement] has ever considered our specific oppression a priority or worked seriously for the ending of that oppres-sion" (15).

[14] Note, though, that the *Ms.* account fails to acknowledge a few key feminist organizations and publications that appeared in France in the mid-sixties. See also Marks and de Courtivron, "Intro-duction II: Histories of France and of Feminism in France," and "Introduction III: Contexts of the New French Feminisms."

May 1968 in France and to the French Communist Party (PCF) rather than by any prior sympathy for an explicitly feminist cause. The audience was composed mostly of students and intellectuals galvanized by the 1968 student-worker strikes who, if such things can be generalized from the Maoist bent of the paper, had opposed and alienated themselves from the huge PCF by endorsing pro-Chinese—that is, pro-revolutionary rather than pro-Soviet/professionalist/humanist—formulations of class struggle and social change: they advocated the ideological education of workers, and they placed great value on both theoretical practice and anti-institutional subversion.[15]

The authors of "Combat" are thus faced with interpolating a call for women's liberation into a heavily theorized (and masculinized) conversation already fractionalized within the French left. In this their problems are in line with those of left U.S. women who, a few years earlier, had struggled to foreground what left leaders saw as a peripheral problem—struggled, that is, with little success. The movement's male leadership was well known for its dismissive contempt of feminist agendas, and even women in the movement "doubted that feminism was comprehensively revolutionary" (Echols, 79).[16] So too must "Combat" preach to an uninitiated New Left that has not yet theorized feminism in any comprehensive way.

The text of Wittig's manifesto remains well within the critical bounds of orthodox Marxism. This is a Marxism that rejects as idealistic the capitalist propagation of individual subjecthood, and insists instead on a universal subject of class consciousness, just as it considers women only as they belong to extant economic classes rather than as constituting a non-economic class of their own. In a later essay Wittig discusses the impossibility of constructing a non-male subject within this ideological framework, and she charges unrevised Marxism with preventing all categories of oppressed

[15] For an overview of the events of May 1968, see Richard Johnson. For the Maoist-PCF split, see Kate Soper. See also Peter Starr's excellent study of the politics of the period, viewed through a '68-Lacanian lens. Starr describes the Maoist position as one that had wide appeal among students because it could play both sides of the left divide: that is, the "Marxist-Leninist-religious" side on the one hand and the "libertarian-communitarian" side on the other. Starr writes that French Maoism eventually "fell victim (in the mid-1970s) to a mounting perception that reformist evolutionism offered a surer means of effecting social change than revolutionary upheaval and that the vocabulary of class struggle was but a poor instrument for analyzing a social order in which power was increasingly fractured and diffuse" (91).

[16] Separatism was a strong alternative to association with the left almost from the beginning of the U.S. women's movement. See Echols's account of New York Radical Women and other separatist groups, especially chaps. 2 and 4. For a critical account of separatism written in 1970, see Claire Moriarty.

people from "constitut[ing] themselves historically as subjects" (18). But "Combat," using the master texts of Marxist writings on women (Marx, Engels, Bebel) and Marxist ideological formulations (e.g., theorizing male chauvinism as a function of class struggle), ostensibly aims to uncover within the logic of Marxism the rightful—and righteous—place of the women's liberation movement. To this end, the bulk of its theorization of women's exploitation under capitalism hinges on Marx's theories of the family. "Combat" argues, for example, that domestic labor reproduces a model of serfdom, insofar as it is unrepresented, unpaid, and devoid of exchange value; and that the family under capitalism yields two workers, husband and wife, for one wage. Ultimately a function of capitalism, the argument goes, "male chauvinism" undoes working women *and* men.

This line of argument is underscored by the published layout of the manifesto itself, which testifies to the dependence of Wittig's discourse on the authority of the interpolated master texts. Those passages are printed in an enlarged boldface type; sometimes they are surrounded by heavy borders and inserted directly into the fabric of the text, and sometimes they are arranged as headnotes that separate sections of the text. The overall visual effect is one of sublation: "Combat" appears to explicate the master narratives, somewhat in the manner of sacred exegesis.[17] But at key points exegesis competes with aphorism, for this manifesto also makes liberal use of Engels's famous formulation that "in the family, man is the bourgeois, woman plays the role of the proletariat." Repeated like a refrain across the six thousand words of this long manifesto, shored up by other excerpts from *Origin of the Family,* Engels's equation comes to imply that *women*'s invitations to the revolution are more legitimate than men's, and that men are part of the ideological apparatus that has blinded women to the legitimacy of their own revolutionary claims. The implication is that

[17] In all likelihood this puzzling layout resulted from an editorial decision, since several other aspects of the manifesto's publication are similarly incongruent. The title, for example, emphasizing the liberation of "woman" (as opposed to women), runs exactly counter to Wittig's efforts, not only in the manifesto but also in *Les Guérillères* and in all of her essays since, to eradicate an essentialized category of "woman." If the original title of the manifesto was "Pour un mouvement de libération des femmes," as the reference in a footnote in "One Is Not Born a Woman" suggests, then surely the change from "women" (which for Wittig signifies "the class of women") to "woman" (which for Wittig signifies "myth") was not made by Wittig. There is a second interesting title shift in this scenario—from "movement" to *combat,* or "battle." The latter term is certainly more spectacular than the former; and the title in the manifesto's layout floats just below the half-page photograph that visually introduces the piece: it is a photo of angry women defiantly marching together, the iconography of which anticipates to an extraordinary degree the photograph featured in the "Dyke Manifesto."

men—radical revolutionaries or otherwise—are party to the worst kind of false consciousness.[18]

Thus the theoretical schism in "Combat," though it remains well within the discursive boundaries of Marxism, seems to reproduce the broad ideological schism of the U.S. women's movement on the left: Is women's oppression a function of capitalism, or is capitalism a function of women's oppression? The manifesto's strategic predicaments inhere in this fault line: the manifesto must convert to activist feminism an audience of Maoist activists wary of commitment to dogma and sectionalism; the manifesto must participate in left theory and activism even as it uses them to test, accuse, and perhaps even alienate the majority of its non-feminist audience. "Combat" thus runs the risk of further splintering an already splintered group. The new group engendered by "Combat" could be less or more radical than *L'Idiot international*'s audience: less if women's liberation is seen, finally, as "domestic, prosaic" (16), an unattractive limb of the true revolution (a response the manifesto writers fear); but more radical if women's liberation is revealed to be the truest enactment of the manifesto's demand for "all power to the people" (paragraph 38). The voice of the manifesto suggests the likelihood of this latter possibility—that feminism *is* revolutionary telos—but since it can do so only at the expense of a feminist-Maoist alliance (which, not incidentally, makes possible the very existence of the manifesto), the suggestion must be floated with the mild breath of deference.[19] Toward the end of the manifesto, for example, paragraph after paragraph begins with an anaphoric "We know that," or "We understand that," often followed by dutifully enumerated Marxist precepts; each respective conclusion partakes of, even as it gently rebukes, the orthodoxy of the as yet non-feminist radical audience.[20]

[18] In noting this tendency in the manifesto, I am not intimating that Engels himself valorized the revolutionary subjecthood of women over that of men; I mean, rather, that the invocation of Engels in "Combat" has a mantra-like effect quite apart from Engels's theorization of women's oppression under patriarchy.

[19] The issue of *L'Idiot international* in which "Combat" appears bears on its outsized cover a fairly surreal drawing of an angry-looking woman with the title of the manifesto emblazoned on her face. She wears the traditional red bonnet of the French Revolution, and, in place of a tricolor cockade, an insignia of a hammer and sickle. Marthe Rosenfeld kindly provided me with photocopies of both the cover and the manifesto itself.

[20] For example, "We well understand that sexual difference and race difference in and of themselves cannot suffice to create class struggle. We know now that there have existed and there still exist cultures where men and women do not live in an antagonistic relation to each other. But we see clearly that all despotic, aristocratic, and totalitarian governments and regimes (Incas, Mayas, Confucian Chinese, Nazis) have used sexual difference—among other divisive elements—to create antagonism between men and women at the level of the family" (paragraph 23). "We know the role private property/means of production have played in our servitude at the economic level of the family unit" (paragraph 24). "We understand that male chauvinism turns back upon itself"

The manifesto grinds its gears at the moments when discursive conjunctures pull in different ideological directions. For example, the assertion, two-thirds of the way into the manifesto, that "we well know that neither sexual difference nor racial difference in and of themselves can suffice to create class antagonism" implies that "class antagonism" is understood to be the primary unit of Marxist political economism. From this perspective race and gender are as subunits, sublated in orthodox Marxist discourse. But the discourses of race and sexual separatism in the manifesto resist any easy integration into this equation: that is, they remain distinct. Black Power slogans appear in a quotation from Bobby Seale and in the manifesto's not infrequent refrain of "power to the people." The separatist language of women's liberation, especially terms such as "male chauvinism" and "sexism," both American coinages, peppers the text, and the rhetoric of "consciousness raising" girds detailed descriptions of the isolation and servitude of domestic life. Taken together, the experiences depicted in and evinced by the text undermine the determinacy of any assertions of a totalizing "class struggle"; they precipitate "woman" out of the category of universal subject and mark her irreducible difference. [21]

In addition to this affective contradiction, the manifesto's insistent reliance on Engels produces in effect yet another internal argument, this time for the existence of a non-economic class of women. [22] We see this registered in the class-gender uncertainty of the manifesto's title-subtitle tension: "Combat pour la libération de la femme: par delà la libération gadget, elles découvrent la lutte des classes" (Battle for the liberation of woman: beyond all this pseudo-liberation, women are discovering class struggle). Does this battle front the *real* struggle? Is women's liberation just a gadget? Does feminism arise out of the primordial substance of Marxism? Is class anterior to *and* constitutive of gender and race? What, then, constitutes class? The *in*determinacy of "class struggle" reveals itself at the intersection of an overabundance of discursive systems—feminism, black activism, neo-Marxism, orthodox Marxism, Maoism, post-

---

(paragraph 25). There are numerous other examples in the manifesto of this rhetoric of agreement/differentiation. All translations of the manifesto are mine.

[21] Drawing on Chantal Mouffe's observation that a group's political struggle is strengthened by its links with the struggles of other groups, Kobena Mercer argues that "signifiers of race" were particularly important in the "radical democratic chain of equivalences" forged in 1968; "the concept of solidarity encoded around representations of race empowered not only black peoples but subordinate subjects within white society itself" (1992, 429). "Combat," like several other manifestoes of the time, makes use of what Mercer calls the "metaphorical character" of racial signifiers in order to amplify its own connection with other sites of democratic antagonism.

[22] Wittig explicitly makes this argument ten years later in "One Is Not Born a Woman."

structuralism, and, not least among these, the discourses that make up the manifesto form.

Where conventional demands are levied by the manifesto form itself, this uneasy relation between sexual difference and class struggle is especially resonant. The manifestic convention of scripting a history of a marginalized group's struggles, for instance, poses at least two difficulties for a group (women) whose oppression coincides, according to Engels, with the formation of patriarchal culture.[23] In the first place, any representation of such a history risks fixing it as a chronically unsuccessful subplot within a master narrative.[24] This quandary is palpable even in the opening epigrammatic declaration of "Combat": "Since time immemorial, we have lived like a people colonized within the people, so well domesticated that we have forgotten that this situation of dependence is not self-begotten." The strategy at the outset is to use a doubled image: women have been colonized by their own people; their domestication produces a state of amnesia that the remainder of the manifesto will reverse. Thus this manifesto begins its hedge against the form's conventional narrative of a group's historical oppression. The very nature of the history of women's oppression ("since time immemorial") appears to necessitate this hedge. By using the image of people who have forgotten themselves, the manifesto creates two ways of resisting historical representation: the first attributes to women a discourse and an existence that precede the historical discourse of patriarchy; the second provides the basis for a feminist etiology on which the manifesto form's rhetoric of inevitability depends (e.g., the women will soon awaken). Thus the chronicity of the oppression ("since time immemorial") is tempered somewhat by a slumbering but labile consciousness of that oppression.

But "Combat" cannot avoid the problem of historical representation for long. It works in the tradition of political manifestoes that appeal to a moral or political ideal against which the oppressive present deviates from a distant past or future of perfection, and thus its task is more complicated: it has to avoid narrating patriarchy as inevitable or immutable. At the same time, its discursive materialism forecloses the option of rendering women's history as mythic history—a tactic that would in any case reify a precarious kind of essentialism.[25]

[23] For an account of the theoretical problems of *Origin of the Family,* see Lise Vogel, chap. 6.
[24] It should be noted that Lyotard's influential theories about modern metanarratives had by 1970 already become an influential and galvanizing discourse for proto-postmodern factions on the left.
[25] Wittig's subsequent activities in the radical feminist editorial collective *Questions féministes* provided her with a forum from which to critique the biological essentialism of *néo-fémininité* theorists such as Hélène Cixous (Wenzel 271–78), while her works of fiction imagine a recalibrated

Ultimately "Combat" constructs, through a series of disconnected historical narratives, something like a concentric model of French history since 1789. The outer circle, the history of the French left, contains within itself the history of women in the French left who supported and sometimes advanced its causes. This narrative structure amounts to an ambiguous recitation of women's supportive roles in men's history (during the French Revolution, the Commune, and so forth)—ambiguous inasmuch as it sets up a dichotomy of acting men and enabling women. Within this circle lies another history of women on the left, one of humiliation, disenfranchisement, persecution, in which "the chauvinist Robespierre . . . dissolves our societies, forbids us to speak in public, he tries to imprison Rose-Claire Lacombe and decrees a law in which 'natural organization' is proper for us and which renders us unfit for public functions. In 1848 the same history begins all over again" (paragraph 16).

I have touched on these events in Chapters 1 and 2, and the description in "Combat" of this innermost circle of history, which resounds with sarcasm and anger, is one of the most powerful parts of the manifesto.[26] But the very next section follows the nineteenth-century socialist practice of narratively conflating women's history with the history of serfdom. The consequent shift from particularity to homology once again mutes the voice of *la femme* in the service of *la lutte des classes*. The manifestic convention of scripting a historical narrative of oppression, in other words, places the status of woman in "Combat" at risk for becoming merely indexical or synecdochal.[27]

The convention of scripting a group's privileged relation to "justice" lands "Combat" in a similarly entangled position. As a Marxist manifesto, it draws on canonical accounts of women's condition, so that here, women are "truly the serfs of history," "slaves who cry their shame and their humiliation" (paragraph 4), prostitutes dependent on men. While these typically

history for women that borders on the mythic. See Fuss, chap. 3, for an interesting discussion of Wittig's "totalizing" anti-essentialism.

[26] Oddly, the text of "Combat" reprinted by Marie Collins and Sylvie Weil Sayre in their anthology *Les femmes en France* (New York, 1974) is a substantially edited version of the manifesto originally published in Paris: long sections, including most of this historical narrative, have been cut, though the text offers no acknowledgment of this editing, and lists a publication date of 1969. Since the only archival copy of this manifesto (Michigan State) has apparently been lost, the version reprinted by Collins and Sayre is, to my knowledge, the only copy of "Combat" available in this country.

[27] Juliet Mitchell is one of many but also one of the first feminists to critique this convention when she argues that, for the early Marx, the status of "woman" was an index of the general state of society, and that in his early writings, "woman becomes an anthropological entity, an ontological category of a highly abstract kind" (13).

socialist images illuminate the ideals of justice against which such classism and commodification transgress, the language of slavery and prostitution (also typically socialist) nevertheless participates in an iconography of women as slaves, prostitutes, even bondage victims "on their knees . . . chained to the coal trolleys in the mine shafts of the nineteenth century," "whores of the workers" and "whores of the foreman and the boss" whose wombs are "branded with the seal of the master" (paragraph 6). Every representation, drafted with a novelist's eye for detail, resonates powerfully within the surrounding text of non-descriptive—and nondescript—political rhetoric. Although they appear only occasionally in the long manifesto, these graphic cameos nevertheless have a curious cumulative impact: they tend to organize the dramatic moments of the sometimes tedious text around images of suffering, mastered women. Nowhere is this foregrounding of representation more evident than when the manifesto attacks representation itself:

> We do not go in the streets as individuals who are free to gaze or exchange glances. We are objects either of use or beyond use. The billboards and ads upon which our gaze casually alights are composed of images that humiliate us and unceasingly remind us of the sexual exploitations of which we are the objects. We clearly see how all products that the capitalist system spreads through its market set out our bodies like publicity aids. We are consumable at every moment. A billboard launches a new beer: "Drink a big blonde," showing the image of a blonde young woman with its product. To advertise the quality of its tobacco, a cigarette billboard invites us to "Taste a redhead for a change." (14)

This passage, intended to protest the sexual commodification of women, participates in an odd way in the promulgation of specularity. The manifesto can only repeat the billboards rather than contesting the regime of representation to which they testify. Judith Butler, and Linda Zerilli after her, have observed that Wittig's critical essays privilege the ontology of language, so that for Wittig, "the practical task that women face in trying to establish subjectivity through speech depends on their collective ability to cast off the reifications of sex imposed on them which deform them as partial or relative beings" (Butler, 117).[28] The billboard passage accom-

---

[28] Butler's and Zerilli's arguments about Wittig ultimately diverge: whereas Butler sees Wittig's invocation of the universal category of the subject through "marked" and "unmarked" language as a form of "confirm[ing] rather than contest[ing] the normative promise of humanist ideals" (25), Zerilli argues that "in Wittig's hands, what Butler calls 'doing gender' as performance becomes

plishes the reverse, however; it relies on a kind of reformist relation according to which "better images" of women should be produced. Indeed, in this otherwise highly theoretical tract it merely invokes, rather than theorizes, sexual reification.

The images of active resistance in "Combat" are also affected by the manifesto form's containment and release of rhetorical violence. I have proposed that implicit violence helps to underwrite a manifesto's rhetorical reliance on its own telos; indeed, this tactic of implying violence—what we might call, in a taxonomical vein, cataplexis—has been rather stunningly carried off by many famous manifestoes. The veiled threat in the Communist Manifesto serves well: "*If* the proletariat during its contest with the bourgeoisie *is compelled, by the force of circumstances,* to organize itself as a class, *if,* by means of a revolution, it *makes itself* the ruling class, and, *as such,* sweeps away by force the old conditions of production, *then it will, along with these conditions, have swept away* the conditions for the existence of class antagonisms and of classes generally, and *will thereby have abolished* its own supremacy as a class" (Marx and Engels, 353; emphasis added). I want to point out how the rhetorical construction of inevitability quietly accomplishes violent change through passive verb constructions: the repeated clusters of "if"–"then"–future tense; the subtle verbs of implied force (the passive construction of "is compelled," for instance); the swiftness of the revolution (which occurs in a single dependent clause); the euphemism for civil war (which "sweeps away" the bourgeoisie). The revolution is made possible, made effortless, by telos and its narratability.[29]

"Combat," by contrast, contains no such assured threats because a power base like "the proletariat" exists for it only analogously. The manifesto acknowledges that women may be united in England (where militant graffiti declares, "The dreams of Freud are the nightmares of women") and in the United States (where the useful phrases "male chauvinism" and "sexism" are already in circulation); but in France in 1969 resisting women are simply "prudes, bitches, shrews, or hysterical feminists" (paragraph 13).

---

what might be called 'doing universal'" (169). That is, Zerilli convincingly shows, Wittig uses the universal strategically, in order to "force the universal to live up to its promise" (169).

[29] Marshall Berman has argued that "some of Marx's most vivid and striking images are meant to force us all to confront [the social and psychological] abyss that the bourgeoisie has created but cannot face." I would add that Marx's images also accomplish most efficaciously the illusion that inevitability inheres in his manifesto—the inevitability, for instance, that "truth will out," or that communism will self-equilibrate. To wit, the passage from Marx quoted by Berman in connection with the bourgeois abyss can be used for my purposes as well: "Modern bourgeois society, a society that has conjured up such mighty means of production and exchange, is like the sorcerer who can no longer control the powers of the underworld that he has called up by his spells" (101). Class war is inevitable from both sides.

"Bitch," "shrew," "hysteric": all terms un-resignified by the text. The litany repeats the dragging oppression that restyles women's anger as the unnatural, the unhealthy, the dangerous. Unmarked by irony, the word "bitch" keeps its masculinist inflection, while the bitchiness of resistance is ironed out on liberation's negotiating table.[30]

When the manifesto attacks the conditions of isolation imposed by patriarchy on women, it does so by representing that isolation. Arguing that housewives are cut off from one another and from nascent feminist communities, the manifesto actually foregrounds a textual representation of isolation. I quote at length in order to illustrate the extraordinary degree of the housewives' absence—despite the text's use of first-person plural pronouns—from the site of political enunciation:

> In reality, it is solitude to which the capitalist society condemns us. Each of us in the familial cell, or part of the "couple," lives in a solitude, in an isolation, which is unique in the history of humanity. Unlike Blacks, we have no ghettoes to bring us together and unite us. If we work solely in the house, we must await the return of our husbands in order to have any human contact. Huddled within ourselves, cut off from the world, we destroy our self. We have no contact with the world in which men live. We have no hold on it, we do not transform it by our activities. For us, society is the family. We exhaust ourselves without benefiting from our lowly task, and without the help of any sort of camaraderie or friendship, which would be for us a weapon against the solitude of our dependence imposed by "the couple." The creation of children should be for us an important social function, but in the context where that production is inscribed, we cannot perceive it as such. When pregnant, we are mocked for "getting fat"; we do not *create* a child, rather it grows of its own in our womb, as if we were merely the eternal fertile vessels of which the Bible speaks. (paragraph 12)

This passage's appearance early in the manifesto sets up a "we" of heterosexual, white, powerless, immobile women.[31] Here the markedness of sex-

---

[30] See Joreen, "The Bitch Manifesto" (1970), for a *tout court* ironization of "bitch."

[31] Many second-wave manifestoes addressed the problem of women's isolation. But compare the passivity of this passage with a similar passage in Mariarosa Dalla Costa and Selma James (1972) in which isolation masks struggle: "The isolation from which women have suffered has confirmed to society and to themselves the myth of female incapacity. It is this myth which has hidden, first, that to the degree that the working class has been able to organize mass struggles in the community, rent strikes and struggles against inflation generally, the basis has always been the unceasing informal organization of women there; second, that in struggles in the cycle of direct production, women's support and organization, formal and informal, has been decisive" (45).

ual difference sets itself apart from the critique of class relations. The manifesto's explication of the "couple" does not include its importance as a strategic unit for capitalism, nor does it open onto a transglobal understanding of the exploitation of classed labor and the role of women in that economy. Rather, the problem of the "couple" remains prominently circumscribed by the realism of experiential critique. "We" is remarkable here as a univocal construction—one that does not contest the normative heterosexuality of this domestic sphere, and therefore one that completely neglects Wittig's arguments mounted elsewhere in the same year for the political potential of radical lesbianism. Given her relentless critiques of heterosexism and her careful theorization of the lesbian subject in *Les Guérillères* (and of course in subsequent writings), the exclusion of the lesbian subject in "Combat" is stunning. We may speculate that its status as a coauthored work involved the collective construction of a subject approximating an "average" (i.e., heterosexual, married, homebound) woman. But, in fact, the "we" here and elsewhere in the manifesto resembles both the "non-subject" that Donna Haraway sees created by a Catharine MacKinnon brand of radical feminism, wherein "another's desire, not the self's labor, is the origin of 'woman'" (77), and the experiential "we" repudiated by Marxist-feminists such as Teresa Ebert. Here absent women are spoken for through a public form whose "we" starkly fictionalizes the discrete and disconnected experiences of oppression.

The housewife passage illustrates the degree to which the speaking "we" of "Combat" remains caught between two competing political directives. While aiming to portray the oppression of women as an incontestible miscarriage of justice, the polemic partakes of the discursive conventions of the old left, most notably in its connection of "woman" with "family." Juliet Mitchell had testily critiqued this Marxist tendency four years earlier in her groundbreaking essay "Women: The Longest Revolution," where she observed that "the position of women . . . in the work of Marx and Engels remains dissociated from, or subsidiary to, a discussion of the family, which is in its turn subordinated as merely a precondition of private property" (15). In Mitchell's analysis, Marx sublated the problem of women within his economic social analysis (for which the bourgeois family as a declining unit is essential), while Engels saw thralldom in the family as the source of women's oppression: abolish the family unit, and women will enter the work force as equal partners and liberated citizens. But, as Mitchell caustically notes, "the complete failure to give any operative content to the slogan of 'abolition' of the family is striking evidence of . . . the vacuity of the notion" (20).

"Combat" frequently participates in the rhetoric of the abolition of the family, but it does so uneasily, as in this passage: "We must [i.e., we shall] . . . struggle at the level of our oppression, inside the family. Following the law of opposites, that which makes us weak also makes us strong. . . . We say that it is in the family, where we are the pillars, that our political force is great. . . . [I]f we refuse to make children for the bourgeois state . . . there will be no more family" (paragraph 26). It is difficult to imagine the isolated housewife raising the flag for a voluntarist domestic strike of this order. In fact, it makes more sense to observe how the passage enters into the troubled neo-Malthusian waters of nineteenth-century debates about the population control of the working class. In short, from our (undoubtedly presentist) perspective, the rhetorical stumbling block here is not the production of children but rather the manifesto's universalized invocation of a bourgeois family.[32] Its call to revolt—like many American feminist polemics of the time—is based on a nineteenth-century construction of "family," a smoothly configured convention of white Western heterosexuality.

This problem of negotiating the woman-family complex refers us once again to the difficulties produced by the multiple discursive intersections in "Combat" between various strains of feminism and neo-Marxism, Marxist polemic, and manifesto discourse. We might well ask at this point why Wittig, well known in 1970 as the author of the polemical fiction *Les Guérillères,* would choose to coauthor a Marxist manifesto, given all of the form's overdetermined discursive difficulties—especially in view of her success with the experimental *nouveaux romans* she had previously produced. *Les Guérillères,* written at around the same time as "Combat," has been aptly described as a "vision/utopia/manifesto/poetic narrative" (de Courtivron, 81), "the first epic celebration of women ever written" (Beauman, 5), and a "new mythology" (Spraggins, 48)—a work bearing little formal resemblance to "Combat." Its mosaic construction adjoins short scenes of the progressive de-gendering of women ("elles") which culminate in a triumphant battle of ungendered lesbians ("nous"—a pronoun used only once, on the final page) against the patriarchy that has invented gender. These scenes are interrupted periodically by lists of women's first names, which add up to a kind of metonymic, neo-nominal roll call of a transhistorical *nous.*

[32] This family neither represents nor accounts for culturally diverse familial structures—including earlier forms of working-class families—that have functioned, in some cases, as refuges from racism and classism for many women, as the manifesto's allusion to the "Black ghetto" community would seem to acknowledge.

The method of *Les Guérillères* enacts on one textual level what "Combat" proposes on another: the emancipation of women from the ideologies that isolate and silence them. *Les Guérillères* is peopled with *les guérillères*—guerrilla fighters who are the literal avant-garde of an unseen collectivity massing together beyond the strictures of patriarchy. Their method is one of unceasing movement, self-revision, camouflage patterns, new names, endless relocations, strategies of disorder, demystification. They resist, in other words, the discursive interpellations that would identify them either within social taxonomies or as anti-collective individuals. The warriors especially resist all stabilizing forms of representation. Wittig's careful handling of metaphor takes account of the subjects it represents, as the following brief speech—one of dozens in the book—demonstrates: "You compare yourselves privately to the fruits of the chestnut cloves mandarines green oranges but you are fruits only in appearance. Like the leaves you fly away at the slightest breeze, beautiful strong light subtle and prompt of understanding as you are. Beware of dispersal. Remain united like the characters in a book. Do not abandon the collectivity" (58).[33] The passage continually undercuts its own tenuous reliance on troping: the women *appear* to be like fruit, but they are not fruit; they behave like leaves, but must guard against the flightiness of leaves; they are exhorted to maintain the collectivity of a group of like fictional characters—which is just what they are. This labile chain of similes comes to rest, finally, at a point beyond troping: a manifesto-like exhortation for unity of purpose. But it is an unfamiliar kind of exhortation: since it is shown to grow out of individual self-comparisons (to sensual fruit), its substance is maieutic rather than oracular. The exhortation to collectivity preserves, in other words, the integrity of each potential member of the group.

The hybridity of Isabelle de Courtivron's term for the genre of this novel which I mentioned earlier says as much about a poststructuralist-

[33] Many of Wittig's readers have noted her abstinence from and demystification of the use of metaphor; see especially Jean Duffy and Diane Griffin Crowder. I find it useful to examine the way that she *does* use metaphor, however sparsely. In any effort toward de-gendering, metaphor threatens, by substitution and amalgamation, to practice upon the referent the same kind of abstraction that heterosexism practices upon the ungendered (and that democracy practices upon the preterite, for that matter). In "One Is Not Born a Woman," Wittig argues that women are a class, "but to become a class we do not have to suppress our individual selves, and since no individual can be reduced to her/his oppression, we are also confronted with the historical necessity of constituting ourselves as the individual subjects of our history as well" (16). In the same way that she charges women with the nearly impossible task of defining "the individual subject in materialist terms" (19), her work with metaphor undertakes to enact a paradox of representation without fixity or substitution. The two tactics are inextricably linked.

feminist distrust of genre generally as it does about the "avant-garde" techniques that undergird the form of *Les Guérillères*. Studies of genre often reduce differences among texts to simple graphs of formal or stylistic difference, as in the "well-known polarity" described by E. Ann Kaplan "whereby the classical realist text, seen as embodying dominant ideology, [is] pitted against the subversive, non-realist, non-narrative and avant-garde text" (30). Later I will have more to say about the inadequacy of this dichotomy for describing a work such as *Les Guérillères,* but here it is easy enough to assert that Wittig wages war on both terms of this literary perspective; one might just as well say that the form *Les Guérillères* obliterates the dichotomy altogether.

I noted earlier that in form *Les Guérillères* is assembled from two kinds of writing: lists of women's first names, printed in capital letters, are inserted throughout the text, into and among self-contained hypotaxic units *about* women. These latter units, which run about a page in length, are connected by only the barest narrative threads, while the lists of names, though noncontiguous, are linked by virtue of their unvarying seriality. Thus the structure of *Les Guérillères* resembles a fugue, and yet there is nothing of the fugue's formal precision, nothing of the preemptive grace of a pas de deux in this work. Rather, its form enacts interruption, revision, political aggregation, political conviction. It does so not by means of dialectics, or even dialogics, or by any systematic method, but by entwining a fragmented narrative with a metonymic roll call of historical, potential, and neo-nominal women warriors. *Les Guérillères'* heterogeneous form of writing preserves open-ended seriality in the service of infinite *in*clusion; unlike "experimental" avant-garde writing, the form of *Les Guérillères* does not seek "purer"—that is, more idiosyncratic, more precise, more original—levels of expression. Instead, the juxtaposition of its narrative and its roll call of women's names is designed to disclose a group's militant autoidentification that takes place well beyond the brightly lit arena of patriarchal discourse. That autoidentification is entirely political, and *Les Guérillères* stages it in a series of settings designed to reveal the potential for collectivity that gathers steam with each new narrative. The characters (if one can call them that) move gradually from "places" to "spaces." They begin as reluctant agriculturalists or reluctant domestic denizens, hemmed in by rain and water, and the narrative moves them to sites of unfixed flow—roadways, river banks, impromptu meeting places—where they become migrating, marching groups, collectives of warriors, guerrillas, triumphant victors against the patriarchal order of gender, commodity, and discourse. But frequently even this sketchy narrative development is deliberately abandoned or broken, for reasons that have to do with the work's insistent evasion of representation. This evasion constitutes a central concern of the work, which seeks, on the one hand, to project women in communities and as individual subjects and, on the other hand, to challenge the representational language in which texts for communities must be composed.

The predicament of representation generates in the work an anxious attention to polysemes and linguistic paradoxes—or to any ambiguous shred of language that can be woven into narrative contexts and then ripped out again. The text's use of "spinning" is a good example of this technique: the word operates throughout as noun, verb, and adjective of identity and self-transformation. The women at one point literally spin their own bodies: "Spinning glands are at work on each of their limbs. From their many orifices there emerge thick barely visible filaments that meet and fuse together. Under the repeated play of movement in the fingers a membrane grows between them that seems to join them, then prolong them, until eventually it extends beyond the hand and descends along the arm, it grows, it lengthens, it gives the women a sort of wing on either side of their body" (132). The ability of the women to transform themselves into winged creatures suggests their association with birds, weapons, artisans, conjurers. For this very reason the women do not rest with their new forms, and "when they resemble giant bats, with transparent wings, one of them comes up and, taking a kind of scissors from her belt, hastily divides the two great flaps of silk. The fingers immediately recommence their movement" (132).

Like the language of the novel, and as with its resistance to iconography, the warriors themselves excel at transmogrification. Earlier associations in the novel among forms of spinning (animals who spin on their heads, weapons that spin in the air, weaving shuttles that spin silk, for instance) are here superseded by an immediate representation of the body *beyond* representation, the body of pure potentiality, moving in defiance of stasis and objectification. This episode enacts the liberation of "congealed" languages of the literary text; it lights up the normal state of linguistic flux within which discourses and identities are continually made and unmade. Wittig is well known for her belief that power is routed through discourse, and that by a change in discourse, power can be deformed. Her understanding of discourse is deeply materialist: discourse is the material effect of ideology, and patriarchal ideology produces subjects and institutions in its own image. But the real question is this: Is the novel merely another example of what Teresa Ebert calls a "ludic" (i.e., nonresistant) practice? Do its interventions on the level of discourse actually bear on the ideological implementation of class war's effects on women? How, if at all, does the novel intervene in the political field of representation? I would argue that discourse does not trump ideology in this novel, nor can this text be read as a showdown between the two terms: the fictional performativity of freedom and equality displayed in *Les Guérillères* places it in a category of political utopianism.

In fact, in the textual freedom of *Les Guérillères*—freedom from the constraints of representation, commodification, linguistic oppression— we may recognize something like a very canny manifesto. *Les Guérillères* achieves the same goals that all political manifestoes pursue: it centralizes, in its own terms, a previously marginalized history; it reconstructs the crimes of the oppressor; it appeals successfully to a violated code of justice; it defines its own potential audience by providing a model for a provisional coalition. Given that *Les Guérillères* and "Combat" were published within a year of each other, it is tempting to judge the two polemics comparatively, especially in light of de Courtivron's editorial comment, in 1980, that Wittig was dissatisfied with and had subsequently disavowed "Combat." De Courtivron goes on briefly to note Wittig's "disillusionment not only with the outcome of May '68 but with what she considered the power-oriented tendencies of some feminist groups," and then, implying a causal relation, reports that "shortly thereafter [Wittig] published *Les Guérillères*" (81). And indeed it is not difficult to situate the writing of the two works in a causal relation, however specious it might turn out to be: *Les Guérillères'* strategic use of disorder, explicit violence, and spatial freedom appears to constitute a response to the claustrophobic order of "Combat." The fictional text's rendering of the agency of groups, masses, collectives, and companions works a fantastic cure on the solitary woman languishing alone at the central section of "Combat."

But however narratively satisfying this chronology of composition might be, it is based on a static symmetry that opposes "bad" Marxist discourse to a "good" postmodern genre, thereby closing down the semiosis of the manifesto precisely where I wish it to be dilated. The fact is that these two works of Wittig's were written alongside each other; for that matter, *Les Guérillères* may have been finished before "Combat." They were written for different audiences with different relations to the semiotics of revolution and with different ideological relations to modernity. *Les Guérillères* projects an image of revolution that targets patriarchal discourse and its instrumental determinism. Its warriors, possessed of an avant-garde sensibility, are acutely aware of the historical range of failures that have disabled revolutions: there is the danger of recuperation—the danger reiterated by Marat and Marx, by Bakunin and Guy Debord, that bourgeois ideology will absorb the shocks of revolution and become its opposite. There is the further difficulty of preventing the revolution from turning back on itself, from turning into Thermidor; this danger involves, in the words of Cornelius Castoriadis, "the enormous difficulty involved in extending critique of the existing order in practical and positive ways, [and] the impossibility of assuming the goal of an autonomy that is at once individual and social" (quoted in Starr, 21). How, in other words, do you make a revolution that is not ultimately overcome by its own police apparatus? And finally there is the danger that a revolution waged with the weapons and the languages of patriarchy will always lead back to new guises of patriarchy.[34] Wittig's warriors therefore craft a revolution issuing in a New Order that "foster[s] disorder"(93). The fabric of this new (dis)order is performative and linguistic: each time the revolution threatens to become institutionally legible, the warriors pull the loose thread that unravels it. Thus, *Les Guérillères'* audience is paradoxically meant to cohere around the *threat* of assimilation and coherence; like the Maoist-anarchist wing of '68, the novel sets into motion a dialectic of revolutionary iconoblasty and iconoclasty within which the warriors are the individual agents of collective and constant change. *Les Guérillères'* fictionality partakes of the future perfect tense of revolutionary manifestoes as well as the avant-garde moratorium against interpretation; in the words of one of its contemporary reviewers, "It must be taken seriously but must not be taken literally" (Durand, 75).

By contrast, the journalistic "Combat," by virtue of its form, is embedded from the beginning in a preexisting conversation on the left about dogma rather than praxis. But for all its hesitations and conflicts, it is at points brilliantly argued, as when it declares, "To revolutionaries who say women will be free after the proletariat seizes power, we say, 'All power to the people.' We *are* the people and we want to be represented when power is seized" (paragraph 29). "Combat," like so many other instances of its genre, aims to reframe the putatively universal revolutionary subject. In the student revolt of May 1968, that subject is still formed and informed by the languages of what "Combat" calls "male chauvinism." In 1970, therefore, "Combat" addresses not the untransformed masses but the still recalcitrant left. Its "we" is neither virtual nor provisional: it is the "we" of

[34] This failure proceeds according to what Peter Starr, working in the body of Lacanian theory, calls "the logics of specular doubling."

women on the left who are turning their knowledge of Marxist theory against masculinist currents on the left. Whereas the New Left is content to assign women to a "secondary" position in class struggle, by virtue of their particularity, "Combat" aims to universalize the representation of a group that has been historically condemned to particularity. Finally, for all of the differences between Wittig's manifesto and her novel, that is also the central method of *Les Guérillères.*

Another way to understand the divergences of these two pieces is to acknowledge the semiotic and structural differences between utopian and political manifestoes. It is Alain Meyer's thesis that a utopian manifesto advocates political change by urging "'all-and-quickly' or 'All in Eternity'" (31), while a political manifesto will forcibly fix "due dates" of action, concerning itself with the actual processes of transformation and specific historical moments. For our purposes we may understand *Les Guérillères* as a utopian manifesto and "Combat" as a political manifesto: following Meyer, the latter defines a particular strategy, whereas the former may merely hold forth an image of the ideal society, created by the ideal audience it has already called into being. Even on this count, "Combat" is not a lapse into programmatism so much as a self-conscious feminist attempt at political and discursive intervention, an intervention in a form that is especially resistant to discursive transformations by women—and, perhaps more important, an attempt to engage, systematically and seriously, with the conflicting currents of New Left praxis *in 1970.* If it is neither so aesthetically nor so politically evocative as *Les Guérillères,* its method must nevertheless be recognized as one that aims to present a thoroughgoing form of historical materialism.

In his translator's note to the 1968 student manifesto, "Rapport interdisciplinaire Nanterre, 11 juin 1968" (reprinted in *Partisan Review* shortly after its distribution in Paris), Peter Brooks described the political events in France during and after May 1968 as a "revolution of the word." Seeded by the circulation, among political communities in the West, of agonistic manifestoes by feminists, black separatists, student radicals, and dissenters within the left, this French "revolution" was characterized by "the proliferation of flamboyant tracts composed, mimeographed and distributed almost instantaneously . . . [and] graffiti that appeared on walls everywhere to give voice to the individual's participation in the new order of things. . . . [The students] seized and exercised a language which had belonged to the 'others,' to the forces of alienation, to the government, to official sources of information, to propaganda and advertising, gave it a new vitality and originality, and made it serve imagination in power"

(1968, 536). Ironically, the textual participation of "Combat" in this revolution of the word records the *resistance* of "the word" and the *overdetermination* of "language which had belonged to others." Ultimately, the same political manifesto that signals a "new order of things," feminists may discover, can easily reiterate the same old order.

## Strategies for New Manifestoes

What, then, characterizes the transformative strategies at work in more recent manifestoes, manifestoes written from a poststructuralist, post-60s paradigm that challenges authoritative discourse, the totalizing "we," Marxist economism, and the rhetoric of foundational wholeness? Donna Haraway's "Manifesto for Cyborgs: Science, Technology, and Social Feminism in the 1980s" (1985) is a manifesto scorched almost beyond recognition by poststructuralist transformative strategies. Part science fiction, part deconstructive fantasy, part social(ist) critique, the tract is less a manifesto than a theoretical preamble to the manifestic speech act. "Cyborgs" mutes the manifesto form's conventional urgency and exhortation, foregrounding instead the cultural contexts that have destabilized identity politics in the postmodern era. By calling her essay a manifesto, Haraway both invokes and plays ironically with the form's status as a foundational text, drawing out of it a new political—and discursive—agility that elasticizes the manifesto's multiple discursive junctures. The "we" of the manifesto is represented by the Cyborg itself, a "hybrid of machine and organism, a creature of social reality as well as a creature of fiction" (65). The Cyborg-speaker repeatedly retools itself according to multiple political affinities (not identifications), coalitions (not "natural" matrices), and discursive shifts (not authoritative transitions), ultimately with the aim of forging a nontotalizing, degendered, anticapitalist global politics. As its opening manifestic flourish announces, "Cyborgs" is an "effort to build an ironic political myth faithful to feminism, socialism, and materialism" (65).

In calling for a complicated ironic myth rather than calling an audience to action, "Cyborgs" in part highlights its wariness about manifestic discourse: it cautions against feminist taxonomies that "tend to remake feminist history to appear to be an ideological struggle among coherent types persisting over time . . . [with the result that] all other feminisms are either incorporated or marginalized" (74).[35] We have seen how manifestic dis-

[35] Haraway is here summarizing Katie King's critique of the tendency of certain feminisms to narrativize and thus institutionalize some select version of "women's culture." This, too, we may notice, is a convention of the manifesto. An interesting comparison may be made with Denise Ri-

course relies on etiologies and teleologies; significantly, Haraway negotiates those currents with a discourse constituted by irony. Irony, that foremost postmodern mode of critique, is "about contradictions that do not resolve into larger wholes, even dialectically, about the tension of holding incompatible things together because both or all are necessary and true. Irony is about humor and serious play. It is also a rhetorical strategy and a political method" (65).

Broadly speaking, then, the irony of "Cyborgs" makes ontological and then displaces the categories that were so problematic in "Combat"—Man, Woman, Labor, Family. Its political myths reconceive the political efficacy of the imaginary; its liminal Cyborg speaking position embodies all feminisms and inhabits or transgresses all boundaries. From this broad perspective we may be tempted, perhaps, to see ourselves as back in the world of *Les Guérillères*. Part of Haraway's point, of course, is to assert a guerrilla poetics rooted in, but stretching beyond, political discourse: to this end, "feminist cyborg stories have the task of recoding communication and intelligence to subvert command and control" (94). But the emphasis on myth, here and elsewhere in the text, raises the question of whether Haraway's utopianization of the manifesto form does not in some way interfere with the formation of audience and the mobilization of passional activism—the very problem that *Les Guérillères* suffers in its purely conceptual utopia.

It is difficult, after all, to locate a specific agenda in Haraway's panfeminism. In part this difficulty is a function of the elusiveness of Haraway's addressees: are they the "women in the privileged occupational categories, and particularly in the production of science and technology" (89), Haraway's colleagues in the scientific academy? Are they Silicon Valley's third world women, who perform the labor of the "homework economy" in "loneliness and extreme economic vulnerability" (85), recalling to us the lonely (and significantly absent) housewives of "Combat"? Are they the readers of *Socialist Review,* who, standing on the shoulders of earlier dissenting Marxist feminists such as Wittig and Juliet Mitchell, no longer struggle so immediately with the exigencies of Marxist discourse (and no longer engage with concepts such as surplus labor and means of production), having long since fashioned instead a less dogmatic and more supple discourse? [36] Might they be the women of "Redstockings"? Or are her ad-

---

ley's historiographic thesis that, like "women," "feminism" is a context-bound entity that cannot be assumed to be a static force throughout history, but is rather a reactive agent of local praxis.

[36] See Terry Lovell, 71–76, for an overview of socialist-feminist revisions of Marxist discourse. Iris Marion Young offered a typical description of dual systems theory in 1990 in *Throwing Like a*

dressees the readers of *Feminism/Postmodernism,* where the manifesto was anthologized, five years after its original publication, as "a viewpoint of our [postmodern] times" (Nicholson, 11)?

I suggest that the ambiguity surrounding the addressee of "Cyborgs" effectively forecloses the possibility of an emergent, active "we" and a politics of contestation, and not only because of its emphasis on plurality. In Teresa Ebert's words, "Haraway's argument for 'a conscious coalition, of affinity, of political kinship' [is] based *not* on the shared commitment to end exploitation arising from the division of labor but on a mutual understanding of a 'postmodernist identity of otherness, difference, and specificity'" (109).

It must be said that Haraway is working a different beat than Ebert, and if Haraway's is less materialist than Ebert would wish, it is because she aims to retool the manifesto by pressing an important question that had not been adequately theorized by second-wave feminists such as Wittig: "Who counts as 'us' in my own rhetoric? Which identities are available to ground such a potent political myth called 'us,' and what could motivate enlistment in this collectivity?" (72–73). Questions like this were necessitated by the historical consequences of the New Left schisms that formed around the issues of the sexing of rights, as we have seen. But if Ebert's critique is somewhat decontextualized, Haraway's stance is ultimately unsatisfying. For it betrays a fundamental skepticism concerning collectivity and federation, a skepticism amplified later in the hermetically poststructuralist observation that "one is too few, but two are too many" (96), which seems to imply that the "potent political myth called 'us'" is always *verboten* because always contingent.[37]

---

*Girl and Other Essays:* "The system of male domination, most often called "patriarchy," produces the specific gender oppression of women; the system of the mode of production and class relations produces the class oppression and work alienation of most women. Patriarchy "interacts" with the system of the mode of production—in our case, capitalism—to produce the concrete phenomena of women's oppression in society" (23). She went on to challenge the efficacy of dual systems theory and to call for a unified Marxist-feminist theory, arguing that "all socialist political work should be feminist in its thrust and . . . socialists should recognize feminist concerns as internal to their own," just as "socialist feminists [should] take as a basic principle that feminist work should be anticapitalist in its thrust and should link women's situation with the phenomena of racism and imperialism" (32).

[37] A contrary model to this postmodern impasse can be seen in a manifesto such as the AIDS ACTION NOW!/ACT UP manifesto issued in Montreal in June 1989, which demonstrates the force that can be delivered by a manifesto's *provisional* collectivity. Printed in three languages, with a rapid preamble, ten brief, sharply worded demands, and a closing announcement of three upcoming "Public Actions," this manifesto never speaks a "we." Yet it creates a "we," across three languages and cultures, that signals its assent when that "we" attends the recommended Public Actions and devotes itself to agitation. Compromise does not issue—at least not discursively—from the contingency of this jointly constructed "identity." Like the "we" invoked in the pre-Peterloo

The late-70s work by the display artist Jenny Holzer provides us with a useful contrasting model, for it systematically exploits the rhetorical possibilities of a nonhegemonic "we." In a 1989 interview Holzer recalled her search, in 1978, for a new discursive art model: "I tried to figure out what kind of [discursive art] form would be uneasy and hot and I went to the manifesto. . . . I wanted to move between, or include both sides of manifesto-making, one being the scary side where it's an inflamed rant to no good end, and then the positive side, when it's the most deeply felt description of how the world should be" (Holzer, 16).[38] Holzer's description of the manifesto—the form on which she based her series of "Inflammatory Essays" (1979–82)—here exposes the rhetorical tensions that make manifestoes both functional and problematic. The formal membrane of the manifesto must hold together an unlikely dyad of idiosyncratic rage and utopian social scripture, for it aims to programmatize anger as it creates audiences. As Holzer intimates, the manifesto's inflated and catachrestic rhetoric renders a slim, spectacular margin of error: the manifesto may be a "passionate exposition of the way the world could be if people did things right" (Holzer, 16), but it may just as easily be the very discursive model of the lunatic.

Holzer's "Inflammatory Essays" are eviscerated manifestoes—freed from all explicit or particularized references—that simulate exactly the rhetorical cadences of any number of political manifestoes. They first appeared anonymously—and, in some neighborhoods ubiquitously—in the public spaces of New York City,[39] where they were wheat-pasted alongside theater ads, appeals to Jesus, band schedules. The apocalyptic resonance of their manifestic discourses of prophecy, exhortation, and adjudication is well illustrated by one essay in particular:

REJOICE! OUR TIMES ARE INTOLERABLE.

TAKE COURAGE FOR THE WORST IS A

HARBINGER OF THE BEST. ONLY

DIRE CIRCUMSTANCE CAN PRECIPITATE

---

manifestoes, this "we" forms itself around direct action. And for the temporary coalition forged in Montreal between AIDS ACTION NOW! and ACT UP, the manifesto's collective identity constitutes an ideological sign (in Volosinov's sense), which can mean "we" and "anger" and "immediate action," even as it accomplishes, and records through its capacity as a performative speech act, that angry collective action. I am indebted to Paula Treichler for bringing this manifesto to my attention.

[38] See this edition for a selection of Holzer's "Truisms," "Laments," "Inflammatory Essays," "The Survival Series," and "Living Series."

[39] Interestingly, the manifesto form often exemplifies the discourse of the public *urban* space; it frequently acts as a challenge to the politics of privatization.

THE OVERTHROW OF OPPRESSORS. THE
OLD AND CORRUPT MUST BE LAID TO
WASTE BEFORE THE JUST CAN TRIUMPH.
OPPRESSION IDENTIFIES AND
ISOLATES THE ENEMY. CONFLICT
OF INTEREST MUST BE SEEN FOR
WHAT IT IS. DO NOT SUPPORT
PALLIATIVE GESTURES; THEY CONFUSE
THE PEOPLE AND DELAY THE INEVITABLE
CONFRONTATION. DELAY IS NOT
TOLERATED FOR IT JEOPARDIZES THE
WELL-BEING OF THE MAJORITY.
CONTRADICTION WILL BE HEIGHTENED.
THE RECKONING WILL BE HASTENED
BY THE STAGING OF SEED DISTURBANCES.
THE APOCALYPSE WILL BLOSSOM. (56)

Here, Holzer's ironization of the form enhances, rather than diminishes, the dramatic spectacle of the manifesto's rhetorical power, cut free as it is here from all contextual exigencies.

It would be easy enough to read the "Inflammatory Essay" either as a lyrical, untethered celebration of the passional states that engender manifestoes, or as a purely cynical mode of (postmodern) conceptuality, an experiment in discourse, a word-painting on a manifesto-canvas. But I think we ought to go in a different direction. Holzer's "Inflammatory Essay" echoes Marxist revolutionary discourse in its use of phrases such as "contradiction will be heightened" and "only dire circumstances can precipitate the overthrow of oppressors"; the specter that haunts the hollows of this manifesto is the specter of hegemony, the mother of all political struggle in modernity. To say that the manifesto is "cut free" from contextual exigencies is not to say that it is apolitical—and though this claim may seem to run afoul of my insistence that manifestoes be must read in the context of their production and for their mode of addressing putative addressees, perhaps a return to my discussion of the form's iterability in Chapter 1 will help to clarify the point. In "Signature Event Context," Derrida challenges J. L. Austin's highly conditional definition of the performative as "serious," "contextual," and "intentional"; he offers instead a "differential typology of forms of iteration," by which he seeks to show that no performative utterance could succeed if it "were not identifiable as *conforming* with an iterable model, if it were not then identifiable in some way as a 'citation'" (18).

Few texts would serve as better illustration of Derrida's point than Holzer's manifesto. For the Holzer manifesto is agenda-less, and therefore neither serious nor contextual nor intentional in the authorial sense. But it nevertheless distinguishes itself, and is readily identifiable, as a manifesto. Holzer highlights its iterability—even caricatures it—by the conceptual form of its production: like all of the "Inflammatory Essays," it is exactly one hundred words long, divided into twenty lines, printed in Times Roman Bold, and visually differentiated from the other "Essays" by paper color alone.

What does it mean, though, to say that Holzer's manifesto is a manifesto by virtue of its iteration of formal conventions? To answer this is to mediate some of the distance between Austin and Derrida. For certainly the effective (intelligible) "iterability" of any manifesto would necessarily presume a political context: as we saw in my discussion in Chapter 1 of the manifesto as ideological sign, the manifesto reiterates the urgency of political conditions. And yet Holzer's manifesto carries some semantic weight as a manifesto, *even without a context*. That is, its performativity functions as a ubiquitous reminder of the immanence of political insurgency—a reminder of the safety hatch, as it were, within modernity, of the avenues of critique that Habermas says are built into modernity. Holzer's manifestoes do not discuss matters nicely; they play the dissonant bass line of unreasonableness in modernity's chord structure.

To further this claim, I would point out that the speaking positions in Holzer's contextless manifestoes are notably ungendered: neither feminist nor masculinist, they evince an absolute avoidance of particularization. The universal subject is the dissident subject in these texts, and no sex-marking mediates the power of that position.[40] This is a form of universalism based on what Étienne Balibar calls the "right to politics": although that right is guaranteed in the ideals of the political institutions of modernity, it is positively asserted only when freedom and equality are withheld.[41] Paradoxically, the sheer assertion of the "right to politics" in Holzer's manifestoes is structured by their lack of context, gender, particularity; what the manifestoes frame instead is the passional state engendered by a witholding of rights. Each manifesto sketches a different response; the "Essay" cited earlier invokes revolution; another vaguely frames a scenario of torture; a third presents a subject position characterized by personal ("me"), rather than social ("we"), insurgency:

[40] Notwithstanding Michael Auping's rather general assertion that "since her first *Truisms*, Holzer has continued to prod us with the female side of reality" (34).
[41] See especially Balibar's illuminating discussion of "ideal universalism" (66–72).

DON'T TALK DOWN TO ME. DON'T BE
POLITE TO ME. DON'T TRY TO MAKE ME
FEEL NICE. DON'T RELAX. I'LL CUT THE
SMILE OFF YOUR FACE. YOU THINK I DON'T
KNOW WHAT'S GOING ON. YOU THINK I'M
AFRAID TO REACT. THE JOKE'S ON YOU. . . . (55)

This remarkably supple subject position demands the upper hand in a speech act situation even as it exploits intersubjectivity as a discursive field for personal or political violence. This frame can be pressed into the service of countless speakers mounting countless antagonisms, within conditions of sexism, racism, classism, authority, family, and so forth; the only ideological inflections inhering in this subject position are of the broadest, most polemical kind. Yet all of these utterances point to—and displace—an a priori power differential which is, or at least should be, antithetical to the modern promises of democracy. They offer instead subject positions unrestricted in their availability to women and men, lesbians and cyborgs and Sister Outsiders; they accommodate, even invite, all species of insurgency; and they do so by cutting to the heart of an inequality they never actually name.

Of course, for all of its celebration of performative counterhegemony, the very status of the "Inflammatory Essays" series *as a series*—as a collection of related art objects—returns us to the predicament of audience that qualifies "Cyborgs." When all is said and done, Holzer's fluid speaking positions bear only a gestural weight. By formalizing the manifesto's conventions, Holzer has exposed the form's aesthetic objectivity, its ideological reversibility, in effect calling its rhetorical bluff, much as her avant-garde forebears had done, but with a critical difference: far from aestheticizing political ideology, as Marinetti and Wyndham Lewis did, Holzer inscribes—and highlights—the aesthetic within the political. And this, finally, is where the focus of the "Essays" rests. Her formalisms shift the manifesto form's "historical urgency" to a *trans*temporal discourse of historical urgency. In short, by exploiting the manifesto's margin of error—between lunacy and social praxis—Holzer displays the "I" in the manifesto's "we." Her manifestoes are her own: there is no movement, no "we," no agenda, no action—only the reminder that a public genre exists for such movements, such "we's," and that the modern "right to politics" secures their universal relevance.

I want to close by making explicit what has only been implicit thus far: like so many second-wave polemics, "Combat pour la libération de la femme" was a pioneering feminist manifesto. Its failures can be judged only in relation to its successes, for its appearance marked the nascent activism of the French women's liberation movement: the women who, in the summer of 1970, placed a wreath of flowers at the Tomb of the Unknown Soldier—in memory of his unknown wife—constituted the document's material "we." Its broad identifications with other radical democratic groups—Black Panthers, leftist students—semantically strengthened the base of its appeal, and the depth and seriousness of its engagement with Marxist discourse revealed the historical determinants working against that discourse's theorization of feminism. For these reasons, and for the manifesto's exhausting negotiations of the paradox described by Ann Snitow at the beginning of this chapter—the paradox under which feminism at times embraces and at times rejects the semiotics of the female body, the social grouping known as "woman," and collectivity—the manifesto ought to be of substantial interest to historians of feminist polemics.

As Claude Abastado has written, the manifesto "prepares and sketches a restructuring of the discursive field, the installation of new forms of expression." (11) Although this description has the unfortunate effect of taking the revolution out of the manifesto, it does illuminate the problems facing second-wave manifesto writers. For them, production of a manifesto was no mere "sketch" job. It was a task undertaken with stolen pens and a palimpsest, a decoding and recoding of inherited discourse, a creation of collective and transitory political subjecthood. In this regard, the biggest liability for "Combat" was perhaps its audience: like those of Olympe de Gouges or Mina Loy, Wittig's attempts to integrate a feminist program into a left avant-garde necessitated an unwarranted involvement with gendered rhetorical traditions. For the authors of all of these works, the mere (and immediately necessary) act of addressing "their own" on the left meant (immediately, necessarily) differentiating themselves from that left. And though Wittig would go on to argue, later in her career, that in order to make a group truly visible one must make it universal, the fact remains that for all of these feminist polemicists, the very notion of the universal required continuous pressure, constant transformation and resignification, in order for it to support the weight of women in modernity.

# Conclusion

## Now and Again

"Combat pour la libération de la femme" and *Les Guérillères* were written a few years after the publication of Guy Debord's influential *Society of the Spectacle* (*La Société du spectacle*), in which Debord, the leading member of the avant-garde Situationist International, meditated on "the spectacle" as a symptom of commodification and alienation in late capitalism. *Society of the Spectacle* is composed of a numbered set of manifesto-like Nietzschean aphorisms, all of them rhythmically compressed and terse with the syntax of condemnation, as illustrated by this proclamation at the end of the sectioned titled "Time and History": "The time officially promoted all around the world as the *general time of society,* since it signifies nothing beyond those special interests which constitute it, is therefore not general in character, but *particular*"(107). Debord's observation about the universalist-particularist contradictions that are strung across modern enunciations of time ("my time is *the* time") anticipates Homi Bhabha's assertion, a generation later, that modernity "is about the historical construction of a specific position of historical enunciation and address. It privileges those who 'bear witness,' those who are 'subjected'" (1994, 243). Modernity privileges, in other words, those who appropriate or who are granted a vantage point from which specific forms of cultural temporality are empowered as universal. Modernity is not a seamless temporal entity characterized by period, progress, and development, though its narratives often prefer that plotline. It is, instead, subject to the very discontinuities of time that its narratives seek to disguise: different "times" coexist within the same discrete historical moment, just as surely as homologous "times" exist across centuries. It has been my argument that, although the mani-

festo form is itself a product of modernity, and although it aims to produce modern change, it also disrupts the smooth temporal surface of
modern history by marking for us precisely those moments when "history" repeats itself, and also, conversely, when seemingly cogent historical
moments break into nonsynchronous shards.

As an example of the latter function, let me return briefly to the French
Revolution. Even as the news of "liberté, egalité, fraternité" was making its
way into the Caribbean colony of Saint Domingue, acts of repression
against slaves and mulattoes were intensified by colonial whites who had,
paradoxically, sworn allegiance to the Revolution. By October of 1790, the
French National Assembly had retracted the Rights of Man for the
colonies, proclaiming, "No laws concerning the status of persons should be
decreed for the colonies."[1] The Revolution, in other words, stopped at the
racialized and gendered borders of "France": under the jurisdiction of the
Revolution, slaves would remain the property of white colonialists;
women, as we have seen, would be *citoyennes* in name only. The subsequent Haitian revolution, which was at least partly born of this act of cir-
cumvention, in turn took its own rhetoric from its hated uncle. On the
first day of 1804, when General Jean-Jacques Dessalines declared Haiti's independence, he commanded its subjects to "swear by the entire universe,
and by posterity, and by our own names, to renounce France forever, and
to die rather than live under its domination, to fight to the last breath for
the independence of our country."[2]

Using precisely the language deployed by French revolutionaries against
the French king, Dessalines's manifesto atomizes a putatively universal and
coherent "moment" of "the revolution": the myth of one-and-the-same
revolution is displaced by the situatedness of these competing bodies of
(temporally related) manifestoes, thereby exposing the varying simultaneous "times" of unevenly developed and unequally valorized revolutions.
Furthermore, it must be said that the *absence* of manifestoes elsewhere in
the European empire at this time suggests even more sharply how uneven
was the implementation of universal rights bodied forth through modernity. Paul Gilroy points out that "particularly in the slave period, but also
after it, there are few committee minutes, manifestos, or other program-

[1] Quoted in Madison Smartt Bell, 507. See Bell's "Chronology of Events" for a precisely re-
searched account of the uneven developments between French republicanism and Haitian independence (505–23).
[2] In *The Black Jacobins*, C. L. R. James puts these words into Dessaline's mouth: "[Toussaint]
still believes in liberty and equality and a whole lot of nonsense that he had learned from the
French. All I have learnt from the French is that without arms in my hand there is no freedom"
(104).

matic documents" (119) that record the human costs among African Americans of the "lag-time" of modernity; autonomy, freedom, and literacy are, after all, the ephemeral conditions of possibility for the successful implementation of dissent. A "revolutionary moment" contains its own conceptual nemeses in the forms of static hunger and static subordination, which are almost always present in some measure. A recognition of this contradiction, however, does not necessarily justify the historical truism that dooms revolution to the fate of eating its children. Rather, and rather more pointedly, to see this contradiction is to recognize history as a cluster of concurrent "times." Manifestoes will remind us, again and again, that the "general time of society" is always subject to particular revolutionary contestation and critique.

The feminist manifestoes produced in the 1960s suggest something slightly different about the universalizing claims made for a "revolutionary moment." The legibility of manifestoes circulating within and among political avant-garde groups was secured through their participation in a long tradition of manifestic dissent that had recently been honed to iconoclastic perfection in the successes of dadaist, surrealist, and situationist manifestoes. But that legibility was also tied to the logic of the nineteenth-century "permanent revolution," according to which all revolution is universal, and the universal subject of all revolution is the product of Enlightenment ideology—that is, putatively "identical" to European male subjectivity. The rapidly splintering "we's" of sixties manifestoes suggest not only that modernity's promises were not being kept, but also that "revolution" itself entailed a level of discursive gatekeeping. And as we have seen, the women's liberation movement was especially vulnerable to this trick of revolutionary discourse: the pervasive voice of "the" revolution, spoken by men, turned out to be partial in the extreme, as the example of "Combat" suggests. While women were invited rhetorically into the revolutionary moment of the sixties (or, for that matter, of the teens), their demands were vetted at the door by New Left leadership. They were told that their time was "not now, not yet," even as the discourse of the manifestoes through which those radical invitations were made promised changes in time "now, immediately."

It is precisely this feature of the manifesto—the emphasis on "now, not later"—that turns modernity on its axis to reveal its history not only as one of progress, but also as one of conflicts and repetitions. When Diggers threaten that they will "stand up now"; when women of the seventeenth- and eighteenth-century bread riots demand a *prix juste* now; when the First International calls for revolution now; when symbolists insist that they hear the call of the tocsin now; when Suffragettes will go to prison to have the vote now, not during the next session or when they have "earned" it; when Fanon declares that now is the time to turn Europe back upon itself; when the mothers of the plaza de Mayo declare that they will have justice for their disappeared children now; and when these insistent themes are spoken again and again, across countries and centuries *in the same locutions,* it can only mean that "history" is always repeating itself. More to the point, it means that history is nonsynchronous and multidirectional. Hunger and injustice and unfreedom persist simultaneously with and against the grain of "modern times."

This is to say, finally, that the discrete and discontinuous experiences of modernity are themselves the conditions of the production of the manifesto, the conditions to which the manifesto answers in the voice of chiliastic prophecy. From the first emergence of the idea of the universal subject until its ever-deferred completion, the time of the manifesto will always be now.

# Works Cited

Abastado, Claude. "Introduction à l'analyse des manifestes." *littérature,* special number on l'Écriture manifestaire, 39 (October 1980): 3–11.

Abraham, Julie. "The Way We Were." Review of *Daring to Be Bad: Radical Feminism in America, 1967–1975,* by Alice Echols. *The Nation,* August 27–September 6, 1990, 209–12.

Alcoff, Linda. "Cultural Feminism versus Post-Structuralism: The Identity Crisis in Feminist Theory." *Signs* 13.3 (Spring 1988): 405–36.

Alexander, Sally. "Women, Class, and Sexual Differences in the 1830s and 1840s: Some Reflections on the Writing of a Feminist History." In Lovell 1990, 28–50.

Anderson, Amanda. "Debatable Performances: Restaging Contentious Feminisms." *Social Text* 54 (Spring 1998): 1–24.

——. "Cryptonormativism and Double Gestures: The Politics of Post-Structuralism." *Cultural Critique* 21 (1992): 63–95.

——. *Tainted Souls and Painted Faces: The Rhetoric of Fallenness in Victorian Culture.* Ithaca: Cornell University Press, 1993.

Apollonio, Umbro, ed. and intro. *Futurist Manifestos.* Translated by Robert Brain et al. New York: Viking, 1970.

Applewhite, Harriet Bronson, and Darline Gay Levy, eds. *Women and Politics in the Age of Democratic Revolution.* Ann Arbor: University of Michigan Press, 1993.

Ardis, Ann L. *New Women, New Novels: Feminism and Early Modernism.* New Brunswick: Rutgers University Press, 1990.

Arendt, Hannah. *On Revolution.* New York: Viking, 1963.

Aronowitz, Stanley. "Is a Democracy Possible? The Decline of the Public in the American Debate." In Robbins 1993, 75–92.

——. "Postmodernism and Politics." *Social Text* 18 (Winter 1987–88): 99–115.

Asian and Pacific Students Association. "Pamphlet." *Samkaleen Janmat.* April 20–May 5, 1990. Reprinted in *The Collective Voice* (November–December 1991): 30.

Augustine, Jane. "A Feminist Modernist Americanizes the Language of Futurism." *Mid-Hudson Language Studies* 12.1 (1989): 89–101.

Auping, Michael. "Reading Holzer or Speaking in Tongues." In *Jenny Holzer: The Venice Installation.* Buffalo: Buffalo Fine Arts Academy, 1990, 25–37.

Austin, J. L. *How to Do Things with Words.* 2nd ed. Edited by J. O. Urmson and Marina Sbisa. Cambridge: Harvard University Press, 1962.

Baker, Keith Michael. "Defining the Public Sphere in Eighteenth-Century France: Variations on a Theme by Habermas." In Calhoun 1993, 181–211.

Bakhtin, M. M. "The Problem of Speech Genres." In *Speech Genres and Other Late Essays.* Translated by Vern W. McGee. Edited by Caryl Emerson and Michael Holquist. Austin: University of Texas Press, 1986, 60–102.

Balibar, Étienne. "Ambiguous Universality." *differences* 7.1 (1995): 48–74.

Battaglia, Salvatore, ed. *Grande dizionario della lingua italiana.* 17 vols. Turin: Unione Tipografico-Editrice Torinese, 1975.

Beauman, Sally. Review of *Les Guérillères* by Monique Wittig. *New York Times Book Review,* October 10, 1971, 5, 14.

Bell, Madison Smartt. *All Souls' Rising.* New York: Pantheon, 1995.

Belsey, Catherine. "Constructing the Subject: Deconstructing the Text." In *Feminist Criticism and Social Change: Sex, Class, and Race in Literature and Culture*. New York: Methuen, 1985, 45–64.

Benhabib, Seyla. "Epistemologies of Postmodernism: A Rejoinder to Jean-François Lyotard." *New German Critique* 33 (1984): 103–26.

Benstock, Shari. *Women of the Left Bank: Paris, 1900–1940*. Austin: University of Texas Press, 1986.

Benveniste, Émile. *Problems in General Linguistics* [1966]. Translated by Mary Elizabeth Meek. Miami: University of Miami Press, 1971.

Berman, Marshall. *All That Is Solid Melts into Air: The Experience of Modernity*. New York: Simon and Schuster, 1982.

Best, Geoffrey, ed. *The Permanent Revolution: The French Revolution and Its Legacy, 1789–1989*. London: Fontana Press, 1988.

Bhabha, Homi. *The Location of Culture*. London: Routledge, 1994.

——, ed. *Nation and Narration*. London: Routledge, 1990.

Blum, Cinzia Sartini. *The Other Modernism: F. T. Marinetti's Futurist Fiction of Power*. Berkeley: University of California Press, 1996.

——. "Rhetorical Strategies and Gender in Marinetti's Futurist Manifesto." *Italica* 67.2 (Summer 1990): 196–211.

——. The Scarred Womb of the Futurist Woman." *Carte Italiane* 8 (1986–87): 14–30.

Brooks, Peter. "The Fourth World, Part II: Documents." *Partisan Review* 35:4 (Fall 1968): 536–41.

——. "The Fourth World, Part III." *Partisan Review* 36:1 (Winter 1969): 11–35.

Broude, Norma. "Miriam Schapiro and 'Femmage': Reflections on the Conflict between Decoration and Abstraction in Twentieth-Century Art." In Broude and Garrard 1982, 315–29.

Broude, Norma, and Mary D. Garrard, eds. *Feminism and Art History: Questioning the Litany*. New York: Harper and Row, 1982.

"The Brunswick Manifesto" [July 25, 1792]. In Stewart, 307–11.

Bürger, Peter. *The Theory of the Avant-Garde* [1974]. Translated by Michael Shaw. Foreword by Jochen Schulte-Sasse. Vol. 4, *Theory and History of Literature*. Minneapolis: University of Minnesota Press, 1984.

Burke, Carolyn. *Becoming Modern: The Life of Mina Loy*. New York: Farrar, Straus and Giroux, 1996.

——. "Mina Loy's 'Love Songs' and the Limits of Imagism." *San Jose Studies* 13.3 (Fall 1987): 37–46.

——. "The New Poetry and the New Woman: Mina Loy." In Middlebrook and Yalom 1985, 37–57.

Burke, Peter, and Roy Porter, eds. *The Social History of Language*. Cambridge Studies in Oral and Literate Culture. Vol. 12. Cambridge: Cambridge University Press, 1987.

Burnett, David Graham. "Sexual Rhetoric and Personal Identity in Théophile Gautier's 'Preface' to *Mademoiselle de Maupin*." *French Literature Series* 7 (1980): 38–45.

Bush, Ronald. "Ezra Pound (1885–1972)." In B. Scott 1990, 353–71.

Butler, Judith. *Gender Trouble: Feminism and the Subversion of Identity*. New York: Routledge, 1990.

Cahm, Caroline. *Kropotkin and the Rise of Revolutionary Anarchism, 1872–1886*. Cambridge: Cambridge University Press, 1989.

Calhoun, Craig, ed. *Habermas and the Public Sphere*. Cambridge: MIT Press, 1993.

Campbell, Karlyn Kohrs, ed. *Man Cannot Speak for Her.* Vol. 2: *Key Texts of the Early Feminists.* New York: Praeger, 1989.

Cheetham, Mark A. *The Rhetoric of Purity: Essentialist Theory and the Advent of Abstract Painting.* Cambridge: Cambridge University Press, 1991.

Chipp, Herschel B., ed. *Theories of Modern Art: A Source Book by Artists and Critics.* Berkeley: University of California Press, 1968.

Cianci, Giovanni. "Futurism and the English Avant-Garde: The Early Pound between Imagism and Vorticism." *Arbeiten aus Anglistik und Amerikanistik* 1 (1981): 17–27.

Clarétie, Jules, ed. *La Commune: Paris—Versailles—La Province, 18 mars–27 mai 1871.* Vol. 2 of *Les Murailles politiques françaises.* 3 vols. Paris: L. Le Chevalier, 1874.

Clark, Suzanne. *Sentimental Modernism: Women Writers and the Revolution of the Word.* Bloomington: Indiana University Press, 1991.

Clarke, Bruce. *Dora Marsden and Early Modernism: Gender, Individualism, Science.* Ann Arbor: University of Michigan Press, 1996.

Collins, Marie, and Sylvie Weir Sayre, eds. *Les Femmes en France.* New York: Scribner's, 1974.

Combahee River Collective. "A Black Feminist Statement" [1977]. In *All the Women Are White, All the Blacks Are Men, but Some of Us Are Brave: Black Women's Studies.* Edited by Gloria T. Hull, Patricia Bell Scott, and Barbara Smith. New York: Feminist Press, 1982, 13–22.

Condorcet, Marquis de [Marie-Jean-Antoine-Nicolas Caritat]. *Condorcet: Selected Writings.* Edited and introduced by Keith Michael Baker. Indianapolis: Bobbs-Merrill, 1976.

Conover, Roger L. "Introduction." In *Mina Loy: The Last Lunar Baedecker.* Edited and introduced by Roger Conover. Highlands, N.J.: Jargon Society, 1982, i–lx.

——, ed. *The Lost Lunar Baedecker: Poems by Mina Loy.* New York: Farrar, Straus, Giroux, 1996.

Cork, Richard. *Vorticism and Abstract Art in the First Machine Age.* Vol. 1. London: Gordon Fraser, 1976.

Cornell, Drucilla. "Comments on Rita Felski's 'The Doxa of Difference': Diverging Differences." *Signs* 23.1 (Fall 1997): 41–56.

Coster, Robert. "A Mite Cast into the Common Treasury: or, Queries propounded (for all men to consider of) by him who desireth to advance the work of publick Community." In Hopton, *Digger Tracts, 1649–50.* London: Aporia, 1989.

Cott, Nancy F. *The Grounding of Modern Feminism.* New Haven: Yale University Press, 1987.

Crowder, Dianne Griffin. "Amazons and Mothers? Monique Wittig, Hélène Cixous, and Theories of Women's Writing." *Contemporary Literature* 24.2 (1983): 117–44.

Dalla Costa, Mariarosa, and Selma James. "Women and the Subversion of the Community" [1972]. In *Materialist Feminism: A Reader in Class, Difference, and Women's Lives.* Edited by Rosemary Hennessey and Chrys Ingraham. New York: Routledge, 1997, 40–53.

Dangerfield, George. *The Strange Death of Liberal England: 1910–1914.* [1935]. New York: Perigee, 1980.

Darnton, Robert, and Daniel Roche, eds. *Revolution in Print: The Press in France, 1775–1800.* Berkeley: University of California Press, 1989.

Dasenbrock, Reed Way. *The Literary Vorticism of Ezra Pound and Wyndham Lewis: Towards the Condition of Painting.* Baltimore: Johns Hopkins University Press, 1985.

Davis, Jill. "The New Woman and the New Life." In Gardner and Rutherford 1992, 17–36.

de Baecque, Antoine. "Pamphlets: Libel and Political Mythology." In Darnton and Roche 1989, 165–76.

de Courtivron, Isabelle. "Women in Movement(s): 1968–1978." *French Literature Series* 7 (1980): 77–87.

de Gouges, Olympe. "The Declaration of the Rights of Woman" [1791]. In Levy, Applewhite, and Johnson 1979, 87–96.

Dean, Tim. "Paring His Fingernails: Homosexuality and Joyce's Impersonalist Aesthetic." In *Quare Joyce.* Edited by Joseph Valente. Ann Arbor: University of Michigan Press, 1998, 241–72.

Debord, Guy, *The Society of the Spectacle.* Translated by Donald Nicholson-Smith. New York: Zone Books, 1994.

Deem, Melissa D. "From Bobbitt to SCUM: Re-memberment, Scatological Rhetorics, and Feminist Strategies in the Contemporary United States." *Public Culture* 8 (Spring 1996): 511–37.

Derrida, Jacques. "Declarations of Independence." *New Political Science* 15 (Summer 1986): 7–15.

———. "Signature Event Context" [1977]. Translated by Samuel Weber and Jeffrey Mehlman. In *Limited Inc.* Edited by Gerald Graff. Evanston: Northwestern University Press, 1988, 1–23.

Dinwiddy, John. "English Radicals and the French Revolution, 1800–1850." In Furet and Ozouf 1989b, 447–66.

Dow, F. D. *Radicalism in the English Revolution: 1640–1660.* Oxford: Basil Blackwell, 1985.

Drucker, Johanna. *Theorizing Modernism: Visual Art and the Critical Tradition.* Interpretations of Art. New York: Columbia University Press, 1994.

DuBois, Ellen Carol. "Woman Suffrage and the Left: An International Socialist-Feminist Perspective." *New Left Review* 186 (March–April 1991): 20–45.

DuPlessis, Rachel Blau, "'Seismic Orgasm': Sexual Intercourse, Gender Narratives, Lyric Ideology in Mina Loy." In *Studies in Historical Change,* ed. Ralph Cohen. Charlottesville: University Press of Virginia, 1992, 264–91.

Duffy, Jean. "Women and Language in *Les Guérillères* by Monique Wittig." *Stanford French Review* 7.3 (1983): 399–412.

Duncan, Carol. "Virility and Domination in Early Twentieth-Century Vanguard Painting." In Broude and Garrard 1982, 293–313.

Dunlavy, John. *MANIFESTO, or a Declaration of the doctrine and practice of the Church of Christ.* Kentucky, 1818. Rare Books Division, Special Collections, University of Virginia Library.

Durand, Laura G. "Heroic Feminism as Art." *Novel: A Forum on Fiction* 8.1 (Fall 1974): 71–77.

Ebert, Teresa. *Ludic Feminism and After: Postmodernism, Desire, and Labor in Late Capitalism.* Ann Arbor: University of Michigan Press, 1996.

Echols, Alice. *Daring to Be Bad: Radical Feminism in America, 1967–1975.* Foreword by Ellen Willis. Minneapolis: University of Minnesota Press, 1989.

Eley, Geoff. "Nations, Publics, and Political Cultures: Placing Habermas in the Nineteenth Century." In Calhoun 1993, 289–339.

Elliott, Bridget, and Jo-Ann Wallace. *Women Artists and Modernist (Im)positionings.* New York: Routledge, 1994.

Ellmann, Richard, and Charles Feidelson, Jr. *The Modern Tradition: Backgrounds of Modern Literature.* New York: Oxford University Press, 1965.

Epstein, James, and Dorothy Thompson, eds. *The Chartist Experience: Studies in Working-Class Radicalism and Culture, 1830–60.* London: Macmillan, 1982.

Fanon, Frantz. *The Wretched of the Earth.* Translated by Constance Farrington. New York: Grove, 1963.

Farge, Arlette. *Subversive Words: Public Opinion in Eighteenth-Century France.* Translated by Rosemary Morris. University Park: Pennsylvania State University Press, 1995.

Farnell, Gary. "A 'Competition of Discourses' in the French Revolution." *Literature and History,* 2nd ser. 2.2 (Autumn 1991): 35–53.

Felski, Rita. *Beyond Feminist Aesthetics: Feminist Literature and Social Change.* Cambridge: Harvard University Press, 1989.

———. "The Doxa of Difference." *Signs* 23.1 (Fall 1997): 1–21.

———. *The Gender of Modernity.* Cambridge: Harvard University Press, 1995.

Ferguson, Moira, ed. and intro. *First Feminists: British Women Writers, 1578–1799.* Bloomington: Indiana University Press, 1985.

Ferguson, Moira, and Janet Todd. *Mary Wollstonecraft.* Boston: Twayne, 1985. Excerpted in Poston 1988, 317–28.

Finn, Robin. "Image Isn't Everything! Agassi Wins Open on Substance." *New York Times,* September 11, 1995, B1.

Fitzsimmons, Linda, and Viv Gardner, eds. and intro. *New Woman Plays.* London: Methuen, 1991.

Flint, F. S. "Imagisme." *Poetry* 1.6 (March 1913): 198–200.

Foner, Philip S., ed. *We, the Other People: Alternative Declarations of Independence by Labor Groups, Farmers, Woman's Rights Advocates, Socialists, and Blacks, 1829–1975.* Urbana: University of Illinois Press, 1976.

Foucault, Michel. *The History of Sexuality,* Vol. 1. *An Introduction.* New York: Vintage, 1978.

Fowler, Rowena. "Documents: Why Did Suffragettes Attack Works of Art?" *Journal of Women's History* 2.3 (Winter 1991): 109–25.

Fraisse, Geneviève, and Michelle Perrot, eds. *A History of Women in the West.* General editors Georges Duby and Michelle Perrot. Vol. 4. *Emerging Feminism from Revolution to World War.* Cambridge: Belknap/Harvard University Press, 1993.

Fraser, Nancy. "Rethinking the Public Sphere: A Contribution to the Critique of Actually Existing Democracy." *Social Text* 25/26 (1990): 56–80.

Friedberg, Anne. *Window Shopping: Cinema and the Postmodern.* Berkeley: University of California Press, 1993.

Fry, Roger. *A Roger Fry Reader.* Edited and introduced by Christopher Reed. Chicago: University of Chicago Press, 1996.

Furet, François. *Interpreting the French Revolution.* Translated by Elborg Forster. Cambridge: Cambridge University Press, 1981.

———, ed. *The French Revolution and the Creation of Modern Political Culture.* Vol. 3. *The Transformation of Political Culture, 1789–1848.* Oxford: Pergamon, 1989b.

Furet, François, and Mona Ozouf, eds. *A Critical Dictionary of the French Revolution.* Translated by Arthur Goldhammer. Cambridge: Belknap/Harvard University Press, 1989a.

Fuss, Diana. *Essentially Speaking: Feminism, Nature, and Difference.* New York: Routledge, 1990.

Gambrell, Alice. *Women Intellectuals, Modernism, and Difference: Transatlantic Culture, 1919–1945*. Cambridge: Cambridge University Press, 1997.

Gardner, Vivien. "Introduction." In Gardner and Rutherford 1992, 1–14.

Gardner, Vivien, and Susan Rutherford, eds. *The New Woman and Her Sisters: Feminism and Theatre, 1850–1914*. Ann Arbor: University of Michigan Press, 1992.

Gilbert, Sandra M., and Susan Gubar. *No Man's Land: The Place of the Woman Writer in the Twentieth Century*. Vol. 1. *The War of the Words*. New Haven: Yale University Press, 1988.

Gilchrist, J., and W. J. Murray, eds. *The Press in the French Revolution: A Selection of Documents Taken from the Press of the Revolution for the Years 1789–1794*. New York: St. Martin's, 1971.

Giles, Steve, ed. *Theorizing Modernism: Essays in Critical Theory*. London: Routledge, 1993.

Gilroy, Paul. *The Black Atlantic: Modernity and Double Consciousness*. Cambridge: Harvard University Press, 1993.

Godineau, Dominique. "Daughters of Liberty and Revolutionary Citizens." In Fraisse and Perrot 1993, 15–32.

———. "Masculine and Feminine Political Practice during the French Revolution, 1793–Year III." In Applewhite and Levy 1990, 61–80.

Gourmont, Rémy de. *The Natural Philosophy of Love* [1903]. Translated and introduced by Ezra Pound. London: Neville Spearman, 1957.

Green, Barbara. *Spectacular Confessions: Autobiography, Performative Activism, and the Sites of Suffrage, 1905–1938*. New York: St. Martin's, 1997.

Greimas, A. J. *On Meaning: Selected Writings in Semiotic Theory*. Translated by Paul J. Perron and Frank H. Collins. Minneapolis: University of Minnesota Press, 1987.

Greimas, A. J., and J. Courtés. *Semiotics and Language: An Analytical Dictionary* [1979]. Translated by Larry Crist et al. Bloomington: Indiana University Press, 1982.

Gullickson, Gay L. *Unruly Women of Paris: Images of the Commune*. Ithaca: Cornell University Press, 1996.

Guralnick, Elissa S. "Radical Politics in Mary Wollstonecraft's *A Vindication of the Rights of Women*." In Poston 1988, 308–17.

Habermas, Jürgen. "Modernity: An Unfinished Project" [1980]. Translated by Nicholas Walker. In *Habermas and the Unfinished Project of Modernity*. Edited by Maurizio Passerin d'Entrèves and Seyla Benhabib. Cambridge: MIT Press, 1997, 38–55.

———. *The Philosophical Discourse of Modernity: Twelve Lectures* [1985]. Translated by Frederick G. Lawrence. Cambridge: MIT Press, 1995.

———. "The Public Sphere: An Encyclopedia Article" [1964]. *New German Critique* 3 (1974): 49–55.

———. *The Structural Transformation of the Public Sphere: An Inquiry into a Category of Bourgeois Society* [1962]. Translated by Thomas Bürger. Cambridge: MIT Press, 1989.

Hall, Stuart. "Racism and Reaction." In *Five Views of Multi-Racial Britain*. London: Commission for Racial Equality, 1978, 27–40.

———. "The Toad in the Garden: Thatcherism among the Theorists." In Nelson and Grossberg 1988, 35–73.

Hall, Stuart, and Bill Schwarz. "State and Society, 1880–1930." In *The Hard Road to Renewal: Thatcherism and the Crisis of the Left*. London: Verso, 1988, 95–122.

Haller, William, and Godfrey Davies, eds. *The Leveller Tracts, 1647–1653*. Gloucester, Mass.: Peter Smith, 1964.

Hanscombe, Gillian, and Virginia L. Smyers. *Writing for Their Lives: The Modernist Women, 1910–1940*. London: Women's Press, 1987.

Hansen, Miriam. "T. E. Hulme, Mercenary of Modernism, or, Fragments of Avant-garde Sensibility in Pre–World War I Britain." *ELH* 47 (Summer 1980): 335–85.

Haraway, Donna. "A Manifesto for Cyborgs: Science, Technology, and Socialist Feminism in the 1980s." *Socialist Review* 80 (1985): 65–107.

Harrison, Brian. *Peaceable Kingdom: Stability and Change in Modern Britain*. Oxford: Clarendon, 1982.

Harrison, Charles. *English Art and Modernism, 1900–1939*. Bloomington: Indiana University Press, 1981.

Hartmann, Heidi. "The Unhappy Marriage of Marxism and Feminism: Towards a More Progressive Union." In *Women and Revolution*. Edited by Lydia Sargent. Boston: South End Press, 1981, 1–41.

Henderson, Katherine Usher, and Barbara F. McManus, eds. *Half Humankind: Contexts and Texts of the Controversy about Women in England, 1540–1640*. Urbana: University of Illinois Press, 1985.

Hennessy, Rosemary. *Materialist Feminism and the Politics of Discourse*. New York: Routledge, 1993.

Higonnet, Anne. "Writing the Gender of the Image: Art Criticism in Late Nineteenth-Century France." *Genders* 6 (Fall 1989): 60–73.

Higonnet, Patrice. "Sans-culottes." In Furet and Ozouf 1989a, 393–99.

Hill, Christopher. *The Century of Revolution: 1603–1714*. New York: Norton, 1961.

———. "Introduction." In *Winstanley: "The Law of Freedom" and Other Writings*. Edited by Christopher Hill. Cambridge: Cambridge University Press, 1975, 1–35.

———. *The World Turned Upside Down: Radical Ideas during the English Revolution*. London: Penguin, 1972.

———, ed. *Pamphlet Wars: Prose in the English Revolution*. London: Frank Cass, 1992.

Holzer, Jenny. *Jenny Holzer*. Edited by Diane Waldman. New York: Harry N. Abrams, 1989.

Hopton, Andrew, ed. *Digger Tracts, 1649–50*. London: Aporia, 1989.

Hufton, Olwen H. *Women and the Limits of Citizenship in the French Revolution*. Toronto: University of Toronto Press, 1992.

Hulme, T. E. *Speculations*. Edited by Herbert Read. Foreword by Jacob Epstein. London: Kegan Paul, 1936.

"The Humble Petition" [Levellers, 1648]. In Haller and Davies 1964, 148–55.

Hunt, Lynn. *Politics, Culture, and Class in the French Revolution*. Berkeley: University of California Press, 1984.

———. "Pornography and the French Revolution." In *The Invention of Pornography: Obscenity and the Origins of Modernity, 1500–1800*. Edited by Lynn Hunt. New York: Zone, 1996, 301–39.

———, ed. *Eroticism and the Body Politic*. Baltimore: Johns Hopkins University Press, 1991.

Huyssen, Andreas. "Mass Culture as Woman: Modernism's Other." In *After the Great Divide: Modernism, Mass Culture, Postmodernism*. Bloomington: Indiana University Press, 1986, 44–62.

Hyder, R., ed. *Swinburne Replies*. Syracuse: Syracuse University Press, 1966.

Hynes, Samuel. *The Edwardian Turn of Mind*. Princeton: Princeton University Press, 1968.

"The Jacobins Denounce the Society of Revolutionary Republican Women" [September 6, 1793]. In Levy, Applewhite, and Johnson 1979, 182–85.

James, C. L. R. *The Black Jacobins.* In *The C. L. R. James Reader.* Edited by Anna
    Grimshaw. Oxford: Blackwell, 1992, 67–111.
Jameson, Fredric. "On Negt and Kluge." In Robbins 1993, 42–74.
———. *The Political Unconscious: Narrative as a Socially Symbolic Act.* Ithaca: Cornell
    University Press, 1981.
Janes, R. M. "On the Reception of Mary Wollstonecraft's *A Vindication of the Rights of
    Woman.*" In Poston 1988, 297–307.
Jaudon, Valerie, and Joyce Kozloff. "'Art Hysterical Notions' of Progress and Culture."
    *Heresies* 4 (Winter 1978): 38–42.
Johnson, Richard. *The French Communist Party versus the Students: Revolutionary
    Politics in May–June 1968.* New Haven: Yale University Press, 1972.
Jones, Gareth Stedman. "The Language of Chartism." In Epstein and Thompson 1982,
    3–58.
Jones, Henry Arthur. *Plays.* Edited and introduced by Russell Jackson. Cambridge:
    Cambridge University Press, 1982.
Joreen. "The Bitch Manifesto" [1970]. In *Radical Feminism.* Edited by Anne Koedt,
    Ellen Levine, and Anita Rapone. New York: Quadrangle, 1973. 50–59.
Kadish, Doris Y., and François Massardier-Kenney, eds. *Translating Slavery: Gender and
    Race in French Women's Writing, 1783–1823.* Kent: Kent State University Press, 1994.
Kadlec, David. "Pound, *BLAST,* and Syndicalism." *ELH* 60 (1993): 1015–31.
Kaplan, E. Ann. "Feminism/Oedipus/Postmodernism: The Case of MTV." In
    *Postmodernism and Its Discontents: Theories, Practices.* Edited by E. Ann Kaplan.
    London: Verso, 1988, 30–44.
Kayman, Martin A. *The Modernism of Ezra Pound: The Science of Poetry.* London:
    Macmillan, 1986.
Kelly, Joan. *Women, History, and Theory.* Chicago: University of Chicago Press, 1984.
Kenner, Hugh. *The Pound Era.* Berkeley: University of California Press, 1971.
Kent, Susan Kingsley. *Sex and Suffrage in Britain: 1860–1914.* Princeton: Princeton
    University Press, 1987.
Kenyon, J. P., ed. and intro. *The Stuart Constitution: Documents and Commentary.*
    Cambridge: Cambridge University Press, 1962.
Klancher, Jon P. *The Making of English Reading Audiences, 1790–1832.* Madison:
    University of Wisconsin Press, 1987.
Kouidis, Virginia. *Mina Loy: American Modernist Poet.* Baton Rouge: Louisiana State
    University Press, 1980.
Kramerae, Cheris, and Paula Treichler. *A Feminist Dictionary.* London: Pandora, 1985.
Krauss, Rosiland. *The Originality of the Avant-Garde and Other Myths.* Cambridge:
    MIT Press, 1986.
Landes, Joan B. *Women and the Public Sphere in the Age of the French Revolution.*
    Ithaca: Cornell University Press, 1988.
Lazarus, Neil, Steven Evans, Anthony Arnove, and Anne Menke. "The Necessity of
    Universalism." *differences* 7.1 (Spring 1995): 75–145.
Le Hir, Marie-Pierre. "Feminism, Theatre, Race: *L'Esclavage des noirs.*" In Kadish and
    Massardier-Kenney 1994, 65–83.
Lesbian Avengers Civil Rights Organizing Project. "Out Against the Right: The Dyke
    Manifesto." New York, ca. 1994.
Levenson, Michael. *A Genealogy of Modernism: A Study of English Literary Doctrine,
    1908–1922.* Cambridge: Cambridge University Press, 1984.

Levy, Darline Gay, and Harriet Branson Applewhite. "Women, Radicalization, and the Fall of the French Monarchy." In Applewhite and Levy 1993, 81–107.
——. "Women and Militant Citizenship in Revolutionary Paris." In Melzer and Rabine 1992, 79–101.
Levy, Darline Gay, Harriet Branson Applewhite, and Mary Durham Johnson, eds. and trans. *Women in Revolutionary Paris: Selected Documents Translated with Notes and Commentary.* Urbana: University of Illinois Press, 1979.
Lewis, Wyndham. *The Letters of Wyndham Lewis.* Edited by W. K. Rose. London: Methuen, 1963.
——. *Wyndham Lewis on Art: Collected Writings, 1913–1956.* Edited by Walter Michel and C. J. Fox. New York: Funk and Wagnalls, 1969.
——, ed. *BLAST* 1 [London], June 20, 1914.
——. *BLAST* 2 [London], July 1915.
Lidderdale, Jane, and Mary Nicholson. *Dear Miss Weaver: Harriet Weaver Shaw, 1876–1961.* New York: Viking, 1970.
London Democratic Association. "To the Masses of Yorkshire about to Assemble En Masse to Demand their Rights." London: *Northern Star,* October 13, 1838, 8.
Long, Michael. "The Politics of English Modernism: Eliot, Pound, Joyce." In Timms and Collier 1988, 98–112.
Longenbach, James. *Stone Cottage: Pound, Yeats, and Modernism.* New York: Oxford University Press, 1988.
Lovell, Terry, ed. and intro. *British Feminist Thought: A Reader.* Oxford: Basil Blackwell, 1990.
Loy, Mina. *The Lost Lunar Baedeker: Poems.* Selected and edited by Roger L. Conover. New York: Farrar, Straus and Giroux, 1996.
——. *The Pamperers* [1916], *The Dial* 69.1 (July 1920): 65–78.
——. *The Sacred Prostitute* [unpublished, ca. November 1914]. Yale Collection of American Literature, Beinecke Rare Book and Manuscript Library, Yale University.
Lyon, Janet. "Mina Loy's Pregnant Pauses: The Space of Possibility in the Florence Writings." In *Mina Loy: Woman and Poet.* Edited by Maeera Schreiber and Keith Tuma. Orono, Maine: National Poetry Foundation, 1998, 379–401.
——. "Women Demonstrating Modernism." *Discourse* 17.2 (Winter 1994–95): 6–25.
Lyotard, Jean-François. *The Postmodern Condition: A Report on Knowledge.* Translated by Geoff Bennington and Brian Massumi. Minneapolis: University of Minnesota Press, 1984.
Macdonell, Diane. *Theories of Discourse: An Introduction.* Oxford: Basil Blackwell, 1986.
MacKenzie, Midge. *Shoulder to Shoulder: A Documentary.* New York: Knopf, 1975.
"Manifeste du Comité Central de l'Union des Femmes: pour la défense de Paris et les soins aux blessés" [May 1871]. In Clarétie 1874, 2:440.
"Le Manifeste de Montréal." Toronto: AIDS ACTION NOW!/ACT UP, June 1989.
*Manifesto: International Committee of the Fourth International.* Fortieth Anniversary of the Fourth International. New York: Labor Publications, 1978.
"Manifesto Issued by the Syndicate of Technical Workers, Painters, and Sculptors, Mexico City, 1922." In Chipp 1968, 461.
Marcus, Jane. "The Asylums of Antaeus: Women, War, and Madness—Is There a Feminist Fetishism?" In *The New Historicism.* Edited by H. Aram Veeser. New York: Routledge, 1989, 132–51.
——, ed. *Suffrage and the Pankhursts.* London: Routledge and Kegan Paul, 1987.

Marcuse, Herbert. "A Note on Dialectic." In *The Essential Frankfurt School Reader.* Edited by Andrew Arato and Eike Gebhardt. New York: Continuum, 1988, 444–51.

Maréchal, Sylvain. "Manifeste des egaux" [1794]. In *Defense of Gracchus Babeuf: Before the High Court of Vendome.* Edited and translated by John Anthony Scott. New York: Schocken Books, 1972, 91–95.

Marek, Jayne E. *Women Editing Modernism: "Little" Magazines and Literary History.* Louisville: University of Kentucky Press, 1995.

Marinetti, F. T. *Marinetti: Selected Writings.* Editcd and introduced by R. W. Flint. Translated by R. W. Flint and Arthur A. Coppotelli. New York: Farrar, Straus and Giroux, 1972.

Marks, Elaine, and Isabelle de Courtivron, eds. *New French Feminisms: An Anthology.* New York: Schocken, 1980.

Marsden, Dora, ed. *The Freewoman.* London, 1911–1912.

——. *The New Freewoman: An Individualist Review* [London, 1913]. New York: Kraus Reprint, 1967.

Marx, Karl, and Friedrich Engels. "The Communist Manifesto." In *The Marx-Engels Reader.* Edited by Robert C. Tucker. New York: Norton, 1972. 335–62.

McEntee, Ann Marie. "'The [Un]Civill Sisterhood of Oranges and Lemons': Female Petitioners and Demonstrators, 1642–53." In Holstun 1992, 92–111.

Melzer, Sara E., and Leslie W. Rabine, eds. *Rebel Daughters: Women and the French Revolution.* New York: Oxford University Press, 1992.

Mercer, Kobena. "'1968': Periodizing Postmodern Politics and Identity." In *Cultural Studies.* Edited by Lawrence Grossberg, Cary Nelson, and Paula Treichler. New York: Routledge, 1992, 424–38.

——. "Traveling Theory: The Cultural Politics of Race and Representation." Interview by Lorraine Kenny. AFTERIMAGE (September 1990): 7–9.

Meyer, Alain. "Le Manifeste politique: modèle pur ou pratique impure?" *littérature* 39 (October 1980): 29–38.

Michel, Walter, and C. J. Fox, eds. *Wyndham Lewis on Art: Collected Writings, 1913–1956.* New York: Funk and Wagnalls, 1969.

Middlebrook, Diane Wood, and Marilyn Yalom, eds. *Coming to Light: American Women Poets in the Twentieth Century.* Ann Arbor: University of Michigan Press, 1985.

Mitchell, Bonner, ed. *Les Manifestes littéraires de la Belle Epoque, 1886–1914: anthologie critique.* Paris: Seghers, 1966.

Mitchell, David. *Queen Christabel: A Biography of Christabel Pankhurst.* London: Macdonald and Jane's, 1977.

Mitchell, Juliet. "Women: The Longest Revolution." *New Left Review* 40 (1966): 11–36.

Mitchell, W. J. T. *Iconology: Image, Text, Ideology.* Chicago: University of Chicago Press, 1986.

Moréas, Jean. "Le Manifeste symboliste" [September 18, 1886]. In B. Mitchell 1966, 23–32.

Morgan, Robin, ed. *Sisterhood Is Powerful: An Anthology of Writings from the Women's Liberation Movement.* New York: Random House, 1970.

Moriarty, Claire. "On Women's Liberation." *New Politics* 8.2 (Spring 1970): 27–36.

Morrell, Caroline. *Black Friday: Violence against Women in the Suffragette Movement.* London: Women's Research and Resources Centre Publications, 1981.

Morris, Meaghan. *The Pirate's Fiancée: Feminism, Reading, Postmodernism.* London: Verso, 1988.

Morrisson, Mark. "Marketing British Modernism: *The Egoist* and Counter-public Spheres." *Twentieth-Century Literature* 43.4 (Winter 1997): 439–69.

Mouffe, Chantal. "Introduction." In *Gramsci and Marxist Theory.* Edited by Chantal Mouffe. London: Routledge and Kegan Paul, 1–18.

Negt, Oscar, and Alexander Kluge. *Public Sphere and Experience: Toward an Analysis of the Bourgeois and Proletarian Public Sphere* [1972]. Translated by Peter Labanyi, Jamie Owen Daniel, and Assenka Oksiloff. Foreword by Mariam Hansen. Theory and History of Literature. Vol. 85. Minneapolis: University of Minnesota Press, 1993.

Nelson, Cary. *Manifesto of a Tenured Radical.* New York: New York University Press, 1997.

Nelson, Cary, and Lawrence Grossberg, eds. *Marxism and the Interpretation of Culture.* Urbana: University of Illinois Press, 1988.

Nevinson, C. R. W. *Paint and Prejudice.* New York: Harcourt, Brace, 1938.

Nevinson, Margaret Wynne. "Futurism and Woman." *The Vote,* December 31, 1910, 112.

Nicholls, Peter. "Futurism, Gender, and Theories of Postmodernity." *Textual Practice* (Fall 1989): 202–21.

———. *Modernisms: A Literary Guide.* Berkeley: University of California Press, 1995.

Nicholson, Linda J., ed. *Feminism/Postmodernism.* New York: Routledge, 1990.

Nicholson, Linda, ed. *Feminist Contentions: A Philosophical Exchange.* New York: Routledge, 1995.

"NOW Bill of Rights" [1967]. In Morgan 1970, 512–14.

O'Brien, Conor Cruise. "Nationalism and the French Revolution." In Best 1988, 17–47.

Outram, Dorinda. "Le Langage mâle de la vertue: Women and the Discourse of the French Revolution." In Burke and Porter 1987, 120–35.

Palumbo-Liu, David. "Universalisms and Minority Culture." *differences* 7.1 (Spring 1995): 188–208.

Pankhurst, Christabel. *The Great Scourge and How to End It* [1913]. In *Suffrage and the Pankhursts.* Edited by Jane Marcus. Women's Source Library. Series Editors Dale Spender and Candida Ann Lacey. London: Routledge, 1987, 187–240.

Pankhurst, Emmeline. "I Incite This Meeting to Rebellion." In *Feminism: The Essential Historical Writings.* Edited by Miriam Schneir. New York: Vintage, 1972, 293–95.

Pecheux, Michel. "Discourse: Structure or Event?" In Nelson and Grossberg 1988, 633–50.

Perloff, Marjorie. *The Futurist Moment: Avant-Garde, Avant-Guerre, and the Language of Rupture.* Chicago: University of Chicago Press, 1986.

"Petition of Right" [1628]. In Kenyon 1962, 83–85.

"Le Peuple de Paris aux soldats de Versailles" [May 1871]. In Clarétie 1874, 2:568.

Pinero, A. W. *Plays.* Edited and introduced by George Rowell. Cambridge: Cambridge University Press, 1986.

Poggioli, Renato. *The Theory of the Avant-Garde* [1962]. Translated by Gerald Fitzgerald. Cambridge: Harvard University Press, 1968.

Popkin, Jeremy D. "Journals: The New Face of News." In Darnton and Roche 1989, 141–64.

Poston, Carol H., ed. *A Vindication of the Rights of Woman: An Authoritative Text, Backgrounds.* 2nd edition. New York: Norton, 1988.

Pound, Ezra ["Bastien von Helmholtz"]. "The Bourgeois." *The Egoist* 1.3 (February 2, 1914): 53.

———. *"Ezra Pound Speaking": Radio Speeches of World War II.* Edited by Leonard W. Doob. Westport, Conn.: Greenwood, 1978.

———. "A Few Don'ts by an Imagiste." *Poetry* 1.6 (March 1913): 200–206.

——— ["Bastien von Helmholtz"]. "John Synge and the Habits of Criticism." *The Egoist* 1.3 (February 1, 1914): 54–55.

———. "The New Sculpture." *The Egoist* 1.4 (February 16, 1914): 67–68.

———["A. M."]. "Review of Valentine de Saint-Point." *The Egoist* 4.5 (May 1917): 61–62.

———. "Salutation the Third." *BLAST* 1 (June 1914): 45.

———. *The Selected Poems of Ezra Pound.* New York: New Directions, 1957.

———. "The Serious Artist." *The New Freewoman* 1.9–1.10 (October 15–November 1, 1913).

———["Bastien von Helmholtz"]. "Suffragettes." *Egoist* 1.13 (July 1914); reprinted in B. Scott, 1990, 367–71.

Proudhon, Pierre-Joseph. *Selected Writings.* Edited and introduced by Stewart Edwards. Translated by Elizabeth Fraser. Garden City, N.Y.: Anchor, 1969.

Pykett, Lynn. *Engendering Fictions: The English Novel in the Early Twentieth Century.* London: Edward Arnold, 1995.

Raeburn, Antonia. *The Militant Suffragettes.* London: Michael Joseph, 1973.

Rancière, Jacques. "Politics, Identification, and Subjectivization." *October* 61 (Summer 1992): 58–64.

"Rapport interdisciplinaire Nanterre, 11 juin 1968." Translated by Peter Brooks. *Partisan Review* 35.4 (1968): 536–41.

"Redstockings Manifesto." Reprinted in Betty Roszak and Theodore Roszak, eds. *Masculine/Feminine: Readings in Sexual Mythology and the Liberation of Women.* New York: Harper, 1969, 272–74.

Reed, Christopher. "Bloomsbury Bashing: Homophobia and the Politics of Criticism in the Eighties." *Genders* 11 (Fall 1991): 58–80.

Riley, Denise. "Does Sex Have a History?" In *Feminism and History.* Edited by Joan Wallach Scott. New York: Oxford University Press, 1996, 17–33.

Robbins, Bruce, ed. *The Phantom Public Sphere.* Vol. 5 of *Cultural Politics,* Minneapolis: University of Minnesota Press, 1993.

Romero, Patricia W. *E. Sylvia Pankhurst: Portrait of a Radical.* New Haven: Yale University Press, 1990.

Rose, Barrie. "Feminism, Women, and the French Revolution." In *The French Revolution in Social and Political Perspective.* Edited by Peter Jones. London: Arnold, 1996, 253–68.

Rose, Jonathan. *The Edwardian Temperament, 1895–1919.* Athens: Ohio University Press, 1986.

Rosen, Andrew. *Rise Up Women!: The Militant Campaign of the Women's Social and Political Union.* London: Routledge, 1974.

Rosenfeld, Marthe. "Language and the Vision of a Lesbian-Feminist Utopia in Wittig's *Les Guérillères.*" *Frontiers: A Journal of Women's Studies* 6 (1981): 6–8.

Roszak, Betty, and Theodore Roszak, eds. *Masculine/Feminine: Readings in Sexual Mythology and the Liberation of Women.* New York: Harper, 1969.

Roudinesco, Elisabeth. *Madness and Revolution: The Lives and Legends of Théroigne de Méricourt.* Translated by Martin Thom. London: Verso, 1991.

Rowland, William G., Jr. *Literature and the Marketplace: Romantic Writers and Their Audiences in Great Britain and the United States.* Lincoln: University of Nebraska Press, 1996.

Russell, Charles. *Poets, Prophets, and Revolutionaries: The Literary Avant-Garde from Rimbaud through Postmodernism.* New York: Oxford University Press, 1985.

Ruthven, K. K. *Ezra Pound as Literary Critic.* London: Routledge, 1990.

Saint-Point, Valentine de [Desglans de Cessiat-Vercell]. "Futurist Manifesto of Lust" [1913]. In Apollonio 1970, 70–74.

——. "Manifesto of the Futurist Woman" [March 25, 1912]. In *Le futuriste: donne e letteratura d'avanguardia in Italia (1914–1944)*. Edited by Claudia Salaris. Milan: Edizioni delle donne, 1982, 31–36.

Sale, Roger. "Keeping Up with the News" Excerpted in Daniel G. Marowski et al., eds. *Contemporary Literary Criticism*, vol. 22 (Detroit: Gale Research Co., 1985), 474–75.

Schama, Simon. *Citizens: A Chronicle of the French Revolution*. New York: Vintage, 1989.

Schiebinger, Londa. "Feminine Icons: The Face of Early Modern Science." *Critical Inquiry* 14 (Summer 1988): 661–91.

Schor, Naomi. "French Feminism Is a Universalism." *differences* 7.1 (Spring 1995): 15–47.

Schreiner, Olive. *Woman and Labor*. London: Stokes, 1911.

Schwarzkopf, Jutta. *Women in the Chartist Movement*. New York: St. Martin's, 1991.

Scott, Bonnie Kime, ed. *The Gender of Modernism: A Critical Anthology*. Bloomington: Indiana University Press, 1990.

Scott, Joan Wallach. *Gender and the Politics of History*. New York: Columbia University Press, 1988.

——. "Universalism and the History of Feminism." *differences* 7.1 (Spring 1995): 1–14.

——. "'A Woman with Only Paradoxes to Offer': Olympe de Gouges Claims Rights for Women." In Melzer and Rabine 1992, 102–20.

"SDS National Resolution on Women" [1968]. In Roszak and Roszak 1969, 254–59.

Segal, Naomi. "Sexual Politics and the Avant-garde: From Apollinaire to Woolf." In Timms and Collier 1988, 235–49.

Servan-Schreiber, Claude. "What French Women Are Up To." *Ms.* (September 1972): 30–31.

Shaw, G. B. *Plays, Pleasant and Unpleasant*. London: Constable, 1898.

Sheppard, Richard. "The Problematics of European Modernism." In Giles 1993, 1–51.

Shumway, Lauren. "The Intelligibility of the Avant-Garde Manifesto." *French Literature Series* 7 (1980): 54–62.

Sledziewski, Elisabeth G. "The French Revolution as the Turning Point." In Fraisse and Perrot 1993, 33–37.

Smith, Nigel. *Literature and Revolution in England, 1640–60*. New Haven: Yale University Press, 1994.

Snitow, Ann. "A Gender Diary." In *Conflicts in Feminism*. Edited by Marianne Hirsch and Evelyn Fox Keller. New York: Routledge, 1990, 9–43.

Snow, Edgar. "Theorizing the Male Gaze: Some Problems." *Representations* 25 (1989): 30–41.

Soboul, Albert. *Understanding the French Revolution*. Translated by April Ane Knutson. New York: International, 1988.

Solanas, Valerie. *SCUM Manifesto* [1967]. London: Phoenix, 1991.

Soper, Kate. *Humanism and Anti-Humanism*. London: Hutchison, 1986.

Spraggins, Mary Beth Pringle. "Myth and Ms.: Entrapment and Liberation in Monique Wittig's *Les Guérillères*." *International Fiction Review* 3.1 (1976): 47–51.

Stallybrass, Peter. "'Drunk with the Cup of Liberty': Robin Hood, the Carnivalesque, and the Rhetoric of Violence in Early Modern England." In *The Violence of Representation: Literature and the History of Violence*. Edited by Nancy Armstrong and Leonard Tennenhouse. London: Routledge, 1989, 45–76.

Starr, Peter. *Logics of Failed Revolt: French Theory After May '68*. Stanford: Stanford University Press, 1995.

Stephens, Winifred. *Women of the French Revolution*. New York: E. P. Dutton, 1922.

Stevenson, Randall. *Modernist Fiction: An Introduction.* Lexington: University of Kentucky Press, 1992

Stewart, John Hall. *A Documentary Survey of the French Revolution.* New York: Macmillan, 1951.

"Suffragist Outrages: Wholesale Window Smashing in London." *The Times* [London], March 2, 1912, 8.

Suvin, Darko, with Mark Angenot. "Demystification, or the Implicit of the Manifested: Laudation before a Limit-Finding of Marx's *Communist Manifesto*." Unpublished ms., 1997.

Swinburne, Algernon Charles. *Swinburne Replies.* Edited by R. Hyder. Syracuse: Syracuse University Press, 1966.

Tickner, Lisa. *The Spectacle of Women: Imagery of the Suffrage Campaign, 1907–14.* London: Chatto and Windus, 1987.

Timms, Edward, and Peter Collier, eds. *Visions and Blueprints: Avant-Garde Culture and Radical Politics in Early Twentieth-Century Europe.* Manchester: Manchester University Press, 1988.

Tisdall, Caroline, and Angelo Bozzolla. *Futurism.* New York: Oxford University Press, 1978.

Toulmin, Stephen. *Cosmopolis: The Hidden Agenda of Modernity.* Chicago: University of Chicago Press, 1990.

"The Tragedy of Enthusiasm." *The Times* [London], March 4, 1912, 9.

Tytell, John. *Ezra Pound: The Solitary Volcano.* New York: Anchor Doubleday, 1987.

Tzara, Tristan. "Dada Manifesto 1918." In *The Dada Painters and Poets: An Anthology.* Edited by Robert Motherwell. New York: Wittenborn, Schultz, 1951, 76–82.

Vicinus, Martha. *Independent Women: Work and Community for Single Women, 1850–1920.* London: Virago, 1985.

Vogel, Lise. *Marxism and the Oppression of Women: Toward a Unitary Theory.* New Brunswick: Rutgers University Press, 1983.

Volosinov, V. N. *Marxism and the Philosophy of Language* [1930]. Translated by Ladislav Matejka and I. R. Tituknik. New York: Seminar Press, 1973.

Walkowitz, Judith. *Prostitution and Victorian Society: Women, Class, and the State.* Cambridge: Cambridge University Press, 1980.

Walzer, Michael, ed. and intro. *Regicide and Revolution: Speeches at the Trial of Louis XVI.* Translated by Marian Rothstein. New York: Columbia University Press, 1992.

Weber, Eugen. "The Nineteenth-Century Fallout." In Best 1988, 155–82.

Wees, William C. *Vorticism and the English Avant-Garde.* Toronto: University of Toronto Press, 1972.

Weininger, Otto. *Sex and Character.* London: Heinemann, 1906.

Wenzel, Helen. "The Text as Body Politics." *Feminist Studies* 7 (Summer 1981): 264–87.

West, Rebecca. *The Young Rebecca: Writings of Rebecca West, 1911–17.* Selected and edited by Jane Marcus. Bloomington: Indiana University Press, 1982.

Wilhelm, J. J. *Ezra Pound in London and Paris: 1908–1925.* University Park: Pennsylvania State University Press, 1990.

Williams, Raymond. *Culture and Society: 1780–1950* [1958]. New York: Columbia University Press, 1983.

——. "The Politics of the Avant-garde." In Timms and Collier 1988, 1–15.

——. *The Politics of Modernism: Against the New Conformists.* Edited by Tony Pinkney. London: Verso, 1989.

Willis, Ellen. "Porn Free." *Transition: An International Review* 63 (1996): 4–23.

Wilson, Anna. "Mary Wollstonecraft and the Search for the Radical Woman," *Genders* 6 (Fall 1989): 88–101.

Winkiel, Laura. "'The Sweet Assassin' and the Performative Politics of the SCUM Manifesto." In *The Queer Sixties*. Edited by Patricia Juliana Smith. New York: Routledge, 1999.

Wittgenstein, Ludwig. *Philosophical Investigations* [1945]. Translated by G. E. M. Anscombe. 3rd edition. New York: Macmillan, 1958.

Wittig, Monique. *Les Guérillères.* Translated by David Le Vay. Boston: Beacon Press, 1971.

———. "The Mark of Gender." In *"The Straight Mind" and Other Essays*. Boston: Beacon, 1988, 76–89.

———. "One Is Not Born a Woman." In *"The Straight Mind" and Other Essays*. Boston: Beacon, 1988, 9–20.

———. "The Straight Mind." In *"The Straight Mind" and Other Essays*. Boston: Beacon, 1988, 21–32.

Wittig, Monique, Gille Wittig, Marcia Rothenburg, and Margaret Stephenson. "Combat pour la libération de la femme." *L'Idiot International* 6 (May 1970): 12–16.

Wolfe, Tom. "Stalking the Billion-Footed Beast: A Literary Manifesto for the New Social Novel." *Harper's Magazine* (November 1989): 45–56.

Wollen, Peter. *Raiding the Icebox: Reflections on Twentieth-Century Culture.* Bloomington: Indiana University Press, 1993.

Wollstonecraft, Mary. *A Vindication of the Rights of Woman* [1792]. Edited by Carol H. Poston. 2nd edition. New York: Norton, 1988.

Women's Social and Political Union. "Votes for Women, New Movement: Manifesto." London, ca. 1909. The Suffragette Fellowship Collection, London Museum, 50-82/549, reel 12.

Wordsworth, William. Preface to *Lyrical Ballads* [1802]. In *The Norton Anthology of English Literature*. 5th edition. Vol. 2. Edited by M. H. Abrams et al. New York: Norton, 1986, 157–170.

Wright, Sir Almroth. *The Unexpurgated Case against Woman Suffrage.* London: Constable, 1913.

Yeo, Eileen. "Some Practices and Problems of Chartist Democracy." In Epstein and Thompson 1982, 345–80.

Young, Iris Marion. "The Ideal of Community and the Politics of Difference" [1986]. In Nicholson 1990, 300–323.

———. *Throwing Like a Girl and Other Essays in Feminist Philosophy and Social Theory.* Bloomington: Indiana University Press, 1990.

Zerilli, Linda. "The Trojan Horse of Universalism: Language As a 'War Machine' in the Writings of Monique Wittig." In Robbins 1993, 142–72.

Zinnes, Harriet, ed. *Ezra Pound and the Visual Arts.* New York: New Directions, 1980.

# Index

Abastado, Claude, 15, 202

Aesthetics: in English avant-garde, 89, 99, 104, 108n. 34, 109n. 36, 112, 124, 165–166; gender in, 76–84; and new women, 84–91; in Omega Workshop, 98, 113n. 47; revolutionary, 66–67

AIDS ACTION NOW!/ACT UP, 197–198

Alcoff, Linda, 169

Aldington, Richard, 133, 139, 143

Alexander, Sally, 170

American Revolution, 27

Anarchism: and revolutionary discourse, 59; and SCUM, 174

Anderson, Amanda, 51n. 11, 87n. 68, 127n. 7, 169n. 2

Anger, 61–62; use of, by militant suffragists and avant-garde, 106; women's, 186

Anti-liberalism, 116–117

"Anti-modern" modernists, 40–41

Anti-sentimentalism, 112–114

"Aphorisms on Futurism" (Loy), 153

Ardis, Ann, 86, 87, 88, 119

Arendt, Hannah, 26–27, 54n. 17, 58, 59, 83n. 62

Aronowitz, Stanley, 35–36, 54n. 17, 172n. 7

Audiences: creation of, 23–29; Pound's antipathy toward, 136

Auping, Michael, 200n. 40

Austin, J. L., 24n. 23, 28, 199–200

Avant-garde, 40–42; and early modernism, 93–94; English, polemics of, 89; and feminism, 102, 165, 171n. 5; and feminist "counterculture" journals, 124–129; and fin de siècle, 81; and futurists, 82–83, 88–89, 97–98; and *Les Guérillières*, 190; and imagists, 128–135; Loy and, 42, 156; masculinity, 142; militancy of, 104–105; and negativity, 158; and New Woman, 88; and plebeian public sphere, 84; political and aesthetic, alignment of, 78–79; popular dismissal of, 111; in prewar England, 94–101; "sanity" of, 103; strains of, 83; vorticists and, 97–101; woman, 148–167; women's participation in, 88–89. *See also* Futurists; Imagism; Vorticists

Aylmer, G. E., 16

Baker, Keith Michael, 54, 57nn. 20, 22, 68n. 36

Bakhtin, M. M., 13

Balibar, Étienne, 35n. 36, 200

Bell, Madison Smartt, 204n. 1

Benhabib, Seyla, 24n. 23

Benstock, Shari, 92

Benveniste, Émile, 25–26

Berman, Marshall, 185

Bhabha, Homi, 31, 35n. 35, 203

Billington-Greig, Teresa, 126

"Black Feminist Statement," 177n. 13

Black Power, 7, 94, 98, 184

*BLAST*, 99, 108–113, 116, 117, 121, 127–129

Bluestockings, 63

Blum, Cinzia Sartini, 150–152

Bourgeoisie: Marx and, 185; Pound's definition of, 135; rhetoric of, 31; and universalism, 32–33

Bourgeois public sphere, 31–39, 47–48, 57, 85

Brooks, Peter, 174n. 9, 194

Broude, Norma, 108n. 34

"Brunswick Manifesto," 49

Bürger, Peter, 80, 83, 89, 171n. 5

Burke, Carolyn, 100n. 16, 148n. 36, 153, 160–161, 164n. 51

Burnett, David Graham, 14, 82n. 58

Bush, Ronald, 140–142

Butler, Judith, 28, 171n. 6, 184–185n. 28

Carson, Sir Edward, 117

Castoriadis, Cornelius, 193

Chartist movement, 35, 77–78, 85

Cheetham, Mark, 109n. 36, 112n. 42

Clark, Suzanne, 112–113, 155n. 44

Clarke, Bruce, 126n. 5, 144n. 32

"Coffeehouse discussion," 31–32

"Combat pour la libération de la femme" (Wittig), 177–195, 201–202

"Communist Manifesto," 27–28, 39, 60, 76–77, 185

Condorcet, Marquis de, 57n. 20, 68n. 36

Conover, Roger L., 100n. 16

Constituency (of manifestoes), 36–37

Coster, Robert, 17

"Dada Manifesto 1918," 41–42

Dadaists, 41–42

Dalla Costa, Mariarosa, and Selma James, 186n. 31

Davis, Jill, 87

de Baecque, Antoine, 48n. 4, 65–66

de Courtivron, Isabelle, 189–192

de Gouges, Olympe, 46–54, 57, 67, 85

de Saint Point, Valentine, 90, 149–153, 156, 163, 166

Dean, Tim, 81n. 56

Debord, Guy, 175, 193, 203

Declaration of Independence, American, 14, 26–28, 60

"Declaration of the Rights of Man and Citizen," 46, 53–54

"Declaration of the Rights of Woman" (de Gouges), 46–54

Deem, Melissa, 120n. 57, 173–174

Derrida, Jacques, 27–28, 199–200

Dessalines, Jean-Jacques, 204

Diggers, 16–20, 85. See also Levellers

"Diggers Song, The," 18

Dinwiddy, John, 78

Discourse, revolutionary, 58–59; and feminism, 67; imagist, 136–138; militant women and, 72–74, 90; in 1960s, 90; reworkings of, 127–129

Doolittle, Hilda (H. D.), 134–135, 137, 138

Dow, F. D., 19

DuBois, Ellen, 78n. 49

Duncan, Carol, 112n. 43

Dunlavy, John, 13

Dunlop, Marian Wallace, 96

DuPlessis, Rachel Blau, 100n. 16, 155n. 45

Dyke Manifesto, 10, 37–39

Ebert, Teresa, 169n. 2, 175n. 10, 187, 191, 197

Echols, Alice, 169, 170n. 3, 172n. 8, 175n. 11, 176n. 12, 178n. 16

Egoism, 126

Egoist, The, 125, 141n. 29

Eley, Geoff, 56

Elliot, Bridget, and Jo-Ann Wallace, 92

Engels, Friedrich, 60, 179–182

England: feminist manifestoes in, 57, 62–68; imperial dissolution of, 116–117; masses in, 85; prewar avant-garde in, 93–101, 165–166; and radical Chartist women, 78; and reform movements in 1640s and 1650s, 16–23; and vorticists, 97–101

"Englands New Chains Discovered" (Levellers), 20

Fanon, Frantz, 14, 29, 35n. 35, 206

Farge, Arlette, 73n. 45, 68n. 35

Farnell, Gary, 65n. 31

Fauchet, Claude abbé, 74–75

Felski, Rita, 40n. 37, 82n. 59, 86n. 67, 92n. 1, 102n. 22, 113, 127n. 7, 171n. 5

Feminism: and avant-garde, 42–44, 148–167; and "counterculture" journals, 124–129; and England, 57, 62–68; and the Enlightenment, 57, 62; and family, 187–188; and French Revolution, 46–47, 52–53, 67–68; futurists and, 100, 148–152; and literary modernism, 92; Marsden's rebuttals of, 141, 145, 147–148; and masculinist polemics, 166; and New Woman, 87; and Nietzsche, 102; and revolutionary discourse, 67, 90, 180; second-wave, 128, 168–202; and use of "we," 23–26, 36, 60, 126–127

"Feminist Manifesto" (Loy), 42–44, 154, 166

Ferguson, Moira, and Janet Todd, 62

Fitzsimmons, Linda, and Viv Gardner, 87n. 69